Hockey FOR THE COACH, THE PLAYER AND THE FAN

by FRED SHERO and ANDRÉ BEAULIEU

Illustrations by GEORGE KARN

SIMON AND SCHUSTER NEW YORK

Copyright © 1979 by Fred Shero Hockey Programs, Inc., and André Beaulieu
All rights reserved
including the right of reproduction
in whole or in part in any form
Published by Simon and Schuster
A Division of Gulf & Western Corporation
Simon & Schuster Building
Rockefeller Center
1230 Avenue of the Americas
New York, New York 10020

Designed by Irving Perkins
Manufactured in the United States of America

1   2   3   4   5   6   7   8   9   10

Library of Congress Cataloging in Publication Data

Shero, Fred.
    Hockey for the coach, the player and the fan.

    1. Hockey coaching.   I. Beaulieu, André,
Date—   joint author.   II. Title.
GV848.25.S53   796.9′62   79-11977
ISBN 0-671-24752-2

Both of us dedicate this book to every hockey player, hockey coach, and hockey fan, and each of us would like to dedicate it especially to our respective wives and children.

To my wife, Mariette, to Rejean and Jean Paul, and to my new family, the New York Rangers organization.

F.S.

To my wife, Kay, to Jacqueline and Jean Paul, and to all the people in hockey with whom I have been associated.

A.B.

Contents

CHAPTER **1** *The Coaching Game*

In a relatively short period of time—since World War II—hockey has developed and grown at an amazing rate due to expansion in professional hockey, keener competition, innovative coaching and training techniques and television. Television? There is no question that TV has had a major impact on the sport as fans of all ages are exposed to the best in hockey in coverage of the National Hockey League, international competition and championship junior and college play.

Television has also brought hockey patrons and participants face to face with the very real fact of the progress—if not domination—of European teams in the sport. If the Soviets, Czechs and Swedes have taught North Americans anything about hockey, it is that there is no one way of playing or teaching the game and that we all have much to learn from each other.

Those who spend a lot of time lamenting about the "good old days," but not enough in keeping up with the changing scene will be left behind. Hockey is undergoing the same process of change that has been seen in football and soccer. As they say, it's becoming a whole new ball game for those who coach, play and enjoy the world's fastest and most exciting team sport.

College and secondary-school teachers often observe that "Johnny can't read." Hockey coaches come up against a similar situation when they get a player at any level who lacks sufficient training in the basics of hockey. This presents a real challenge to coaches of young players. They can't, and shouldn't, expect too much of their young charges. But they must expect enough. Youngsters who grow up in hockey should get an early start on the fundamentals of stickhandling and passing. This is also the time to encourage good habits and an understanding of discipline.

Part of the fun of hockey—and it should be fun—is growing with and into the sport and accepting new challenges as strength, size and ability mature. This puts a demand on the coach to be effective on whatever level he is active. A coach should use drills and exercises appropriate to his players' skills, so that the players will be able to participate and execute the drills. Keep it simple in working with youngsters, and stress exercises that will keep them interested while improving their basic skills. The game becomes more complex as systems and strategy become more difficult. Go gradually to more difficult drills and strategy as skills develop. In general, drills should be hard enough to present a challenge to the players on any level, and practices should be more demanding than the game.

Players can learn in different ways, so the coach should consciously use several avenues of communication: visual (player has to see in order to understand), oral (player has to hear in order to understand), and mechanical (player has to participate in order to understand). Utilize all of these forms of communication in working with players of all ages and ability.

One of the most important, and more difficult, challenges in coaching is that of installing a system. The oldest systems in North America are the 1-2-2 and 2-1-2 systems. The 1-2-2 is the one-man-in pattern, while the 2-1-2 is the two-man-in system. These are covered in this book, along with other systems that have been developed and used with success. It is up to the coach to find a system that fits his players and then to work the team on the system with the persistence of a drill sergeant. The key in playing against any system is to find its weakness and take advantage of it.

The material in this book is directed to the thinking, innovative coach who is a student of the game as well as a teacher. Material has been drawn from many sources—high schools, junior programs, colleges and the professionals, in North America and Europe. The purpose is to help broaden the coach's repertoire by offering a wealth of ideas, drills and exercises that he can adopt or adapt. There is literally something for everyone, and the coach can pick and choose and experiment to find what will benefit his players and him. Nothing, after all, is so good that it can't be improved on. And that is our challenge.

One Coach's Creed

I will never hesitate giving credit where credit is due. It's better to recognize a good performance than criticize a poor one.

I will look on each day as a new opportunity.

I will attack my daily work with boldness, enthusiasm and confidence, and I will persist until I achieve my goal.

If I fail, it is because I have chosen to fail.

By helping others to do their best and attain their goals, I help myself.

I recognize that each obstacle and defeat I must face and overcome sharpens my skill, strength, courage and understanding.

I will never forget how I got where I am today.

I consider sacrifice not as giving something up, but gaining something important toward the attainment of a personal goal.

I will live this day as if it is my last, not looking back to yesterday's mistakes or successes, and not worrying about what might come tomorrow.

I will not mix my personal problems with my work problems. I will work them out where they belong—at home and at work.

I will attempt to be honest and objective with myself and my players, and will try to give each individual the treatment he earns and deserves.

I believe that a man may make mistakes, but that he can't be considered a failure until he blames his mistakes on someone else.

By my actions and comments, I can influence my players and fellow workers, because one teaches by example.

I believe that winning and losing are in the guts and mind of a coach. Outwardly, he accepts success with equanimity, and defeat without criticism.

I will maintain a positive attitude. I will praise rather than put down, be hopeful rather than hopeless, be helpful instead of selfish, and be enthusiastic rather than complaining.

I will accept constructive guidance and suggestions when they are offered, and when I feel that I need help or support I will ask for it, not because I am weak or indecisive, but because I see a healthy dependence on others as a sign of strength and independence.

I believe that what really counts is what you learn after you know everything.

I will constantly remind myself to "do it now."

Philosophy

1. Set reasonable, short-term goals for yourself and your players. When they have been achieved, set new goals. Trouble starts when there is too large a gap between expectation and realization. It's better to keep your expectations in the realm of reality and to set goals that offer a challenge, but realistically can be achieved.

2. No one coaches to lose, or plays to lose, for that matter. Players, teams and coaches go out to win. Unfortunately, someone has to lose, and it's up to the coach to put things in their proper perspective. A good coach gives his players the tools with which to win and the will to win, but also helps them to deal with defeat. The most important consideration should be the game itself as a battle of wits, strength, skill and determination.

3. The superior coach is a *teacher and student of the game.* You don't have to have been a superstar to excel as a coach, although this can and does happen all the time. What is more important than the coach's past glories on the rink (or court, or field) is his ability to instruct, inspire, prepare and challenge his players.

4. Just as coaches aren't all alike, players require individual attention. The *coach as a lay psychologist* understands his players and what it takes to elicit the best performance from each of them—whether it's a pat on the back or a period on the bench. He knows when and where to apply the heavy hand, and when and how to encourage and offer support. For an individual or a team, a slump is a lonely place to be. The coach is in a position to know what it will take to help—not force—a player on his way. He can be guided out of a slump with understanding and hard work. Get the player's mind off himself and his misery by getting him back into his role as an important contributing member of the team. After all, when someone is drowning, it's no time to give him a swimming lesson or point out the deficiencies of his backstroke. He needs support. A team losing streak calls for a pulling together into a "we're in this together and we'll get out of this together" relationship. This is the time to lighten up on the players, not to crack down, and to leaven work with some fun on the ice. On the other hand, when things are going well, don't go overboard with praise or flattery. That's the time for giving proper credit and then piling on the work.

5. The *coach is a salesman.* Take a tip from the sales experts, who work at keeping a positive mental attitude. Urge, encourage, sell: your system,

your principles, your philosophy, your methods, your objectives. Act now—not tomorrow, or next month, or next season. Be confident and enthusiastic (it's contagious).

6. The *coach is a teacher*. Like a good instructor in the classroom, the coach is well prepared for each day's work. Approach practice with a lesson plan and incorporate your strategy for the next game into the day's practice session. Zero in on your objectives. Encourage your players to set their own personal objectives (have them write them down and give them to you in a sealed envelope to be opened at some point in the season). Encourage them to measure their own efforts, not against other players, but against themselves at their best. Comparisons with other players are self-defeating. Urge your players to do as well as they are capable of doing, but demand that they always try to do their best. Help mold your players into what they can and should be and refuse to allow them to let themselves down. As a teacher, find satisfaction in seeing your players develop and mature in the game.

7. *Coach as a parent figure*. In some respects, a hockey team is like a family. Members of the team spend a lot of time together for six to eight months of the year, and must work out satisfactory relationships among themselves and with the coach. They share in the responsibility for the success or failure of the group effort. In a positive team environment, there is a unique kind of caring and sharing that goes on. Anyone who has ever played on a winning team knows the thrill and fulfillment of the experience and the close relationship among teammates that was a part of it.

If a team can be considered a family of sorts, the coach is elected to the role of parent. He should be sensitive to his players' hopes, needs, limitations and problems, but must be firm in sticking to his principles and fair in dispensing justice. For openers, define what is expected of the players, on the ice and off. Be certain that you are heard and understood. Players should recognize clearly that the coach is interested in them as individuals and will do the best he can for them, but that he must ultimately act in the best interests of the team. Like a parent, a coach doesn't like everything he has to do, but he must act on what has to be done without excuses or hesitation.

The coach can also encourage an atmosphere conducive to positive interaction among members of his player family. It's basically a matter of meshing talents and personalities. A group that establishes this rapport generally develops its own lines of authority, internal discipline, mutual trust, respect, spirit and pride. The problem player, the so-called bad apple, must be identified early and dealt with, because constant grumbling and fault-finding, from even one player, can cause dissension and contaminate team togetherness.

8. The *coach as public relations practitioner*. Public relations is a necessary part of the coaching bag, and comes into play in dealing with players, fans, officials, the media, parents, management and the public at large. Follow these guidelines: be courteous, be accessible, be fair and, most important, be honest. Remind yourself that as a public spokesman for the team, you set the image and personality of the team in the public eye.

9. Being human, we all make mistakes. The important thing is not to make the same mistakes over and over again, but to learn from them and go on. Don't lash out at players when they lose or make honest mistakes. Deal with the problem at hand, firmly and fairly. There's nothing wrong with getting angry. Go ahead and let the players know how you feel. But confine yourself to anger without insult.

10. Each coach has to work out for himself how he is going to approach his players and his job. He can be easygoing or tough; a taskmaster or a buddy. The main thing is to be consistent, which can mean being easy or tough as the situation requires. If everyone knows what is expected of him, it makes the coach's role easier in the long run. Communicating in a meaningful way is the key. The coach's role isn't an easy one. He is not really a part of management, whatever the organizational structure he works within, and yet he is not a member of the team either. And while a coach necessarily becomes very involved with his players, getting too close can interfere with his effectiveness. Finding the right balance in his relationship with the players is necessary if the coach is to be successful.

Organization of Practice

Because practice time is always limited, make good use of every minute at your disposal. Plan practice before you arrive at the rink, and go over your lesson plan with the players before going on the ice (in the dressing room, if possible). Spending practice time giving instructions or explaining a drill, or stopping practice to talk to a player eats up time that could be put to better use. It's best if drills can be run without the active participation of the coach (use captains or assistants). From a position in the end or by the side boards, the coach can observe what's going on and talk to players, if necessary, while the rest of the team works.

When planning the day's practice, the first question is "What should we accomplish today?" The next consideration is what to do to obtain maximum benefit for the players and team. Practices will vary depending on the level of the players (peewees to pros) and upon the time of the year (early season, midseason, late season). But practices generally consist of individual drills (skills, conditioning), positional drills and team drills. Exercises can include all of these elements.

PRESEASON ON-ICE PRACTICE

OBJECTIVES: Conditioning.
Building endurance, speed, strength and agility.
Brushing up on skills.

A TYPICAL PRACTICE: Warmups, skill drills, positional play drills (breakout patterns, forechecking patterns), team drills, goalie drills. If practice includes a scrimmage, make it as gamelike as possible, conducted at a gamelike pace. A controlled scrimmage gives the coach an opportunity to judge each individual's skills.

EARLY-SEASON ON-ICE PRACTICE

OBJECTIVES: Placement of players.
Balancing the team.
Working on a system.
Developing team unity.
Pinpointing individual and team strengths and weaknesses.

A TYPICAL PRACTICE: Skating, puck control and passing, breakout patterns, forechecking patterns and positional play.

MIDSEASON ON-ICE PRACTICE

OBJECTIVES: Juggling talent where necessary.
Work with team and individuals on weak points.
More emphasis on teamwork and strategy.

A TYPICAL PRACTICE: Skating, passing and stickhandling, offensive and defensive plays, power play and/or penalty killing drills, goalie drills, individual checking game, work on faceoff patterns.

LATE-SEASON ON-ICE PRACTICE

OBJECTIVES: Get ready physically and mentally for playoffs.
Run a check on each individual (time off for some, work for others).
Reinforce the system.
Try out new strategy in consideration of the playoffs.
Work on team and individual weaknesses.

A TYPICAL PRACTICE: Offensive and defensive zone strategy, power play and/or penalty killing, skating, passing and stickhandling, special assignment work for each line with a pair of defense.

These are merely some guidelines. What works well with one group of players may not get the job done with another group of players on the same level. The coach must set his own general guidelines, but should be flexible within that framework. Do whatever is necessary to produce results. As in the case of selecting a system, it's up to the coach to decide what will fit his players and team objectives.

PRACTICE NOTES

1. Teach new material at the beginning of practice when players are alert and receptive.
2. Correct major errors immediately, but save minor matters until after practice.
3. Keep practices lively and challenging by changing tempo, introducing new drills from time to time and allowing for some playtime (games, keep-away, shinny).
4. Take into consideration the composition of the team, and its strengths and weaknesses, as well as your game plan for the next game, when planning practice.
5. Keep players busy and don't let them stand around. If you are using 2 zones for drills, set up another activity in the neutral zone.
6. In any drill, insist on good positioning and good execution.

Training Methods

Everyone's got a theory on off-ice training and most of the methods work most of the time for most players. Whether it's isometrics, isotonics, aerobics, anaerobics, weight work, calisthenics or whatever, the primary axiom is work. Daily work at something, alone or as part of a team. A player's performance on the ice reflects what he does (and is) off the ice. Being an athlete implies a commitment to the training required of an athlete. This may mean sacrificing some self-indulgences, but it comes with the territory. It's no different if you are a ballet dancer, brain surgeon, concert violinist. To be successful, you have to work, practice and pay the price.

Ideally, an athlete should never get out of shape. Some effort every day should be easier in the long run than a crash program right before the season starts. A youngster who stays active will stay in condition. A normal amount of running, biking, gym work and seasonal sports participation will do the job.

Being active isn't enough for the older, serious athlete. Training programs, individual and team, are a necessary part of the picture. Here we can learn much from European training methods, and in particular, from the Soviets and Czechs, who make training (conditioning) a year-round endeavor. And it shows in their endurance, agility, stamina and strength. In the off-season, in North America at any rate, training is mostly an individual thing. The coach can recommend, urge, advise and insist, but the player will make his own decisions. When training camp begins, it's not difficult to pick out the players who have been conscientious in their own self-interest over the summer.

As in the case of practice planning, here are some suggested training methods:

OFF-SEASON AND PRESEASON DRY LAND TRAINING

OFF-ICE OBJECTIVES: Physical conditioning.
Increase strength and speed.
Develop stamina and endurance.
Build attitude and confidence.
Prevent injuries.
Develop mobility and agility.

OFF-ICE ACTIVITIES: Track and field events (including sprint running and hurdles).
Team sports (soccer, basketball, football, floor or street hockey).
Individual sports (tennis, squash, handball, golf, racketball, bicycling, swimming).
Weight lifting (begin with a comfortable weight and add X pounds a week working every other day).
Calisthenics.
Obstacle courses.

IN-SEASON TRAINING

OFF-ICE OBJECTIVES: Serve as a warmup before going on the ice.
Maintain fitness.
Increase endurance and speed.
Improve agility, balance and strength.

OFF-ICE ACTIVITIES: Calisthenics.
Weight lifting.
Isometrics, isotonics.
Team sports (basketball, floor hockey, soccer).
Individual sports (tennis, squash, racketball, golf, handball, rope jumping, running).
ON-ICE OBJECTIVES: Maintain fitness.
Building endurance, stamina, strength.
Increase agility, balance and mobility.
ON-ICE ACTIVITIES: Calisthenics with sticks.
Conditioning drills, such as resistance drills, tandem drills, power and endurance skating drills.

Nowhere is it written that because hockey is an athlete's major interest (or career choice), he shouldn't be involved in other sports. In fact, it's recommended. Sports participation keeps a player fit and strong. And most athletes find a game of soccer or basketball more fun than a session of calisthenics.

Keeping Tabs

Game statistics provide information on team and individual performance the coach can't get from behind the bench. There is undoubtedly a point of overkill in keeping statistics, but some information is essential:

Number of shots on goal by period (team and individual)
Power play, shorthanded, tying and winning goals
Goals scored by and against each line and defensive unit (plus–minus)
Goaltender's averages

A compilation of this information will give the coach specific direction in planning practices and also in setting team goals and measuring achievement. Break the season into periods of measurement of performance and put the statistics to work in pinpointing areas that need special attention in practice.

Other interesting team and individual statistics:

Number of shots at the goal
Faceoffs won and lost (especially in the defensive zone)
Number of rushes
Number of attacks broken
Number of fast attacks

Number of rebounds controlled/lost
Penalties (number of "good" and "bad" penalties and by whom)
Shots blocked by the defense
Giveaways (defensive, neutral and offensive zones)
Bad passes (defensive, neutral and offensive zones)
Hits (defensive, neutral and offensive zones)
How are goals scored against the team (charted)

From time to time, do an evaluation in these areas:

Forechecking system (control/weaknesses)
Breakout system (number controlled/stopped)
Power play unit (strengths/weaknesses)
Penalty killing unit (strengths/weaknesses)
Individual performances (shooting, passing, checking, aggressiveness, playmaking, recovery after being taken out of the play)

Thought Provokers

1. Do you use a system?
2. What are your priorities at the beginning of each period?
3. Would you pull your goaltender for an extra skater with 5 to 10 seconds left at the end of the period when you have a man advantage and the score is tied or you trail?
4. Are you prepared for your practices? Do you take into consideration your next game (opponent and strategy)?
5. Do you give players specific guidelines to follow on the ice whether they are on the offense or defense?
6. Keep your comments in the locker room generalized. Specific comments for individuals should be made in private.
7. What do you do with a player who is having a "hot" night? Or with the line or star that is having a "bad" night?
8. If things are going sour, don't hesitate to make changes that will stir things up and generate new life.
9. Behind the bench, keep criticism constructive.
10. Do you ask the players' opinions on how the opposition is playing against them?
11. Make sure when you instruct that the players are ready to listen and learn and aren't tired or distracted.
12. Do you consider yourself a creative and innovative coach?
13. Consider having regular "office hours" when players are welcome to stop by and talk.
14. Be what you ask of your players—self-disciplined, responsible and organized.

CHAPTER **2** *Skating and Stickhandling*

Skating is, of course, the foundation upon which all hockey is built. Elements of skating ability include speed, balance, stamina, agility, mobility and strength.

This chapter includes skating drills designed to improve skating on every level of hockey. With variations, the coach will have nearly one hundred drills available to his players and him. While skating drills are an integral part of each practice session, variety on a day-to-day or week-to-week basis keeps players interested and challenged, and gives the coach the means of changing the tempo of practices and improving the overall conditioning, skills, effectiveness and attitude of his charges.

All skaters, including goaltenders, should participate in skating and stickhandling exercises.

Warmup Exercises

1. Forward weaving
2. Backward weaving
3. Single leg weaving
4. Groin stretching
5. Single leg kick
6. Single leg pivot
7. Glide and touch heels (2 hands)
8. Leg spread (in and out)
9. Leg crossovers (forward)
10. Leg crossovers (backward)
11. Knee lift to chest
12. Slalom skating
13. Running or walking on toes or heels
14. Interval jumping (alternate 1 foot + 2 feet)
15. Trunk rotation
16. Alternate toe touching
17. Lateral side stepping
18. Mirror drill (2 players)
19. Skate on 1 leg around circle (alternate pushing leg as you change direction backwards and forward)
20. Stationary pivoting (1 leg is immobile while the other leg circles around it; alternate forward and backwards)
21. Skate, drop to knees
22. Skate, drop to stomach
23. Running on skates
    a. Straight forward
    b. Around circles

Optional Activities to Improve Balance, Strength and Stamina

1. Resistance pushing (2 players)
2. Stationary resistance (2 players)
3. Stick pulling (side to side, 2 players)
4. Back to back pushing (2 players)
5. Rope pulling
6. Rope jumping
7. Chasing (2 players)
8. Wrestling (2 players)

Offensive player

Offensive player carrying puck

Defensive player

Defensive player carrying puck

Offensive player skating forward

Direction of pass

Defensive player skating forward

Shot on goal

Defensive player skating
backward

Crossover or lateral movement

Checking or screening
opposing player

9. Shoulder bumps (2 players)

Most of these are familiar enough to coaches, but mixing and matching not only adds variety to practices, but gives added dimension to overall skating skills.

Drills

DRILL

1. All of the players are grouped together without pucks. One player, who is designated as the leader, skates off with the other players falling into line behind him.

2. The leader may skate anywhere he desires, in any pattern. Obviously, sharp turns or moves which recross the original path aren't recommended because of the line of following skaters.

VARIATIONS

A. Anyone may take over the lead by overtaking the current leader.

B. The coach may speed up or slow down the drill with whistle signals.

C. The drill becomes a stickhandling exercise with the addition of pucks for all skaters.

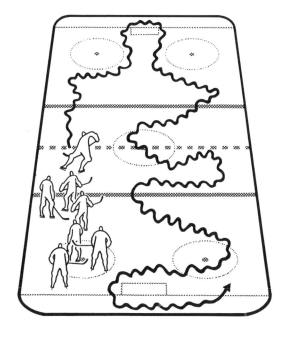

DRILL

1. Players take up positions along the skating pattern. Each player has a puck.

2. Players skate the pattern, at the coach's signal, maintaining a distance of about 20 feet apart. To complete the drill, players should skate the entire circuit 2 or 3 times.

3. This is a good exercise for developing balance, agility, mobility and edge control. It is also useful in working on turns, lateral movements and crossovers.

VARIATIONS

A. The pattern can be reversed so that the drill starts and ends on the right instead of the left side.

B. Coach may use the whistle to speed up or slow down the drill.

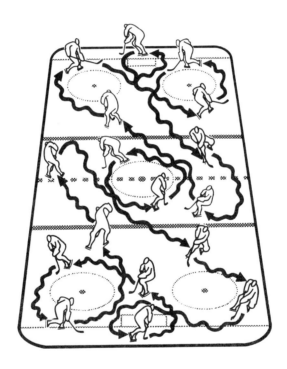

DRILL

1. Have all the players in one zone with pucks for everyone. The players maneuver around the zone without circling or following one another.
2. The purpose of this drill is to teach players to stickhandle, keeping their heads up while controlling the puck. Because movement is confined, players will also work on dekes, lateral movement, left and right turns, stops and starts and speed variation.

VARIATIONS

A. To make the drill more challenging, take the puck away from one player, who must then fight for another player's puck.
B. Take away a number of pucks. This will make the drill more difficult because players with pucks will either have to maintain control or give up their pucks to other skaters.
C. Expand the drill to 2 or 3 zones.
D. Have the players stickhandle with only 1 hand on the stick. The puck will be harder to control in traffic in the zone, thus the exercise serves to strengthen the players' wrists and forearms.

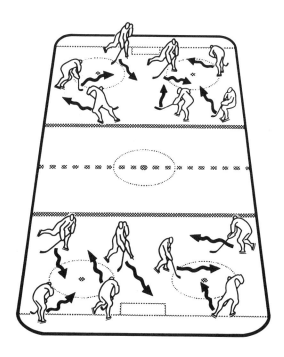

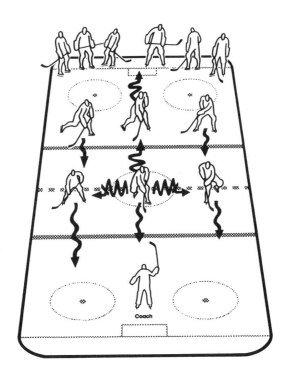

DRILL

1. Coach leads the drill by stick or hand signals.

2. Six players take the ice at one time for the drill and may use 1, 2 or 3 zones, at the coach's discretion.

3. At the coach's signal, skaters execute these maneuvers: forward and backwards skating; forward and backwards weaving while skating; right and left crossovers, and dropping to their knees and up.

VARIATION

Drill may be done with or without pucks.

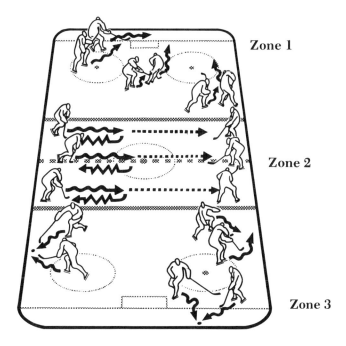

Zone 1

Zone 2

Zone 3

DRILL

1. Team is split into 3 groups; each group works in 1 zone for a specified length of time.

2. At the whistle, groups rotate zones. The drill is completed when each group has taken part in the exercise in each zone.

Zone 1: Puckhandling games. Skaters would work individually, or in pairs (a) controlling the puck along the boards, (b) controlling the puck in open ice and (c) controlling the puck with the use of the net against opponent.

Zone 2: Passing game. Players at the boards on the left side skate to mid-ice, pass to the skater opposite, and return to position skating backwards. The players on the right side repeat the same exercise once they have received the pass from their partners. Drill should include skate and stick passes and catching passes off-ice with the gloves, skates or body and forehand and backhand passes.

Zone 3: In pairs, players work on the use of the body along the boards, in open ice and in the corner in keeping the puck away from an opponent.

DRILL

1. Team is divided and players are grouped on opposite corners of the rink.

2. Players on the right of the ice work on board passing. As they complete that drill, they line up with the group utilizing the other half of the ice.

3. The second drill going on simultaneously has the players stickhandling in a weaving pattern down the ice.

4. After each group has gone the length of the ice 2 or 3 times, reverse the drill so that the group on the left is board passing and the stickhandling group is on the right. This gives players the opportunity to work on both forehand and backhand passes.

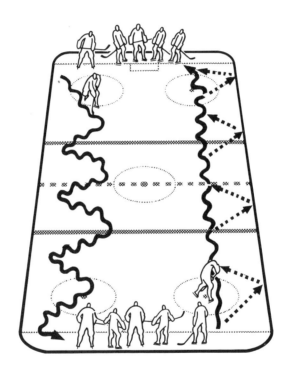

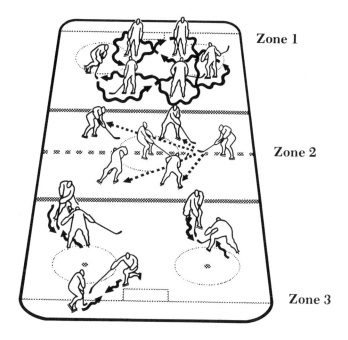

Zone 1

Zone 2

Zone 3

DRILL

1. Split the team into three groups. Each group works in a zone.
2. After a specified length of time, the coach whistles rotation of the groups from one zone to the next. Drill is completed when each group has worked in all 3 zones.

Zone 1: Each player takes a turn at skating and stickhandling in a weaving pattern between the other players. Exercise should be done clockwise and counterclockwise.

Zone 2: Five players form a circle in the neutral zone. One player in the middle of the circle chases the puck, as the others attempt to keep it away from him. Two pucks may also be used in this game.

Zone 3: Three players skate with pucks; 3 are without pucks and work to take away a puck from another skater.

DRILL

1. Team is divided and players are lined up in groups of three at opposite ends of the rink.
2. One group of three players skates forward to the middle circle, pivots, skates around the circle backwards 3 or 4 times and finishes by skating to the goal line.
3. Alternate ends in going through the drill.

VARIATIONS

A. Players may begin the drill skating backwards, pivoting to forward position at the circle, or may go through the entire drill in a forward or backward position, eliminating the pivot turn.
B. Drill may be done with or without pucks.

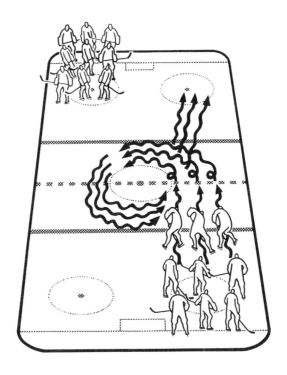

DRILL

1. Team is divided into 5 units and each unit is situated at one of the circles.
2. One by one, players at each circle skate the circle pivoting from forward to backward around the circle.
3. The first round has the players pivoting while facing the faceoff point (or into the circle).
4. In the second portion of the drill, the skaters pivot while facing the boards (or looking out of the circle).
5. Drill should be done clockwise and counterclockwise.
6. Coach may use the whistle to speed up or slow down the drill.
7. Purpose of the drill is to work on control of left and right pivoting turns while increasing agility.

VARIATION

Drill can be done with pucks.

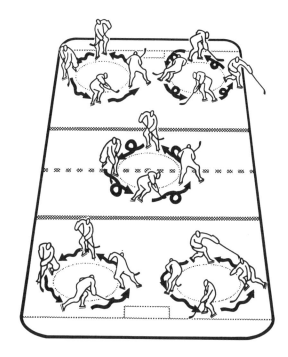

DRILL

1. Divide the team and have the units line up by the boards at opposite ends of the rink.
2. Group A goes first, with players proceeding to skate around the circles 2 or 3 at a time.
3. Players should skate each circle twice before moving to the next circle in the pattern.
4. Drill should be done skating forward and skating backward.
5. Group B executes the drill when Group A has completed the circles.

VARIATIONS

A. Skaters may shift from forward skating to backward skating on the second time around each circle.
B. Drill becomes a good stickhandling exercise with the addition of pucks.
C. Coach may use the whistle to speed up or slow down the drill.

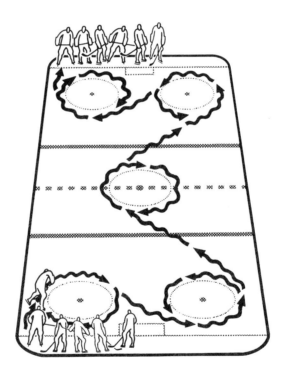

DRILL

1. Split the players into 5 groups, situate a group at each of the faceoff circles, as diagramed.
2. In rotation, each player in each group works on a small figure eight inside the circle. He should skate the figure eight forward and backward 4 to 8 times, according to the coach's instructions, before being replaced by the next player.

VARIATIONS

A. Figure eights may be done with or without pucks.
B. Coach may decide pattern of the exercise, such as 4 forward figure eights and 4 backward, or 2 forward, 2 backward, and so on.

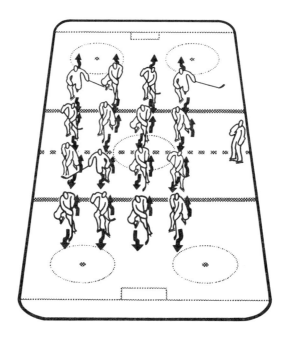

DRILL

1. Skaters spread out in 4 or 5 rows on the ice. The coach takes up a position by the boards at the red line.

2. At the coach's whistle, everyone skates forward. At the next whistle, players stop and reverse direction.

3. Do the drill in 2 sets of 8 whistles and 2 sets of 5 whistles, pausing for a minute after each set.

VARIATIONS

A. Have the players skate forward when they hear the first whistle and backwards on the second whistle, continuing the procedure for four sets.

B. Use the same setup, but have the players face the coach. At the whistle, the players take lateral steps or crossover steps to the left. At the next whistle, players take lateral steps or crossover steps to the right, and so on for a designated number of sets.

C. Drill and variations may be done with or without pucks.

DRILL

1. Divide the team and have each group line along the boards on opposite corners of the rink.

2. Following a leader and maintaining a distance of 10 to 15 feet, players in Group A skate to the middle of the first blue line, stop, and skate backwards to the opposite side from where they started.

3. Alternating between groups A and B, players skate the same triangular pattern to blue line, red line, and finally, to the far blue line. In each case the players skate forward to the line and backwards to the other side.

VARIATIONS

A. This drill can be done with or without pucks.

B. Drill may commence with backward skating and shift to forward skating at the lines.

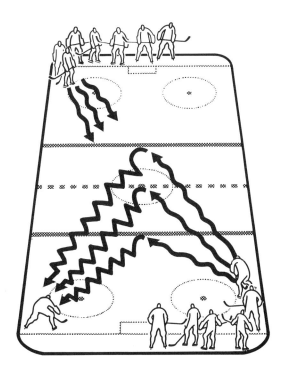

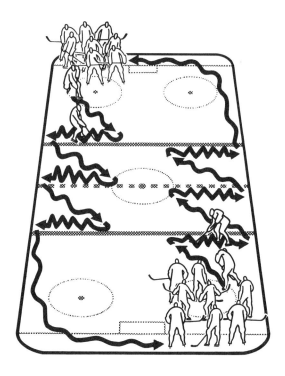

DRILL

1. Divide the team and situate each unit in 3 rows in opposite corners of the rink (see diagram).
2. At the signal, 1 player from each corner skates forward to the middle of the blue line, stops and skates backwards to the boards, stops and skates forward to the middle of the red line, stops and skates backwards to the boards, stops and skates diagonally to the middle of the far blue line, where he stops again and skates backwards to the boards. The players complete the drill by stopping at the boards and skating forward around the net to the end of the line in the corner.

VARIATIONS

A. Drill can be done with or without pucks.
B. Switch groups to the corner on the other side of the ice after each player has done the drill once.

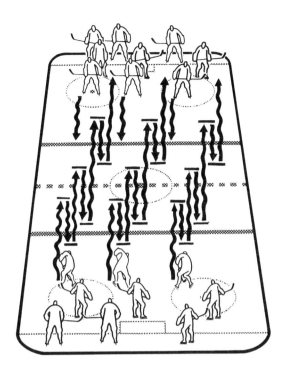

DRILL

1. Players line up in groups of 3 at both ends of the rink.
2. One group of 3 skaters opens the drill by skating forward at full speed. At the coach's whistle, the skaters stop and reverse direction. In a set of 5 to 7 whistles, the players should skate the length of the ice.
3. Coach should vary the distance skated between whistles.
4. When the first group has completed the drill, the first threesome on the opposite end of the ice executes the exercise, and the drill goes on, alternating ends, until all skaters have participated.

VARIATIONS

A. Using the same pattern of whistled commands, have the skaters go forward, stop and skate backwards until the next whistle, when they proceed forward, and so on.
B. Drill may be done with or without pucks.

DRILL

1. Players line up in groups of 3 at both ends of the rink.

2. First group of 3 skaters skates forward as fast as they can. When the coach whistles or shouts "turn," skaters turn sharply and continue skating forward in the opposite direction. At the next whistle or voice command, players again turn and continue the forward progress.

3. Each group of skaters should have a set of 5 to 7 turns. Players should alternate right and left turns.

4. Distance skated between shouts or whistles should vary.

5. Groups on each end alternate skating the pattern until the drill is completed.

VARIATION

Drill may be executed with or without pucks.

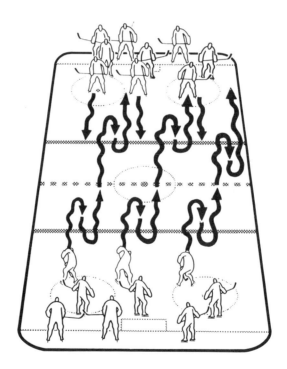

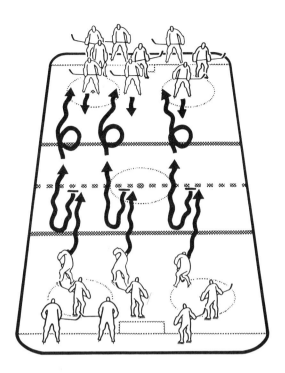

DRILL

1. Divide the players and situate groups in lines in both ends of the rink (see diagram).
2. At the coach's signal, a unit of 3 players starts from one end, skates to the red line, stops, returns to the blue line, makes one-half control turn, skates to the far blue line, makes a full control turn and then skates to the goal line.
3. The next group starts from the end in which the first group finished, and the drill alternates back and forth.

VARIATIONS

A. As many as 5 players can participate in each run-through.
B. Each starting unit could go down the ice and back, returning to starting position.
C. Drill can be executed with or without pucks.

DRILL

1. Players are situated around the rink in the skating pattern.
2. At the coach's whistle, players skate the pattern, going from the left side to the middle to the right side and so on.

VARIATIONS

A. Coach may vary the drill by whistling for sprint skating between the blue lines.
B. Coach may alternatively speed up the drill on the sides only, or on one side only, or in the middle.
C. Coach may alter the drill by having the players reverse from forward to backward skating between the blue lines.
D. Drill may be done with or without pucks.

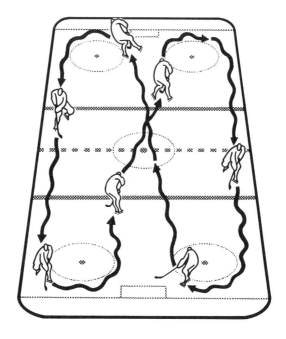

DRILL

1. Split the team into 2 groups and situate groups in opposite corners of the rink as illustrated.

2. The drill begins at one end when 3 players skate out at the coach's signal. The outside pair of skaters skate forward, while the inside player skates forward one way, pivots and skates backward on the return. Side by side the players skate the length of the ice, make the swing to the other side of the rink and return to the goal line. They remain in that corner as the next 3 skaters start out from the opposite end of the ice.

3. Keep the drill going, with groups coming from alternate ends, until each player has skated backwards once.

VARIATIONS

A. The coach may have all 3 players skate forward on one side and backwards on the other (return) side.

B. The drill may be run with or without pucks.

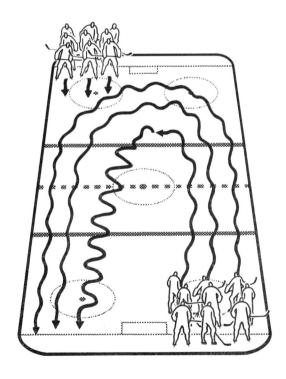

DRILL

1. Team is divided and each group of players lines up by the boards at one end of the rink.
2. Maintaining a distance of about 10 to 15 feet apart, skaters weave across the ice single file, changing from forward to backward skating, backwards to forward, etc., on each turn.
3. Drill begins and ends with forward skating.

VARIATIONS

A. Drill may be repeated as many times as the coach desires.
B. Begin with backward skating, changing to forward skating on the turn, and so on through the pattern.
C. Drill may be executed with or without pucks.

DRILL

1. The players are split into 4 groups and a group is situated in each of the corners of the rink.

2. At the coach's whistle, the first group of skaters comes out from one corner single file and follows the pattern illustrated: goal line to blue line to the opposite goal mouth returning down the middle, around the original goal to the blue line and then a full circle of the ice.

3. When the first group returns to position, the unit in the next corner goes out. Rotation continues—clockwise or counterclockwise—until all of the players have skated the pattern.

VARIATIONS

A. Drill may be executed with or without pucks.

B. The drill may be timed the first time it is done, and the players can be required to attempt to cut the time on successive run-throughs of the drill. This can be done unit by unit, taking the best time as the time to be beaten when the drill is executed again. Suggest that this drill be done once a week.

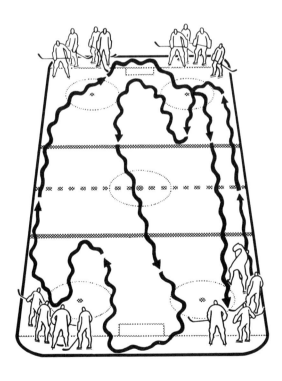

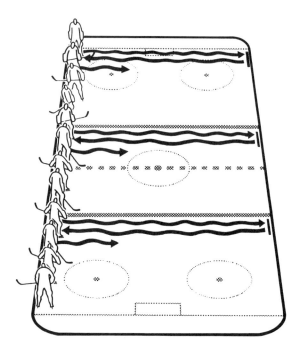

DRILL

1. Players are lined up along the boards on one side of the rink.
2. At the whistle, first player in each zone skates across the ice, stops and returns. When he returns, the player next to him repeats the routine, and so on until all of the players have skated.
3. Repeat the drill.

VARIATIONS

A. Coach may have any number of skaters going at one time: every other player, every third player, and so on. Drill may also be done with all skaters in 1 zone going together.
B. Have skaters skate forward to the boards and return skating backwards.
C. Repeat the drill any number of times.
D. Drill may be done with or without pucks.
E. Have all the skaters in 1 zone go out at once and skate 4 times across and 4 times back without stopping. Time the exercise (the pros do the 8 laps in about 35 to 40 seconds) and require the groups to better their time each run-through of the drill. Once a week is good for this exercise.

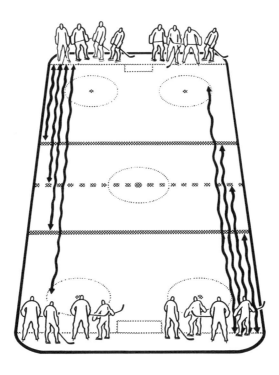

DRILL

1. Team is divided and players line up behind the goal line on each end of the rink.

2. One or more players on opposite ends of the rink skate to the blue line, pivot and return.

3. In rotation, each skater takes his turn skating to and from the blue line, the red line, the far blue line, and finally to the goal line.

VARIATIONS

A. One, 2, 3 or 4 players may skate from each end at once.

B. Entire drill—to and from all four lines—may be executed without pause by each player or group of players.

C. Skaters may go to and from each line twice.

D. Drill can be executed by having players skate forward one way and backward on the return.

E. Drill may be done with and without pucks.

DRILL

1. Team is divided and players are situated along the goal lines on both ends of the rink.
2. At the whistle, first and second skaters in opposite corners of the rink skate to the red line, stop and come back to the blue line, stop, skate to the far blue line, stop, come back to the red line, stop, and go on to the goal line, stop, and come back to their original positions.
3. The next two skaters in each line continue the drill by repeating the same pattern. Skating continues until all players have gone through the drill.

VARIATIONS

A. Alternate ends of the rink by having every other player on one end of the rink go through the drill; when they have completed the pattern, alternating players on the other end of the rink skate. Everyone skates in 2 sets in this variation.
B. The coach may have the players skate forward to the line, and backwards when returning to the blue or red line.
C. Entire drill may be executed skating backwards.
D. Drill may be done with or without pucks.

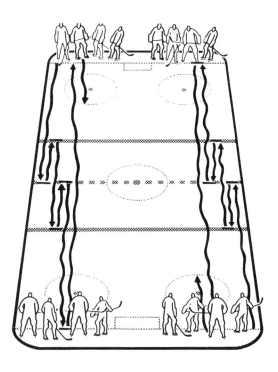

DRILL

1. The entire team is at one end of the ice grouped into 4 units of players at the goal line.

2. The first unit goes out at one time, skating to the goal line and back, to the blue line and back, to the red line and back and finally to the near blue line and back.

3. As the first unit returns, the next unit goes out. Each unit should repeat the exercise 3 times.

NOTES

A. Coach may time the drill in the team's daily practices and may require that the time of execution be cut each successive time the drill is run (once a week is suggested).

B. The pros do this drill in around 35 to 40 seconds. It is a speed drill to help build endurance, speed and stamina and requires both repetition and maximum effort by the players if it is to be effective. If the players are to improve, they must go all out.

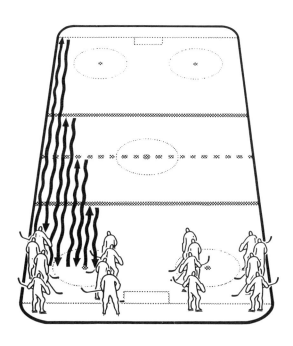

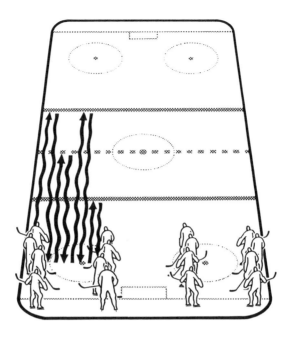

DRILL

1. The team is at one end of the rink and split into 4 units of 4 or 5 players.
2. At the coach's signal, the first unit starts out, skating two-thirds the length of the ice to the far blue line and back, to the red line and back, to the far blue line again and returning and finally, to the near blue line and back. The drill is executed without stopping.
3. When the first unit completes the exercise, the next unit goes out.
4. Each unit should repeat the exercise 3 times, resting as the rotation continues.

NOTES

A. The pros do this drill in around 30 to 35 seconds. It is a speed drill designed to build endurance, speed and stamina. In order to improve themselves, players should go all out, exerting maximum effort, in the exercise.
B. The coach may keep times on the drill, and challenge the players to better the last timing each time the drill is done in practice, probably once a week.

DRILL

1. The players are split into 4 groups and situated at one end of the ice at the goal line.
2. At the coach's signal, the first unit goes out and skates to the near blue line and back 3 times and finishes by skating to the far goal line and back. As 1 unit completes the exercise, the next unit starts out.
3. Each unit should repeat the drill 3 times in rotation.

NOTES

A. The coach may require the players to speed up in order to cut down the number of seconds used to complete the drill each time it is run in practice, possibly 1 time weekly.
B. The pros do this drill in around 25 to 30 seconds. It is a speed drill, and to be effective in building endurance, speed and stamina, it demands that the players go all out in a maximum effort.

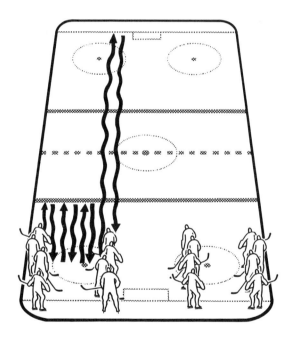

DRILL

1. Four "goals" are set up on each side of the rink in the 4 zones, as illustrated. The goals may be chairs, gloves, highway cones or boxes.

2. Players are situated on each goal, 3 on each side in the ends, 2 on each side in 1 zone in the middle and 1 on each side in the other middle zone.

3. This is a shinny type activity game which can be used as a warm-up exercise before practice. The object is to skate, stickhandle and pass in a confined area and to attempt to score by hitting the target set up as a goal. Players get practice in working in 3 on 3, 2 on 2 and 1 on 1 situations and in developing good puck control.

4. This game is an excellent activity for competition between lines and sets of defensemen. The coach may use it as a showdown competition, allowing the winners from each zone to play other winners to decide an overall winner for the day.

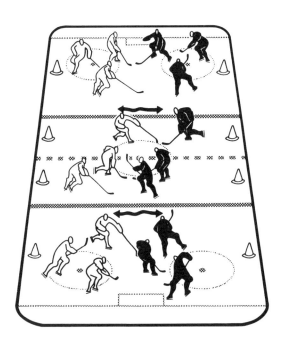

Thought Provokers

1. How much ice time do you ask of your players? Are you encouraging "one-hour" hockey players?
2. Goaltenders need to participate in skating drills as much as your skaters do.
3. High tempo skating drills keep players sharp and help develop an aggressive, quick and agile team.
4. Do you only emphasize forward skating?
5. How much emphasis do you place on backwards skating and lateral movement?
6. Do you organize your skating drills into the overall framework of practice in order to accomplish specific goals?
7. When you add pucks to a drill, see that the momentum of the exercise is maintained and does not slow down.
8. Skating drills can be overdone, but generally are underemphasized.
9. Are your skating drills competitive and challenging, or do the players find them predictable and monotonous?
10. Do you know how to condition and build endurance in your players through skating drills?
11. Do your players clearly understand what they are to do and why they are to do it before they begin a new drill?
12. What drills do you turn to to develop quickness and agility in your players?
13. A scrimmage should never displace skating drills in your overall practice program.
14. Consider having your players use weighted sticks in certain drills.
15. Consider using weighted belts or life-preserver-type vests on your players when they practice.

CHAPTER **3** *Passing, Shooting and Stickhandling*

With skating, the skills of passing, shooting and stickhandling comprise the basics of hockey. No hockey player ever reaches the point where he can say that he has completely mastered these skills. Mastery is a goal, and the struggle to achieve it, or even approach it, requires unflagging determination, constant practice and continual learning.

International competition on all levels of hockey has set a new standard of achievement in passing, shooting and stickhandling. International play is a classroom, as well as an occasion for competition and comparison. Teams and countries learn from one another, and there is no question that North American players can take their cue on the basics from the fleet, slick and smooth Europeans.

In many of the drills, I have stipulated that the players change sides of the ice halfway through an exercise. If the group starts on the right side, it should go over to the left side for the remainder of the drill. The reasoning behind this is that this system gives the players the opportunity to skate and attack from different sides and angles, to make cuts and dekes and turns, to give and receive passes from both sides—and from forehand to backhand positions—and to make different shots (wrist, snap, backhand and slap) from varying distances and angles.

In hockey, practice may not make perfect, but it offers the only route to approach perfection. The progressive and innovative coach will find in this chapter a great variety of shooting, passing and stickhandling drills—including a number of European exercises—that will make practice fun, challenging and productive.

Drills

1 ON 0 DRILL (1 pass, 1 shot)

1. Divide the team into 2 groups. Position groups in opposite corners of the rink.
2. At the coach's signal, 1 player from each end starts out carrying a puck. In the neutral zone, the players pass off, exchanging pucks, and then go in on the net for a shot on goal.
3. As the players skate in for the shot, the next pair of skaters start out, and so on.
4. Have the groups change to the opposite corners halfway through the drill.

VARIATION

The drill can be modified to utilize the four corners of the rink. The team is then divided into four groups. The first players in line in the right-hand corners start the drill. As they complete the passes, the first players in the left corners start out and the drill continues with the corner teams alternating.

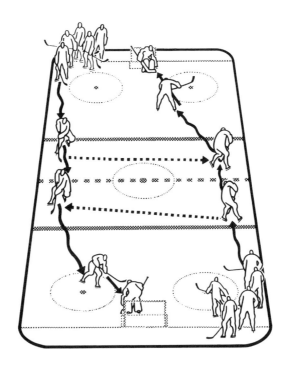

1 ON 0 DRILL (1 pass, 1 shot)

1. Players are split into 4 groups. Each group is positioned along the boards on each side at the blue line, as illustrated.
2. At the coach's signal, 1 skater breaks out at the blue line and, skating in the neutral zone, receives a pass from the first player in line on the other side of the ice in the same zone and skates in alone for a shot on the net.
3. The next player comes out from the group in the other zone diagonally across center ice. Rotation goes on in an X pattern, with players breaking out from the 4 corners of the neutral zone.
4. After taking the shot on goal, the player joins the group in that end which has the next skater starting out.
5. The coach may have the team go through the drill once or twice.

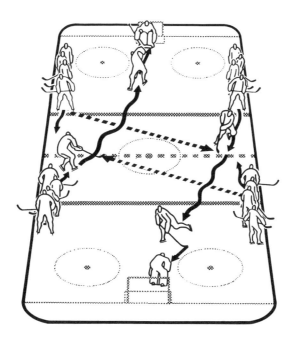

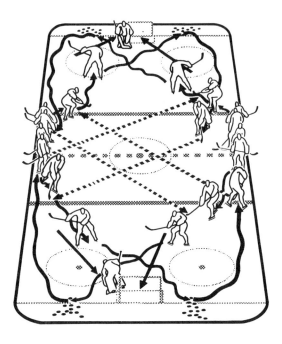

1 ON 0 DRILL (1 pass, 1 shot)

1. Split the team into 2 groups, with each group positioned in a line along the boards on either side of the neutral zone. Pucks are placed in the 4 corners of the rink.

2. The drill begins with 4 players, the first skaters in line facing each end zone, carrying a puck into the slot area and taking a shot on goal. They should start seconds apart in each zone, and work the puck so that they don't shoot at the goalie at the same time. After shooting, each skater goes into the corner opposite that from which he started, grabs a puck, carries it outside the zone and makes a diagonal pass to the player starting out from the line across the ice.

3. The drill continues as skaters start out, receive a diagonal pass across the neutral zone, stickhandle in for a shot on goal, take a puck and carry back and make a pass to the next skater. Timing is important in this drill, as skaters have to follow the pattern, watching the other player in his zone as they stickhandle, shoot and pass. As players become familiar with the drill, have them pick up the tempo.

1 ON 0 DRILL (6 passes, 1 shot)

1. Players are located along the side boards on one side of the neutral zone. Two defensemen are situated behind the goal line in one end of the rink, and another pair of players is placed in the neutral zone, as diagrammed.

2. The drill begins with a forward skating with a puck into the zone and passing to the defenseman on that side. He, in turn, passes to his defensive partner behind the goal line while the skater makes a swing on that side. That same defense behind the goal line passes to moving player, who goes into the neutral zone and passes to the designated receiver located outside the blue line. That player makes a diagonal pass to the player located at the other blue line, but opposite side of him. He then makes a return pass to the player that started the play at the other end of the rink and now is breaking in the middle for a shot on goal, before returning to his original position.

3. Have the forwards change sides of the ice halfway through the drill.

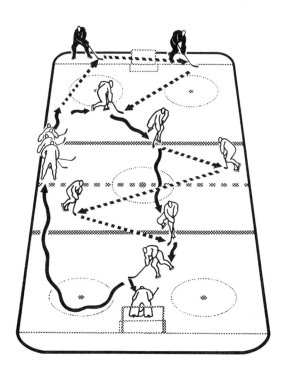

1 ON 0 DRILL (5 passes, 1 shot)

1. Divide the players into 2 groups with a group in one corner of the rink and the other unit along the opposite side boards in the neutral zone.

2. A player from the corner starts the exercise by carrying the puck behind the net. At the same time, a player by the boards starts skating along the boards into the zone. He cuts to the middle, as illustrated, to take a pass from the player behind the net, then quickly makes a return (drop) pass and breaks toward center ice. In the middle, the skater receives a second pass from the corner and before going in for a shot on goal, the player makes a pass to a player coming back from a shot on goal on the opposite side of where the play started (see diagram). The player behind the goal should move around the corner as he passes, receives and passes again.

3. As the player goes in for a shot on goal, the next pair comes out to go through the drill.

4. Have both units change sides of the ice halfway through the drill.

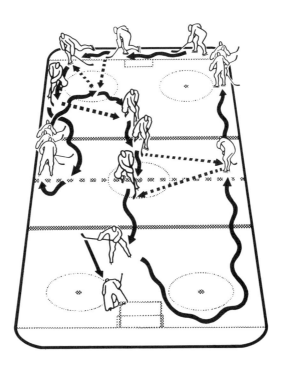

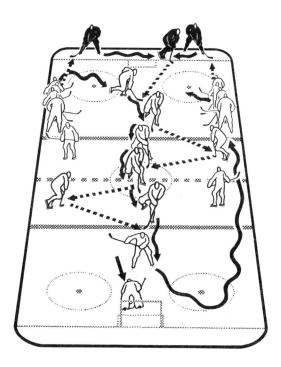

1 ON 0 DRILL (6 passes, 1 shot)

1. Players make a line along each board at the blue line at one end of
the rink. Six players take up positions: (1) two in the corner behind the
goal line, (2) two more along the boards on the opposite side of the
neutral zone, and (3) two more opposite the two in the neutral zone. (See
diagram.)

2. At the coach's signal, the first player in line passes a puck to the
player behind the goal line, who carries the puck behind the net as
the player who made the pass swings in front of the net. As he makes the
swing, he gets the puck back from the player behind the net, and passes
it to one of the players by the boards in the neutral zone. Still skating,
the player gets a return pass, makes a swing toward center ice, passes to
the player located opposite side diagonally of the one where the previous pass was made, then takes a return pass, and goes in for a shot on
the net. After making the play, the skater returns to the group in the
other end, as the drill continues (see diagram).

3. The next play starts from the other side of where the previous one
started and the execution of the drill is the opposite way of the previous
play ahead as the drill continues.

1 ON 0 DRILL (short passes, 1 shot)

1. The players form 2 groups, which take up positions in diagonal corners of the rink. One defenseman from each group is situated in the circle by the players in each end.

2. The drill begins with the first players in line in each corner skating down the ice and making a swing in the other end. As they make the swing, they each take a pass from the defenseman in the circle. At the same time as the pass is made, a player at the boards in each corner starts out down the ice, and the pairs on either side of the rink make short passes back and forth as they skate to the other zone. As they come into the end, the players who take the passes from the defense initially, and who are in the middle, take a shot on goal.

3. After making the play, the players skate to the end of the line in the corner where they finish as the drill continues. This exercise should be run at a brisk tempo so that it works the players on crisp pass execution on the move, as well as timing.

4. Have the groups change sides of the rink halfway through the drill, and have 2 players who have skated relieve the passers in the circles.

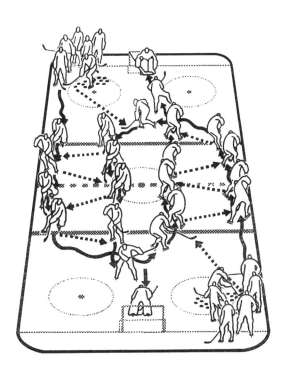

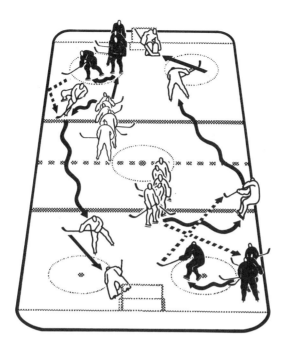

1 ON 0 DRILL (2 passes, 1 shot)

1. The forwards form 2 groups at center ice, with each group facing one end of the rink. The defensemen are situated in each end zone, as diagrammed. On one side, the defense are near the side boards and in the other end they are inside the faceoff circle near the slot.

2. The drills are run simultaneously on each side with the same pattern, but slightly different positioning. The player at the head of the line passes to a defenseman, who moves laterally with the puck until the forward has made his swing and is ready to receive a return pass from the defense and skate into the zone for a shot on goal. After shooting, forwards return to center ice. On the side where the defensemen are located on the side of the slot, the passes to the forwards can be banked off the boards.

3. Have the forwards and defensemen change sides halfway through the drill.

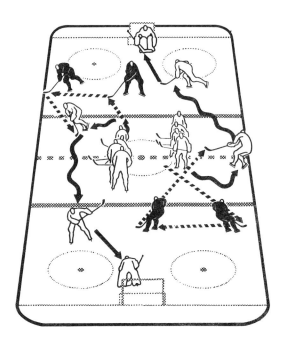

1 ON 0 DRILL (3 passes, 1 shot)

1. Put the forwards at center ice in 2 lines, with a line facing each end zone. Two defensemen are situated in each end zone just inside the blue line.

2. The drill starts on each side of the rink at the same time; each forward has a puck. On one side, the forward skates ahead and passes to the defensemen in front of him and makes a swing toward the boards. The defense passes to his partner, who returns the puck to the skater in the neutral zone. The puck carrier goes into the zone for a shot on goal and returns to his group at center ice. The first player on the other side passes from standing position to the defenseman on the side, who gives the puck to the defenseman in the middle. After passing, the forward starts out, swinging across to the boards, where he gets the puck from the second defense and breaks for a shot on the net.

3. Groups may switch patterns after a certain period of time, and should switch sides halfway through the exercise.

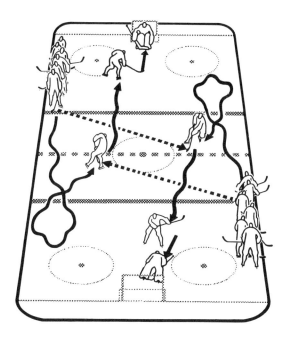

1 ON 0 DRILL (1 pass, 1 shot)

1. Divide the team into units situated along the side boards at the blue lines on opposite sides of the rink, as shown. Both groups face center ice.

2. At the coach's signal, 1 player from one side skates into the opposite zone, makes a swing to the outside, and breaks toward the middle. As he approaches the red line, he receives a pass from the player in line on the other side of the ice and goes in on the net for a shot.

3. After taking the shot, the player returns to the group from which he started as the next player begins the pattern.

VARIATIONS

A. The coach can have 1 player from each side starting out at the same time, following the pattern outlined above.

B. The drill may also be run as a rotation exercise, with 1 player from each group going out at a time, and play rotating from group to group until everyone has participated.

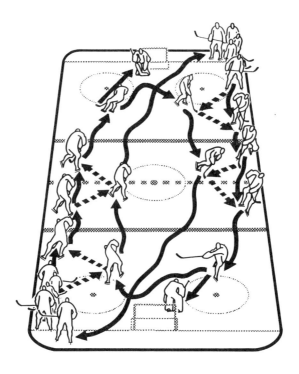

1 ON 0 DRILL (4 passes, 1 shot)

1. The team splits into 2 groups and each group takes up a position along the boards in 1 corner of the rink, as illustrated. Two players from each group take up positions in the middle, 1 in the slot area and 1 inside the red line in the neutral zone.

2. At the coach's signal, the first player in line at each corner skates out, carrying a puck, and passes to the player in the slot area. The puck is returned from the slot and the player makes a second pass to the player located in the middle in the neutral zone. After the puck is returned, the skater goes in on the net for a shot on goal.

After the shot is taken, the shooter goes to replace the player in the slot, who moves to the spot in the neutral zone. The player who was in the neutral zone goes to the end of the line.

This rotation continues throughout the drill. Players must move quickly in order to be in position to receive and make passes as pairs come out from the corners.

3. Players in both groups in the corners should switch to the opposite side of the ice halfway through the drill.

1 ON 0 DRILL (4 passes, 1 shot)

1. Divide the players into 2 groups and situate the groups by the boards in opposite corners of the rink.
2. Two players from each group are positioned along the boards, 1 midway in the defensive zone and 1 in the neutral zone, as illustrated.
3. In turn, players in each end skate around their net, pick up a puck, pass to the teammate in the defensive zone, get a pass back, pass to the teammate in the neutral zone, get the pass back and go in for a shot on goal.
4. Players should keep skating as they make and receive passes.
5. Switch players to the other side of the ice halfway through the drill and make substitutions in the stationary players.

VARIATIONS

A. After the player has taken his shot, he goes to replace the player along the boards in the defensive zone. After taking a pass and making a pass in this position, he moves to the neutral zone to replace the player there. After taking and making a pass in the center he goes to the end of the line. Everyone rotates positions in this manner throughout the drill.
B. The coach may have only 1 player along the boards, or may have 2 as shown in the diagram, or even 3 players ready to receive and make passes from the boards.

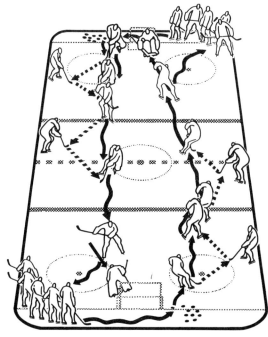

1 ON 0 DRILL (pass from corner, 1 shot)

1. Divide the team into 2 groups, with each group situated in a line along the boards in the neutral zone, as illustrated.

2. One player from each group is located in the corner with a quantity of pucks.

3. The drill begins with 1 player from each side of the rink skating into the slot of the zone he is facing, taking a pass from the corner, and skating into the opposite zone for a shot on goal. After shooting, the skater goes into the corner, and makes the pass to the next player coming into the slot. He then goes to the end of the line that he came from.

4. Allow each player to take his shot on goal and get to the corner before the next skater goes out.

5. Halfway through the drill, switch the pucks and passers to the opposite side of the rink.

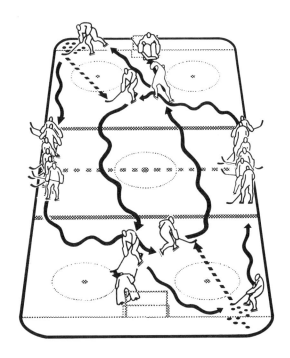

1 ON 0 DRILL (pass from corner, 1 shot)

1. Divide the team into 2 groups with each group lining up along the boards in zones on opposite sides of the rink (see diagram).
2. Have 1 player from each group (usually a defenseman) situated in the corner of the same zone with a quantity of pucks.
3. The drill begins when the first player in line in each group skates to center ice at the coach's signal. There he takes a pass from the corner, makes a swing toward his zone and skates into the far zone for a shot on goal. As he moves out of the neutral zone, the next player in line goes, and the drill continues.
4. Switch the pucks and passers to the other side of the rink halfway through the drill. Make substitutions in passers at the same time.

VARIATION

After the player takes the shot on goal, he can go to the corner to replace the passer instead of going back to the end of the line. When he makes the pass to the next skater, he then returns to the line.

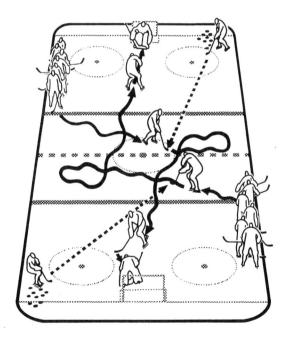

1 ON 0 DRILL (pass from side, 1 shot)

1. Divide the team into two groups. Each group takes a zone and lines up along the boards at the blue line on opposite sides of the ice.
2. The first player in each line skates to the far blue line, makes a swing to the middle and takes a pass from the first player in the line at the boards on the opposite side. He then skates back into his zone for a shot on the goalie (wrist, slap, snap or backhand shot).
3. Switch players to the other side of the ice halfway through the drill and simply reverse the skating pattern.

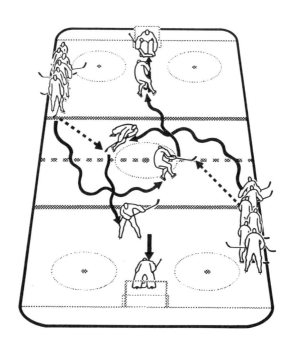

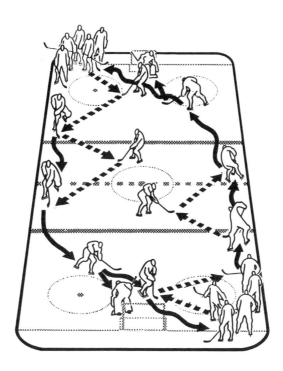

1 ON 0 DRILL (4 passes, 1 shot)

1. Team is split into 2 groups and players take up positions along the boards in opposite corners of the rink.

2. Two players from each group are stationed in the middle, 1 in front of the net and 1 over the near blue line, to receive and make passes.

3. The drill begins with 1 player from each end skating along the boards, passing to the player in the middle, getting the puck back and skating into the zone for a shot on goal. After taking the shot, the players stop in front of the net, receive a pass from the corner, and then pass to the skater breaking out from the line along the boards.

4. After passing off to the skater just beginning the drill, the player goes into the corner to get a puck and makes a pass to the following player who is coming in for a shot on goal and who stops in front of the net to take the pass.

5. Move both groups to the opposite ends of the ice halfway through the drill.

1 ON 0 DRILL (2 passes, 1 shot with backchecker)

1. Divide the team into 2 groups and set up the groups in opposite corners of the rink. One player from each group takes up a position in the slot inside the blue line.

2. At the coach's signal, 1 player from each corner passes to the stationary teammate in the middle, skates forward to receive a return pass and goes into the far zone for a shot on goal. At this point, he becomes the backchecker for the next player starting out on that end, and backchecking, returns to his original position.

3. Only 1 player from each end goes at one time, starting the drill when the player he follows has taken his shot.

4. Groups should change sides of the rink halfway through the drill; substitute passers.

VARIATIONS

A. Two players from each end start out at the same time. The outside player carries the puck, makes a pass to the stationary player in the slot, receives a return pass and goes in for a shot on goal. The inside skater is the backchecker who covers his partner without interfering with the progress of the drill.

B. On the second run-through, the outside and inside skaters switch positions so that the former puck carrier becomes the backchecker and the former backchecker carries the puck.

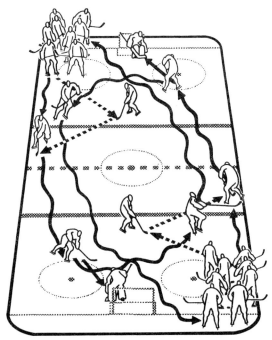

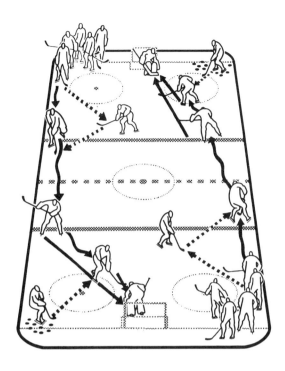

1 ON 0 DRILL (3 passes, 2 shots)

1. Team is split into 2 groups; each group is situated in opposite corners of the rink.

2. Two players from each group are located as indicated on the diagram: 1 player at the blue line to receive and return a pass and 1 player in the corner to pass to players skating into the zone.

3. At the signal, players from both corners pass to the teammate in the slot, skate down the ice as they receive the pass from the slot. At the blue line, they take a slap shot on goal and keep skating until they receive a pass from the corner, which they shoot at the goal with a wrist, snap or backhand shot.

4. After taking the second shot, players take the corner positions, make the passes to the following skaters, and then go to the end of the line to repeat the drill.

5. Switch sides of the ice halfway through the drill.

VARIATION

Instead of having each player making the pass from the corner in rotation, use 1 player in each corner throughout the drill. They may be replaced by 2 other passers halfway through the drill.

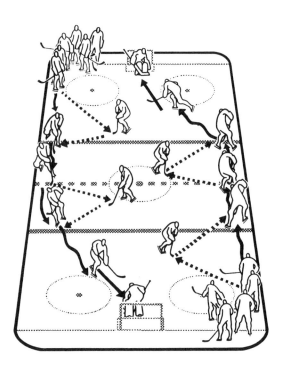

1 ON 0 DRILL (4 passes, 1 shot)

1. Team is divided into 2 groups with the groups situated by the boards in opposite corners of the rink.

2. Two players from each group are located in the middle: 1 inside the near blue line and 1 just beyond the red line. The stationary players face the group skating towards them.

3. At the coach's signal, the first skater in each group carries a puck along the boards, passes to the stationary player in the zone, gets the puck back as he crosses the blue line, passes to the other stationary player, gets it back and goes in for a shot on the goal.

4. Players in both groups should switch to the opposite side of the ice halfway through the drill.

1 ON 0 DRILL (4 passes, 1 shot)

1. Divide the players into 2 groups; groups take positions on either side of the center circle facing opposite ends of the rink.

2. One player from each group stations himself inside the faceoff circle ahead, as shown.

3. The drill begins when the first player in each line at mid-ice passes his puck to the player in the faceoff circle. When the pass is completed, the skater goes into the zone, skates around the faceoff circle and catches a return pass from the player in the circle as he approaches the blue line. The player then passes to the second player in line at mid-ice, gets it back, and goes in on the net for a shot on goal.

4. After taking the shot, the player goes back to take the place of the player in the faceoff circle nearest the goal. After he receives and makes a pass to the next skater, he joins the line opposite that from which he started.

5. Change sides of the ice halfway through the drill.

NOTE

The drill demands concentration from everyone on the ice. At the same time, it keeps everyone busy and involved in what is going on.

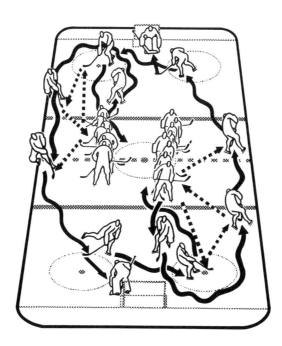

1 ON 0 DRILL (1 pass, 1 shot)

1. Split the team into 2 groups and put a group on each side of the rink at the blue line along the boards.
2. At the coach's signal, the first player in line in each group starts out carrying a puck. They make a swing in the neutral zone exchanging passes across the center faceoff circle and proceed into their own zones for a shot on goal.
3. After taking the shot, players go back to the groups from which they started as the next players go out.

NOTE

Have the lines change sides of the ice halfway through the exercise.

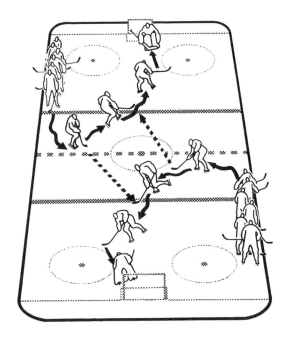

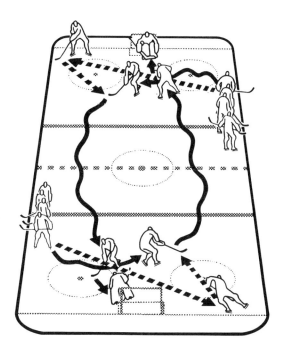

1 ON 0 DRILL (2 passes, 1 shot)

1. Divide the players into groups and situate each group along the side boards near the blue lines facing opposite ends, as shown. One player from each group goes to the corner across the ice from the skaters.
2. The drill starts with 1 player from each side making a pass to the player in the corner as they start a swing toward the slot area of the zone. As the player makes his swing, he receives a return pass from the player in the corner and skates on into the opposing zone for a shot on goal.
3. After taking the shot, each player returns to the side from which he started.

NOTE

Halfway through the drill, have the groups change sides of the ice in the same zone.

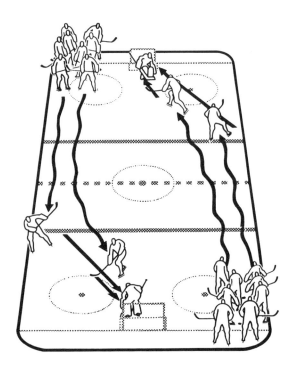

2 ON 0 DRILL (2 shots)

1. Divide the team into 2 groups and situate each group in opposite corners of the rink.
2. At the coach's signal, 2 players from each corner start out carrying pucks. They skate down the ice side by side, about 10 feet apart.
3. The outside player of each pair shoots a slap shot on the goal from the blue line; the inside player shoots the wrist shot from the slot.
4. As the first skaters cross the blue lines into the offensive zones, the next pairs start out, and so on.
5. On the second run-through, have the players change inside–outside positions so that those who did the slap shot the first time will take the wrist shot and vice versa.
6. Switch the players to the other corner of the rink halfway through the drill.

2 ON 0 DRILL (wide passes, 1 shot)

1. The team goes into 4 units, and each unit is situated along the boards at the blue line facing center ice, as shown.

2. The drill begins at the coach's signal with the first 2 players in line on one end skating out together. As they go down their sides, they pass the puck back and forth across the ice. When they reach the top of the faceoff circles, the player who is in control of the puck takes a shot on goal. After completing the exercise, they skate to the end of the lines on that end of the ice where they finish, as the next set of players go out.

3. The play switches from one end to the other and continues until everyone has participated. This is a fast tempo passing drill, so everyone should be sharp in passing and shooting, and then getting out of the way for the next set of players.

NOTE

This is also a good exercise for the goaltenders on each end in that it gives them work in cutting down their angles on shots from the circles.

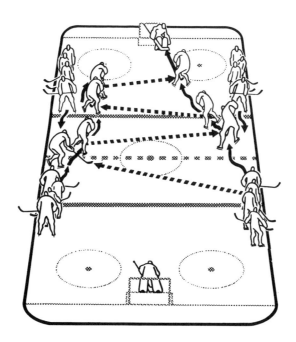

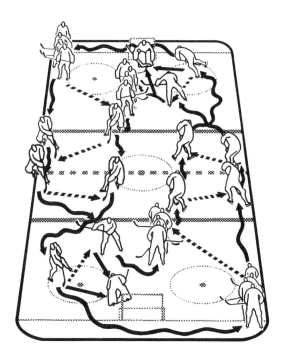

2 ON 0 DRILL (drop pass, 1 shot)

1. Divide the team into 4 groups. Situate 2 groups by the boards in opposite corners of the rink; put the remaining 2 groups in the slots, as indicated on the diagram.

2. The first player in each group along the boards passes a puck to the first skater in line in the slot. The two skate down the ice 2 on 0, passing the puck once or twice (at the coach's instruction) in the neutral zone.

3. At the far blue line, the skaters cross paths. The puck carrier then either drops the puck to his teammate, who takes a shot on the net, or he moves in to take the shot himself.

4. The player who does not shoot goes to the net for the rebound.

5. While drop passing is the key to this drill, if the players are not in position for the drop, the puck carrier should fake a drop pass and shoot rather than disrupt the drill.

6. Change sides of the ice halfway through the drill.

7. Since this is a drop pass drill, the shooter, after taking the shot, usually goes to the slot area and the player looking for the rebound goes to the corner. This way, on one side the player is the shooter and on the other side goes for the rebound.

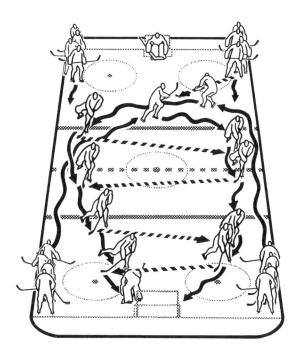

2 ON 0 DRILL (passing)

1. Split the team into 4 groups and situate each group in one corner of the rink, as illustrated.

2. The drill starts at one end as 1 player from each corner skates along the boards. After they cross the far blue line, the skaters switch side each other. As the outside skater is making the swing, he receives a pass from the first player in line at the near corner. They return skating 2 on 0, passing the puck back and forth and conclude with a shot on goal and a return to position. The next pair of players start from the other end when the shot has been taken.

VARIATION

Leave a quantity of pucks at each blue line, and have the players grab a puck as they skate by instead of receiving a pass.

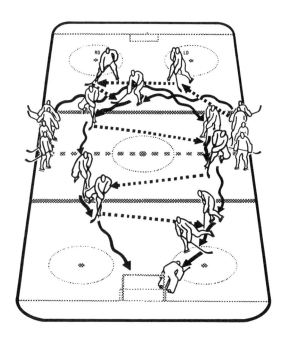

2 ON 0 DRILL (breakout pass situation with 2 defense inside the defensive zone)

1. Players are divided and grouped along the boards on each side of the ice in the neutral zone, as shown. Two defensemen are situated at the top of the circles in the defensive zone facing the skaters.
2. The drill starts with a player on one side in the neutral zone passing to the defense on his side of the ice in the defensive zone. As the defense passes to his partner, the 2 forwards start out and make a swing to the opposite side of the ice. The second defense returns the puck to the player who made the initial pass as he makes his swing across the middle. The forwards rush 2 on 0 against the goalie, moving the puck back and forth and setting up a play for a shot on the net.
3. After taking the shot, the forwards go to the ends of the lines from which they started as a new pair of players start out.
4. The starting pass should alternate from one side of the ice to the other, so that passes are made from left to right defense and then from right to left defense.

VARIATION

Put 1 or 2 defense against the 2 forwards as they come in for a shot on goal.

2 ON 0 DRILL

1. The team is at one end of the rink with half of the players along the boards on one side and the other half in line along the boards on the opposite side.

2. To start the drill, a player comes out from each corner towards the middle. One player carries a puck. As the players skate down the ice 2 on 0, they make short passes back and forth between them and take a shot on the net.

3. After the shot is taken, both players make a short swing to the outside. One player grabs a puck in the corner, and as they skate along the side, they make wide passes back and forth before taking a second shot on goal as they return to their original positions.

4. The next pair of skaters comes out as the pair in front of them begins the return skate.

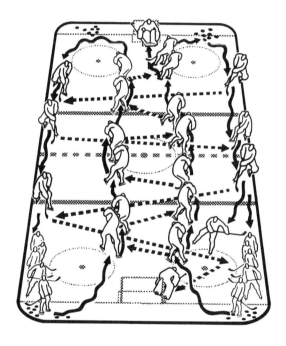

2 ON 0 DRILL (breakout pass situation from defense inside of his defensive zone)

1. The team is split into 2 groups with 1 group located on each side along the boards in the neutral zone. One defenseman takes up position at the top of the circle in the zone facing the lines of forwards, as shown.
2. To start the drill, the first player in line on one side passes to the defenseman on his side in the defensive zone. After passing, he and the forward on the other side start out and make a swing to the opposite side of the ice. As the forward from the other side comes by, the defense passes to him. The forwards move the puck between them as they go 2 on 0 against the goaltender.
3. After the play is completed, the skaters return to the ends of the lines from which they started and the next pair of players come out.
4. The defensemen should rotate passing position. The left defense should pass from the left side and the right defense from the right side of the zone.

VARIATION

Put 1 or 2 defense against the 2 forwards as they come in for a shot on goal.

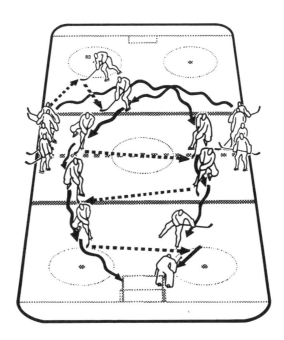

3 ON 0 DRILL (passing)

1. Divide the players and situate them in 2 groups at the ends of the ice, as diagramed.

2. At the coach's signal, 3 players from one end start out. Two players skate along the boards, the puck carrier makes the swing around the net to center ice. They skate the length of the ice, passing the puck between them as many times as possible and conclude with a shot on the net. At that point, they join the skaters on that end of the ice, as the next line starts out. Alternate ends of the ice.

3. If the coach desires, the line may return to the end of the ice it started from. In this case, the line will skate the length of the ice twice (or more), passing 3 on 0 before the next line goes on.

VARIATIONS

A. If each line makes 2 rushes at once, you may want them to form a 2 on 1 situation on the second rush using 1 forward as a defenseman.

B. You may want to do the same thing for a 2 on 0 situation under this arrangement. You will have a 2 on 0 situation going one way and 1 on 1 situation coming back the other way.

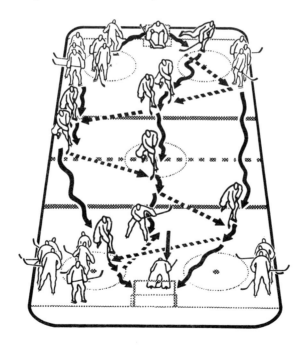

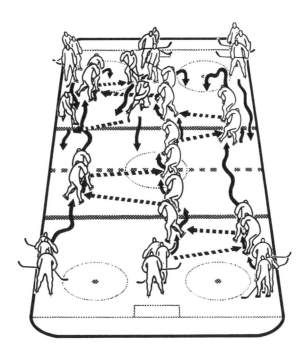

3 ON 0 DRILL (passing with 3 backcheckers)

1. Divide the players into 2 groups and split each group into 3 units as shown on the diagram.

2. A unit of 3 players (or a line) will start at one end at the coach's signal and will skate the length of the ice while passing the puck among themselves.

3. When they arrive at the other end, a new unit of 3 players (or a line) takes over the puck and will start skating down the ice passing the puck back and forth. The unit that has just completed this portion of the drill will turn and go back down the ice backchecking the new passing unit and then return to their original position as the passers become backcheckers for the next line. The rotation continues until everyone has had a turn passing and backchecking.

4. The coach may repeat the drill as many times as he wishes.

3 ON 0 DRILL (breakout pass situation with 2 defense inside the defensive zone)

1. Divide the players and situate 1 group on each side of the ice along the boards in the neutral zone. One defenseman is positioned at the top of each faceoff circle in the defensive zone, as illustrated.
2. The play begins as a wing on one side in the neutral zone passes to the defense on the side in the defensive zone. As he makes the pass, a center comes out to the middle and forwards on both sides start out. The wing who started the play makes a swing to the middle and as he does so, takes a pass from the defense, who has received the puck from his partner. The far winger stays on his side, while the center moves to the side left vacated by the wing who has swung to the middle for the pass from the defense.

The forwards make a 3 on 0 rush against the goalie while passing the puck back and forth. After taking a shot on the net, the forwards return to the ends of the lines from which they started.
3. The drill continues as the forward on the other side of the ice starts the play with a pass to the defense. Wingers should alternate the pass to the defense from one side of the ice to the other throughout the exercise. After a time, replace the defense with another pair of defensemen.

VARIATION

Put 1 or 2 defensemen against the 3 forwards coming in for a shot on goal, thus creating a 3 on 1 or 3 on 2 situation.

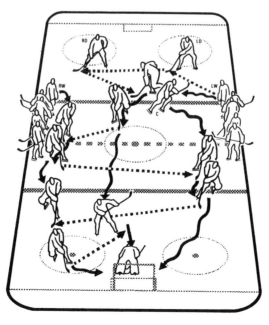

3 ON 0 DRILL (passing, pass from corner)

1. Split the team into 2 groups and situate groups in opposite corners of the ice.
2. At the coach's signal, 1 unit (or line) of 3 skaters starts from one end. The players skate to the far blue line, where 1 of the skaters receives a pass from the opposite corner. The skaters swing back and return to their zone passing the puck between them and finishing with a shot on goal. They return to their original positions as the next line comes out from the other end.
3. Switch the groups of players to the other side of the ice halfway through the drill.

VARIATION

Leave the pucks at the blue lines and have the players take a puck when they skate by to the far blue line instead of receiving a pass from the corner.

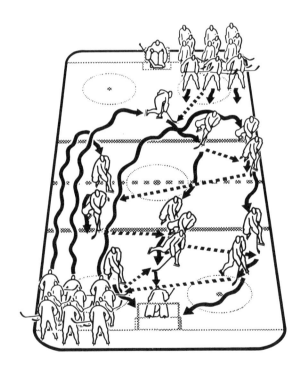

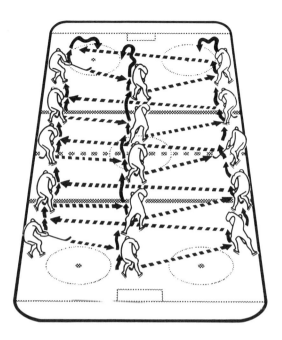

3 ON 0 DRILL (passing with 1, 2, 3 pucks)

1. Team is divided and a group is situated at each end of the ice.
2. One unit of 3 players (or a line) starts from one end and skates the length of the ice 3 on 0, passing the puck between them. At the goal, the players turn and continue skating and passing until they return to their original position.
3. When 1 line completes the drill, 3 players from the opposite end of the ice start the drill. Alternate ends until everyone has participated.
4. Repeat the drill using 2 pucks, then 3 pucks.
5. The diagram indicates the passing pattern, which could be used with 3 pucks.

3 ON 0 DRILL (passing, weaving)

1. The team is divided into 2 groups. Each group is situated at one end of the ice in 3 skating units.

2. At the coach's signal, 3 players start out from one end and go the length of the ice and back to position moving the puck between them while crossing paths.

3. In this drill, the plan is to give the puck to the player cutting in front of the passer. It is a give-and-take drill.

4. When the first line returns to its zone, the second group starts out from the other end, and so on.

5. Drill may be repeated, and positions in each end may be switched.

4 ON 0 DRILL (passing)

1. Divide the team into groups at each end of the ice. Situate the forwards and defensemen as shown on the diagram.

2. At the coach's signal, the drill starts from the corner or behind the net, when 1 defenseman passes to a forward, then joins the forwards in skating down the ice, passing the puck and setting up a shot on goal.

3. The players can end the drill after skating 1 length of the ice and taking the shot, or can return to position by continuing the passing exchange and taking another shot on goal.

4. When the first unit has completed the drill, whether it is skating, 1, 2 or more lengths of the ice, the first unit on the other end of the ice begins, and so on.

VARIATION

All of the players can be situated at one end of the ice, rather than in 2 groups alternating turns.

NOTE

All 4 players should have touched the puck before the shot is taken on goal on this drill. This means there should be at least 4 passes.

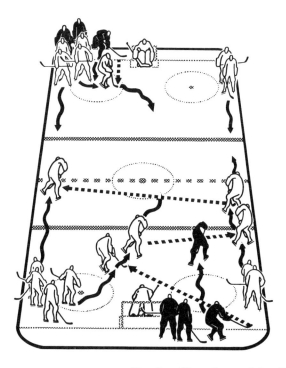

5 ON 0 DRILL (passing)

1. Split the team into 2 groups with 1 group set up at each end of the rink.

2. At the coach's signal, 3 forwards and 2 defensemen from one end start out with a puck, passing the puck between them as they skate the length of the ice and set up a shot on goal.

3. Passes, as indicated on the diagram, can go either clockwise or counterclockwise and should involve all 5 skaters.

4. As the first group finishes with a shot on goal, the next unit of 5 starts out from the opposite end of the ice.

VARIATIONS

A. Have all of the players grouped on one end of the ice.

B. Have each unit of 5 skate and pass 1, 2, 3 or 4 lengths of the ice.

C. Add up to 4 pucks to the drill. As pucks are added, the drill becomes more difficult to execute.

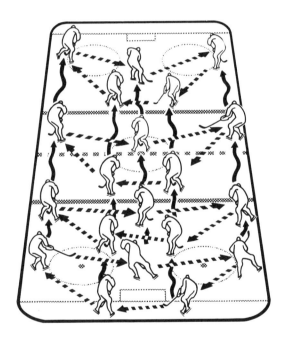

Thought Provokers

1. Lessons in the hockey basics are learned and polished in practice sessions, then put into practice in scrimmages and games. Game situations are a time for execution rather than instruction.
2. Quick tempo drills help develop quickness, agility and timing.
3. Does your stock of passing and stickhandling drills need replenishing? Variety does add spice to practices and helps keep players sharp.
4. Consider having your players use weighted sticks or pucks in certain drills.
5. An objective look at your players in the game situation should give you clues as to which areas need emphasis in practice.
6. Passing, shooting and stickhandling drills can come into play in improving other aspects of the game, such as breakouts, power play and penalty killing.
7. Do you make use of one end of the rink or do you utilize both ends in practice?
8. Do you make sure your players have a chance to practice their forehand, backhand, snap and flip passes in their daily workouts?
9. Do you generally use the same shooting drills? If so, are they effective in developing the players' skill in a variety of shots (wrist, snap, backhand, forehand and slap)?
10. Don't fall into the habit of working passing and shooting drills from the same corner. Switch corners halfway through the drill.

CHAPTER 4 *The Positional Game*

Over a long season, positional play drills become the most important element in daily practice sessions. Positional play exercises give the individual—forward or defenseman—an opportunity to work on the fundamental game skills of offensive and defensive maneuvers. Everyone on the team must learn to move the puck properly offensively and to contain the puck carrier defensively. And whether the drill is an individual exercise or a team drill—working with a defensive partner or a line mate or line—the goal is mastery of defensive and offensive maneuvers.

This chapter offers ideas for improving the basic skills that are required of a player, set of players, line or a unit of 5 players, in the execution of offensive and defensive maneuvers in different situations.

Individual maneuvers for the offense bring into play, and develop, the player's skating agility, quickness, drive, strength, finesse, timing, aggressiveness and hockey sense. For the defense, the emphasis is on checking ability and blocking shots, which require quickness, mobility, good positioning, strength, timing, instinct and aggressiveness.

In most team offensive situations, the rule is to pass the puck—the "give and go" approach. In other words, make the pass before you get into trouble and not when you are in trouble. The player or players without the puck should always move into an open area so that the puck carrier can execute the play, rather than leaving it all up to the puck carrier. There are special situations offensively when you outnumber the opposition, as in 2 on 1, 3 on 1, 3 on 2, 4 on 3, 5 on 4 or 5 on 3 situations. Here you have to rely on proper execution of team play in order to take advantage of the situation and capitalize on it for goals.

In most team defensive situations, the rule is to pressure the puck carrier at all times. One defense should take the body, while the player closest to that play is the backup who will pick up the puck and regain control of the play. In defensive situations when you are outnumbered by the opponent (e.g., 2 on 1, 3 on 1, 4 on 3, 5 on 4 or 5 on 3), you have to rely on playing the zone rather than falling back on the 1 on 1 approach where the idea is to keep the play to the outside until help arrives.

In every situation, the key to success is teamwork. This comes through (1) awareness of each situation, (2) knowledge of what is required by every member of the team and (3) the ability to execute the proper maneuvers.

Drills—Individual Maneuvers

DRILL 1 (1 on 1 situation—full ice)

1. Split the forwards into 4 groups and have each group line up along the boards by the circle in each corner of the rink, as shown.
2. The defense is divided and lined up on either side of the ice in the neutral zone.
3. A player starts from one corner, takes a pass from the first player in line on the opposite side of the ice and goes up against a defenseman who has moved to the center to challenge the puck carrier.
4. After the first player has taken a shot on goal or been taken out of the play, the next player comes from the other end for the next 1 on 1 exercise. Skaters alternate ends, and defensemen alternate at center ice.

VARIATION

Defensemen go through the drill without sticks, or turn their sticks upside down.

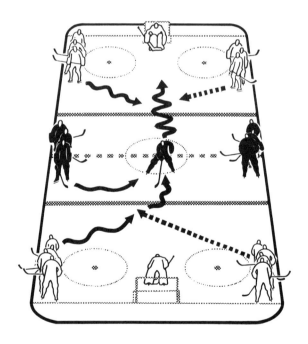

DRILL 2 (1 on 1 situation)

1. Players are grouped along the boards in the four corners of the rink. Groups on each side go through the drill simultaneously using half of the ice.

2. The first 2 players in line in opposite corners of the ice start out simultaneously with pucks, carry them to the red line, stop and pass the pucks to the players facing them in the corner on the same side. They then skate backward, playing a defensive role as the new puck carrier starts out.

3. At the completion of the play, the skaters switch starting ends so that the defense moves to the end of the line of forwards and the offensive player changes to defense the next time around.

4. Halfway through the drill, have the ends change roles, that is, the defensive line becomes the offense and the offensive group becomes the defense and initiates the drill.

VARIATION

Instead of having the two sides go through the drill at the same time, have the sides alternate.

DRILL 3 (1 on 1 situation—2 passes to defense)

1. Divide the forwards and situate them along the boards in opposite corners of the rink, as diagramed. The defense is split along the boards at center ice.

2. Play begins in one corner as the first forward in line starts out with a puck and passes to a defenseman waiting at the blue line. The defenseman skates backward, handling the puck, and passes back to the forward coming at him. This time the forward attempts to go around the defense for a shot on goal.

3. After the play is completed, the first forward in line on the other side starts out, and the sides alternate. The drill can be run simultaneously from both sides also.

4. Have the players change sides of the ice halfway through the drill.

DRILL 4 (1 on 1 situation with a pass to the defense)

1. Divide the forwards and situate the groups along the boards in opposite corners of the rink. Defensemen are situated at center ice, as diagramed, and are prepared to receive and return passes and to move on an alternating basis into the zone to challenge attacking players 1 on 1.
2. The drill begins when the first player in line in one corner starts out with a puck. He passes to a defenseman in the middle, gets it back from him in the neutral zone, and then goes against a defenseman waiting for him in the slot area and attempts to get a shot on goal.
3. When the exercise is completed, play moves to the other side of the ice, and sides alternate thereafter. The drill can be run simultaneously from both sides also.
4. Change lines to the opposite side of the ice halfway through the drill.

DRILL 5 (1 on 1 situation)

1. Team is split into 2 groups, which are situated in opposite corners of the ice. Groups form 2 lines in each corner; each pairing should include a forward and a defenseman, as indicated.
2. The drill begins at one end as the first pair of skaters come out. As they circle at the far blue line to come back, the forward takes a pass from the corner at that end, and goes against his defensive partner, attempting to get a shot on goal.
3. The next pair of skaters come from the opposite end of the ice, and the drill continues alternating ends.
4. On the second run-through, the partners exchange roles, with the forward going to defense and the defenseman becoming the puck carrier.
5. Have the groups change sides of the ice halfway through the drill.

VARIATIONS

A. The defensemen can execute the drill without sticks or with their sticks turned upside down.
B. Instead of having a pass from the corner, leave a quantity of pucks at the blue line and have the forwards pick up a puck as they come back.

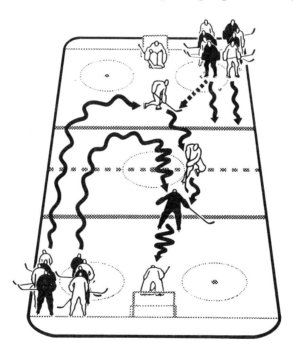

DRILL 6 (1 on 1 situation)

1. Divide the forwards and situate them along the boards in opposite corners of the rink. The defense is split into 2 groups at center ice, with each group facing a forward unit in the corner.
2. A forward from each group starts the drill by making a pass to a player located in the slot area, then receiving a return pass as he skates down the side. Moving into the neutral zone, the forward goes against a waiting defenseman, who will try to contain the forward to the outside, with or without interfering with the puck carrier.
3. Halfway through the drill, have the groups change sides of the ice.

VARIATION

Defensemen can execute the drill with or without sticks, or with their sticks turned upside down.

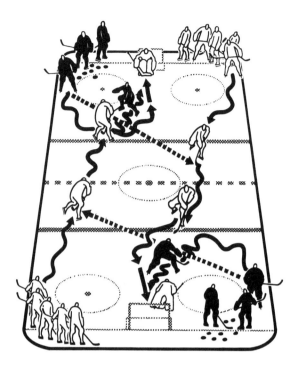

DRILL 7 (1 on 1 situation)

1. Divide the forwards and situate them in groups along the boards in opposite corners of the rink. The defensemen are split into 2 units and situated in the corners across from the forwards.

2. The exercise starts with a defenseman starting out with a puck from each corner and making a pass to the forward skating across from him. After passing, the defense positions himself to try to contain the puck carrier coming at him from the other end for a shot on goal.

3. After finishing the play, the defense returns to his original group in the corner, while the forward joins the group in the end where he finished.

4. Halfway through the exercise, have the forwards and defense change sides of the ice in the same end.

DRILL 8 (1 on 1 situation)

1. Have all the players at center ice except for 2 players (or coaches), who go into opposite corners of the rink. The players at center ice should be split into 4 units, 2 groups of forwards and 2 groups of defensemen, with a defensive and offensive unit on each side of the red line, as diagramed.

2. The drill starts with 1 forward from each group shooting the puck into the corner where the player or coach is situated. The player in the corner takes the puck and gives the puck back to the forward, who is making a swing in the zone toward the boards. After taking the return pass, the forward goes against a defenseman from the unit on his side. The defense tries to contain the puck carrier, playing him in a 1 on 1 situation.

3. The play ends when the puck is forfeited or when the forward gets a shot on the net.

4. Halfway through the drill, the units in the middle and the players in the corners should change sides.

VARIATION

In this drill, the defense can work with or without sticks or with sticks turned upside down.

DRILL 9 (1 on 1 maneuvers—2 zones)

1. Divide the team into 2 groups. Each group will use half of the ice.
2. After each group has completed the exercise in 1 zone, they will switch zones and run through the second drill.

   Zone 1: Defensemen are situated in front of the goal and forwards form 2 lines inside the blue line.

   Two defensemen start the drill by picking up pucks, going behind the net and trying to come out of their zone against 2 forecheckers—forwards who have moved up from the blue line (see diagram). By poke checking, stick checking or body checking, the forwards attempt to take the pucks away from the defensemen.

   Zone 2: Forwards form 2 lines outside the blue line; 2 defensemen are located behind the goal lines, as illustrated.

   As in the drill in Zone 1, the defensemen are the puck carriers while the forwards move up 1 on 1 to take the puck away by body checking, poke checking or stick checking maneuvers.

VARIATION

Have the forwards execute the drill without sticks.

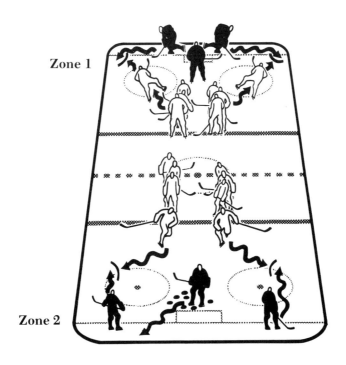

DRILL 10 (individual checking maneuvers—2 zones)

Divide the team and situate groups in each end of the ice.

Zone 1: Forwards form lines along the boards on both sides of the ice at the blue line; the defense is placed inside the blue line at center ice.

The drill begins when the first forwards in line take a puck and shoot it into the corner ahead of them. Both forwards skate to the corners, as do 2 of the defense, and the 2 players in each corner then fight for control of the puck.

Zone 2: Forwards line up along both sides of the boards midway in the zone facing the goal line. The defense sets up in the slot between the circles.

The first forwards on either side take pucks and shoot them ahead into the corners. The forwards and 2 defense skate into the corners after the pucks and each pair of players maneuvers for puck control. The object of these drills is to practice proper use of the body in the corner to gain puck control.

VARIATION

The defense can execute the drills without sticks or with their sticks turned upside down.

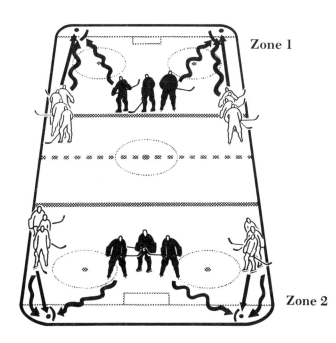

Zone 1

Zone 2

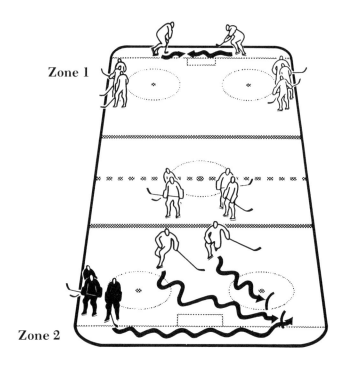

Zone 1

Zone 2

DRILL 11 (individual checking maneuvers—2 zones)

Divide the players into groups of equal size and situate 1 group in each end of the rink.

Zone 1 (1 on 1 situation behind the goal line): Players line up on either side of the ice along the boards facing the goal line.

The drill begins when the first player in each line skates over the goal line. One of the skaters is carrying the puck and the other player is charged with trying to get the puck away from him by using the body. They must stay behind the goal line for 30 to 60 seconds.

The object of the drill is to learn to take the body properly and to gain control of the puck after body contact.

Zone 2 (1 on 2 forechecking situation): The forwards form 2 lines at center ice facing the goal (see diagram) and the defense is situated along the boards in one corner.

As a defenseman carries the puck behind the net and prepares to break out of the zone, 2 forwards move up to try to stop him.

The first forechecker should attempt to force the defense into the corner where he can take him out of the play while the second forechecker picks up the puck. If the first checker misses the puck carrier, he backs up the second checker, who makes his move.

A goalie should be in the net so that the checkers can try to score if they gain possession of the puck.

Switch the defense to the opposite corner of the ice halfway through the drill.

NOTE

After a specified amount of time, have the groups change ends (and drills).

DRILL 12 (1 on 1 situation)

1. The forwards form lines along the boards at each blue line on opposite sides of the ice. They face into the zone, where the defensemen are situated. In one end, the defense is in the middle of the zone; in the other end, the defensemen are near the side boards inside the blue line. The purpose of locating the defense differently is to give them experience in reacting to a puck carrier going to the outside and to the inside.
2. The drill starts with a forward in each group carrying the puck into the zone and trying to beat a defenseman (on the outside, or on the inside, depending on the zone) for a shot on goal. After taking a shot, the forward goes to the corner, grabs a puck, carries it out of the zone and passes across to the next player starting out.
3. Have the groups change sides of the ice halfway through the drill. The coach may wish to reposition the defense in each zone after a certain period of time.

VARIATION

The defense can work with or without sticks, or with their sticks turned upside down.

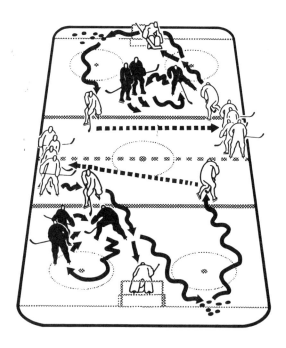

DRILL 13 (1 on 2 situation—2 zones)

Half of the forwards and half of the defense are assigned to Zone 1. The remaining players set up in Zone 2.

Zone 1 (double-teaming in the corner): The forwards form 2 lines at the blue line. The defensemen are situated in front of the net.

The drill begins when the first forwards in line skate toward the corner. The outside player is the puck carrier; the inside skater is the backchecker.

Deep in the corner, the puck carrier is met by 1 of the defensemen, who takes the body in an attempt to halt the play. The checker backs up the defense. If the defense is beaten, or if the puck comes loose, the backchecker moves in to play the body or take control of the puck and the defense becomes the backup.

Defensemen alternate throughout the drill and the forwards switch positions on each run-through.

Zone 2 (double-teaming along the boards): The forwards form 2 lines

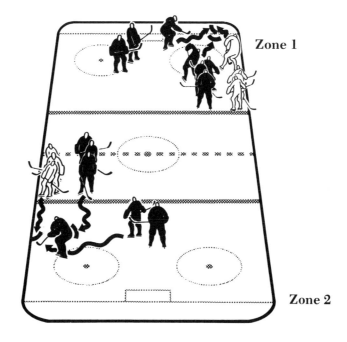

Zone 1

Zone 2

facing the goal at the blue line; the defense is located in the slot area.

The drill starts with 2 forwards, who skate into the zone. The outside player is the puck carrier and the inside player is the checker. A defenseman moves to the boards to intercept the puck carrier and take him out along the boards.

The backchecking player will back up the defense in the event that he is beaten or that the puck comes loose on body contact.

The forwards switch positions on following turns.

NOTE

Groups should move to the opposite side of the ice halfway through the drills.

VARIATION

Defense may play without sticks or with sticks turned upside down.

DRILL 14 (1 on 1 situation)

1. Divide the forwards and situate each group along the boards in opposite corners of the rink. The defense is split on each side along the boards in the neutral zone. A single player, or coach, is positioned in the corner opposite each group of forwards.
2. The drill starts with 1 forward from each corner making a pass behind the net to the player in the opposite corner. After passing, the forward makes a swing toward the middle to receive a return pass from the corner, and goes against a defenseman who comes off the boards to try to contain the puck carrier (with or without interference). The forward attempts to beat the defense and go in for a shot on goal.
3. Halfway through the drill, have the forwards and the player in the corner change sides of the ice.

VARIATION

The defensemen can execute the drill with or without sticks, or with their sticks turned upside down.

DRILL 15 (individual checking maneuvers—2 zones)

Split the players into 2 groups and situate a group in each end of the ice.

Zone 1: The forwards are grouped at the red line on one side of the rink. Defensemen work in pairs from inside the blue line.

One forward starts from mid-ice with a puck and attempts, by using finesse and speed, to beat the defense and get off a shot on net.

Teamwork between the defensemen is the key to the drill. As the forward approaches, 1 defense has to force the puck carrier one way or the other. The next defensive maneuver is to take the playmaker out. As each defenseman makes his move, the other backs him up in case the forward beats him or in case the puck comes loose. Communication between the defensemen is important.

The goalie should be in the net so that the puck carrier can try to score.

Zone 2: The forwards line up with pucks inside the blue line, as shown; 2 defensemen are set in front of the net with a forward between them.

One at a time, the forwards at the blue line try to pass the puck to the forward in front of the net, who will try for a shot on goal.

The defensemen's role is to take the forward out of the play, either by checking him, knocking him down or by moving him out of position.

NOTE

After a specified amount of time, have the groups switch zones.

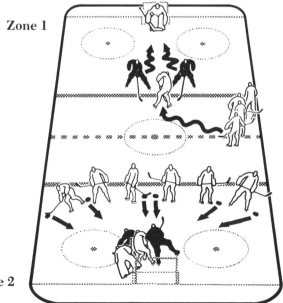

Zone 1

Zone 2

Team Offensive and Defensive Maneuvers

DRILL 16 (2 on 1 situation—pass to the middle)

1. Split the forwards into 4 groups and situate each group in a corner of the rink along the boards.
2. Defensemen are set up at center ice as indicated on the diagram.
3. The drill starts in one corner where a forward passes the puck to a defenseman at the blue line, who in turn passes off to a forward breaking from the other corner. The 2 forwards then go against a second defenseman, who is waiting for them at the far blue line, and attempt to score.
4. The next 2 players come from the opposite end of the ice and this rotation, plus the rotation of defensemen, continues throughout the drill.

NOTES

A. OFFENSIVE MANEUVERS—The forwards should stay wide enough so that they always have 2 alternatives, either taking a shot on goal or passing to their partner. The forward who doesn't take the eventual shot on net should break for the net for the rebound.
B. DEFENSIVE MANEUVERS—Timing and good body position be-

tween the forwards are the key to the defense in a 2 on 1 situation. The defenseman attempts to stay in the middle and between the 2 forwards. In this position he retains several options: forcing the puck carrier to pass, containing the puck carrier's shooting room, keeping the puck carrier to the outside or forcing a player on his forehand to go to his backhand. Because the defenseman is at a disadvantage in a 2 on 1 situation, it's best to avoid taking any unnecessary chances and to play conservatively. In front of the net, the defense must not interfere with his goaltender and must play the man, leaving the goalie to handle the puck.

DRILL 17 (2 on 1 with breakout situation—half ice)

1. Divide the forwards and defense and situate 1 group of forwards and defensemen in each end of the ice.
2. Forwards in each end are grouped along the boards in the corners. Defensemen are behind the goal line and alternate in working with pairs from the corners.
3. The defense starts the play from the side of the net by passing the puck to 1 of the forwards who are starting out of the corner.
4. The forwards pass the puck between them as they skate to the red, turn and start back on the same sides. At the same time, the defenseman who started the play skates to the blue line, stops and skates backwards while trying to break up the forwards' 2 on 1 play for a shot on goal.
5. Groups in the other end of the ice execute the same drill on half ice.

NOTE

See Offensive and Defensive Maneuvers under Drill 16.

VARIATION

Instead of using half ice, have the groups alternate ends of the ice in executing the drill. In this case, have the forwards skate to the far blue line and the defenseman to the red line before turning around and coming back 2 on 1.

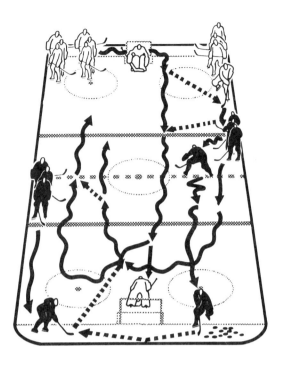

DRILL 18 (2 on 1 and 2 on 0 situations with breakout passes)

1. The forwards are situated in the corners on one end of the ice. Defensemen are split into 2 groups on the blue lines on opposite sides of the ice (see diagram).

2. The drill starts in the forwards' end with 1 forward carrying the puck behind the net and passing to his partner along the boards. The forwards go down the ice 2 on 1 against a defenseman who has started on that side from the blue line.

3. When the play gets into the zone, the defense lets the forwards break on the net in a 2 on 0 situation while he turns and skates to the corner on his side, takes a puck and passes to a defenseman who has moved into the other corner from the blue line.

4. The second defender takes the pass and in turn passes it to 1 of the 2 forwards who have completed their 2 on 0 play. The forwards exchange the puck as they skate back down the ice for a shot on the net.

5. The forwards go to the end of the line opposite that from which they started; the defensemen also change sides after the play.

DRILL 19 (2 on 1 situation)

1. Divide the forwards and defense into 2 groups. Situate the forwards along the boards in the corners. The defense line up by the forwards on one side (see diagram) in each end.

2. The drill starts from one end as 3 players—2 forwards and a defenseman—skate into the opposite end. As they cross the far blue line, the forwards make the swing to the opposite side of the ice, and as they do so, 1 of the forwards takes a pass from the corner. The forwards cross each other and come back on the defenseman, who has stopped at the blue line and is skating backwards, trying to contain the attack. (Note: See Drill 16 for Offensive and Defensive Maneuvers.)

3. The next 3 players start from the opposite end of the ice, and the units continue this rotation throughout the drill.

VARIATIONS

A. Instead of taking a pass from the corner as the forwards cross to come back, the coach may have pucks at the blue line for the forwards to pick up as they make the swing.

B. Defense may execute the drill without sticks or with their sticks turned around.

DRILL 20 (1 on 1, 2 on 1 situations—half ice)

Divide the forwards and defense and situate a group in each zone.

Zone 1: 1 on 1. The forwards are in lines along the boards in both corners, while the defensemen are at the goal line by the faceoff circles, as illustrated.

The drill begins with the first skaters on one side—a wing and a defenseman—coming out. The defense carries the puck, which he passes to his wing enroute to the blue line. The wing skates to the red line, makes a swing and comes back against the defense 1 on 1. The defenseman, after passing, skates to the blue line and pivots to a backward position. The next pair comes out from the opposite side of the ice after the wing has made the swing and has come back to the blue line. Sides alternate throughout the drill. Timing is important in order to avoid collisions and interference.

Zone 2: 2 on 1. The forwards line up along the boards in the corners; the defense is out from the circles at the goal line.

A defenseman starts the drill by carrying the puck and passing it to the winger on his side. While the defense skates to the blue line and pivots

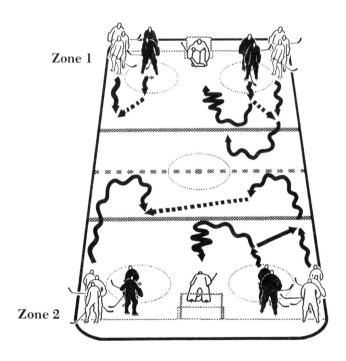

Zone 1

Zone 2

to a defensive position, the forwards skate down their sides to the red line. They make the swing and come back, passing the puck back and forth, in an attempt to outmaneuver the defense for a shot on goal.

The next play starts with the defenseman on the opposite side of the goal, and the defense continues this rotation throughout the drill.

NOTE

After a specified amount of time, have the groups switch drills.

DRILL 21 (2 on 1 situation)

1. Split the forwards and defense into 2 groups and situate groups in opposite corners of the rink. Players set up in 2 on 1 formations along the boards.

2. At the coach's signal, the first group in each corner goes down its own side of the ice, with the forwards attempting to make a play for a shot on goal and the defense trying to stop, contain or control the play.

3. When play on each side is stopped, units join the groups in the ends where they finish and the next skaters start out.

4. Have the groups in the corners change sides of the ice halfway through the drill.

DRILL 22 (2 on 2 situation)

1. The forwards are split into 4 groups and situated in the corners. The defense is divided into units along the boards on each side at center ice.

2. The drill starts at one end with forwards from each corner starting out and moving out of the zone passing the puck back and forth. At the blue line, the forwards go against 2 defensemen who have moved out from the boards and attempt to contain the 2 forwards.

3. The forwards go to the end of the line at the end where they have finished while the next 2 forwards start out from that same end. Defensive pairs alternate.

NOTES

A. OFFENSIVE MANEUVERS—Forwards have 2 key options in a 2 on 2 situation:

1. They can play very wide to give the puck carrier a 1 on 1 situation where his speed and stickhandling ability come into play, while his partner breaks for the net.

2. The player who does not have the puck may cross over to the same side as the puck carrier and attempt to get in front of the defenseman who is trying to contain the attacker. By interfering, the forward gives the puck carrier an opportunity to slip around the defense and to get the

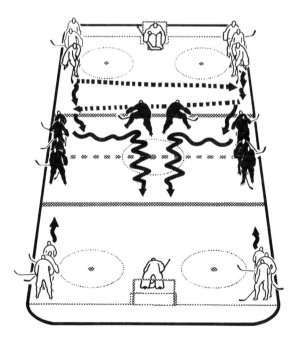

puck deeper into the zone. At this point, the screening forward can break for the net and the second defenseman must cover the goal.

B. DEFENSIVE MANEUVERS—Teamwork between the 2 defensemen is all-important. Options and suggestions include:

1. Defensemen should stay on their sides and not get caught either on one side or chasing around the ice.

2. Defense should attempt to force the play at the blue line. Keep the puck carrier on the outside or force him to his backhand. One defender should force the puck carrier and play the body while his partner keeps an eye on the man he is covering and at the same time looks for a chance to intercept a pass or catch a loose puck.

3. Defensemen should help each other by talking through the situation.

DRILL 23 (2 on 1 or 2 on 2 with breakout situation from defense inside their defensive zone)

1. The team is split into 2 groups; each group is situated on one side of the ice along the boards in the neutral zone. One defense is set at the top of each circle in 1 zone, as illustrated. The other 4 defensemen are positioned at the blue line ready to take on the oncoming forwards.

2. The drill starts with a player on one side in the neutral zone passing the puck to the defense on his side in the defensive zone. After making the pass, the forward makes a swing across ice while the forward first in line on the other side does the same thing. The defenseman who received the pass passes on to his partner on defense, who in turn passes to the skater coming from the opposite side as he makes the swing. The 2 players then rush 2 on 1 or 2 on 2 against the defense waiting for them at the blue line. (Either 1 or 2 defensemen may come out.) The forwards try to make a play for a shot on goal and then return to the lines from which they started.

3. The starting pass to the defense should come from each side of the ice on an alternating basis (from left to right defense then from right to left defense and so on).

4. After a time, have forwards change sides of the ice and have the defensemen rotate positions.

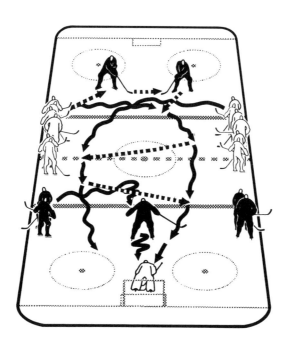

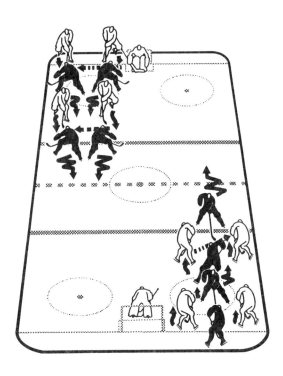

DRILL 24 (2 on 2 situation)

1. Pairs of defense and forwards line up along the boards in opposite corners of the rink. On one side, players are arranged in regular 2 on 2 formations; on the other side, the setup is for a 2 on 1 with a backchecker.
2. At the signal, the first group of 4 on each side start out and go down the ice, the forwards trying to make a play for a shot on goal, and the defense trying to contain or control the play. On the side with the initial 2 on 1 situation, the backchecker comes from behind and helps the defenseman.
3. After play is completed with a shot on the net, or a turnover or goal, each unit joins its respective group on the end where play finished and takes the next shift on that side.
4. Halfway through the drill, have groups change sides of the ice.

DRILL 25 (2 on 2 situation)

1. Split the forwards and defense into 4 groups and position groups in the corners with the forwards lined up along the boards and the defense inside (see diagram).

2. The drill starts at one end with 2 forwards and 2 defense starting out. They skate to the blue line, where the defensemen stop and prepare to back-skate while the forwards make a swing to come back. One of the forwards takes a pass from the corner as he makes the swing, and the forwards exchange the puck as they go up against the defense and attempt to score.

3. Skaters go to the end of the lines by the goal where they finish, and the next players start out from the other end.

NOTE

See Drill 22 for Offensive and Defensive Maneuvers.

VARIATIONS

A. Defensemen can execute the drill without sticks or with their sticks turned around.

B. Instead of passing from the corner as the forwards cross to come back, the coach may have pucks at each blue line for the forwards to pick up as they make the swing.

DRILL 26 (2 on 2 situation with breakout pass—half ice)

1. Divide the forwards and defensemen into groups in each zone. The forwards line up along the boards in each corner; the defensemen are situated behind the goal line as illustrated.

2. The drill starts behind the net. One defenseman passes to his partner, who in turn passes ahead to the first forward in line on the same side of the ice. With the pass, the forwards on either side start out. The puck carrier passes to the other forward at the blue line. Forwards skate to the red line and turn to come back on their sides while the defensemen move to the blue line. Forwards attempt to make a play against the defenders for a shot on goal.

3. Players return to line and the drill continues at both ends.

NOTE

See Drill 22 for Offensive and Defensive Maneuvers.

VARIATIONS

A. The forwards handle the puck themselves, eliminating the breakout pass from the defense and the defensemen play without sticks.

B. Have the forwards skate to the far blue line and the defense to the red line before turning around, thereby making this a full ice drill. Play alternates from one end to the other.

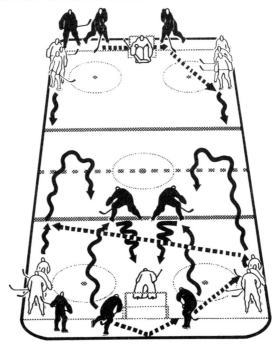

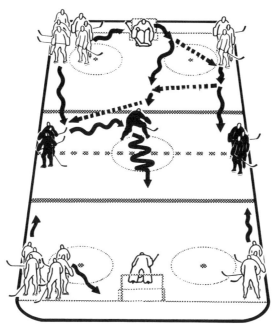

DRILL 27 (3 on 1 situation)

1. Divide the forwards and situate groups along the boards in the ends (see diagram) with 2 lines on one side of the ice and a single line on the opposite side. The defense is along the boards on either side of center ice.

2. The drill begins at one end with a unit of 3 players or a line. The center goes behind the net carrying the puck, then passes to the forward along the boards. The 3 skaters move the puck between them as they go against a defenseman who has moved out to attempt to contain the play.

3. Forwards finish with a shot on the net and go to the ends of the lines in that end as the next forward unit goes out. Ends alternate.

VARIATIONS

A. The 3 on 1 can go down the ice and back. In the two-way drill, forwards return to the lines they started from.

B. Have the defensemen play with their sticks turned around.

NOTES

A. OFFENSIVE MANEUVERS—The forwards should spread out and move the puck ahead taking care not to go offside. Once they are in the offensive zone they should be in a triangular formation where each player has 3 options—a pass to either partner or a shot on goal. The 2 forwards who do not have the puck take positions at the net (for a deflection or rebound) and in the slot area.

B. DEFENSIVE MANEUVERS—The defenseman is definitely at a disadvantage in this situation and must play carefully and conservatively until the play is at the net. The defense should stay in the middle and be careful not to back up so fast as to interfere with his goaltender. He keeps his stick on the ice, tries to keep the puck carrier to the outside or forces him to his backhand and generally attempts to minimize shooting space. Timing and body positioning are crucial. As the play gets closer to the net, the defenseman could (1) challenge the puck carrier or (2) put himself between the 3 forwards, thereby forcing the puck carrier to pass through his body, stick or skate. The odds are good that the defenseman can stop the play at this point, assuming that the goaltender is aware of his intentions.

DRILL 28 (3 on 1 situation)

1. Divide forwards and the defense and group them in 3 lines in opposite corners of the rink, as illustrated.
2. The drill starts at one end with a line and a defenseman. All 4 skate to the far blue line, where they will make a swing and come back. One of the forwards takes a pass from the corner as he makes his swing. The forwards pass the puck among themselves as they go 3 on 1 against the defense, who has pivoted to a backward position and is prepared to defend his goal.
3. The next play comes from the other end.

NOTE

See Drill 27 for Offensive and Defensive Maneuvers.

VARIATIONS

A. Have 3 defensemen play as a line and use a forward from 1 line as defense. Forwards in the line can alternate at the defensive roles as the units of defensemen come up.
B. The defensemen may play with their sticks turned around.
C. Instead of passing from the corner as the forwards swing at the far blue line to come back, the coach may have pucks at each blue line for the forwards to pick up.

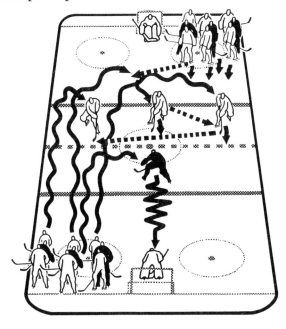

DRILL 29 (3 on 1 situation)

1. Split the players into 2 groups of forwards and defensemen, and have each group set up in 3 on 1 formations in opposite corners of the rink, as illustrated.
2. At the coach's signal, the first unit in each corner goes down their side in a 3 on 1 situation and tries to make a play for a shot on goal.
3. After completing the play, units go to the corner in the end where they finished as the next groups go out.
4. Halfway through the drill, have the units in each corner change sides of the ice.

DRILL 30 (3 on 1 situation; breakout pass—half ice)

1. Divide the forwards and defensemen and situate them in each zone, as illustrated. Forwards are along the boards in the corners; defensemen are split 2 and 1 on either side of the goal behind the goal line.
2. The single defense in the corner begins the drill by passing to 1 of the 3 forwards starting out, usually the center. As the line skates to the red line moving the puck around, the defenseman skates to the blue line and pivots to backward position in the middle. The forwards turn at the red line and come back 3 on 1 against the defenseman and attempt to score.
3. After the play, forwards skate back to their starting positions and another defenseman moves to the corner to start the next run-through.

VARIATION

The forward line can go to the far blue line and the defense to the red line before turning around. In this case, play alternates from one end to the other.

NOTE

See Offensive and Defensive Maneuvers in Drill 27.

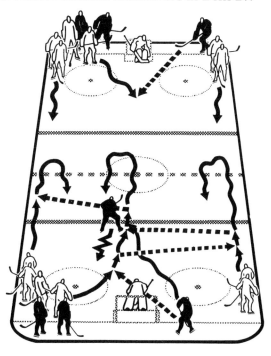

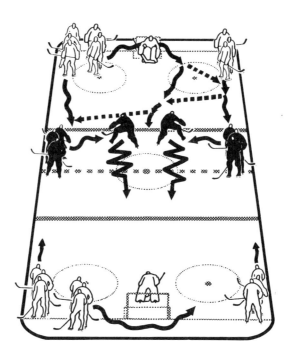

DRILL 31 (3 on 2 situation)

1. The forwards are divided into units in each end of the ice; lines are set up in the corners, as illustrated. The defense is located along the boards on each side of the rink at center ice.

2. The drill starts from one end with the center carrying the puck behind the net and passing to 1 of his linemates. Two defensemen come from the boards to the middle to go against the line as the skaters move out of the zone. The 3 forwards try to set up a play for a shot on goal.

3. Defensemen return to center ice; the forwards go to join the groups in the corners in the end where the play finished. In this case, play alternates from one end to the other.

VARIATIONS

A. The 3 on 2 can also go two ways—down and back. In this instance, forwards go back to the corners from which they started out.

B. In the two-way variation, after the defense stop or control the play in the opposite end, the 2 defensemen may rush the puck with the center-man, or 1 of the forwards, on the way back to the end. The other 2 forwards will act as defensemen.

C. Defense may play with their sticks turned around.

A. OFFENSIVE MANEUVERS—The basic pattern is for the forwards to spread out as much as possible as they move the puck around, especially in the neutral zone, making it more difficult for the defense to maneuver. Once inside the offensive zone, try to force the defense out of position. The key players in a 3 on 2 are the 2 forwards who don't have the puck. Usually 1 forward will go on the side of the puck carrier to put the defenseman into a 2 on 1 situation, while the other forward goes wide to the net, forcing the second defense to cover him. It's important to stay in balance, with a player on each side and in the middle, even if the puck carrier is a wing who cuts to the middle as the centerman moves to the wing's spot to maintain the balance. Other options are outlined in the next chapter, "Team Strategy—the Offensive Game."

B. DEFENSIVE MANEUVERS—The defensemen should also spread out. They must make every effort to keep their positions and not be caught running around, as they are already at a man disadvantage. One defense will try to force the puck carrier to the outside or to a backhand position at his blue line, while the other defense goes against the other forwards 2 on 1. Another option the defense on the same side as the puck carrier has is to attempt to force the play. His backup, however, must play carefully and conservatively here as he has 2 players to cover. Some musts for the defense include: talking to each other, trying to keep an eye on both the puck and the players, and good positioning with the puck in view. Sometimes it is possible for the defense to place himself between 2 forwards where there is a chance of a pass interception.

DRILL 32 (3 on 2 situation; breakout pass—half ice)

1. Offensive and defensive units are set up in both ends. In each end, the defense is behind the goal line and the forwards are in lines at the faceoff circles.

2. The drill starts behind the net as 2 defensemen pass the puck, then headman the puck to 1 of the 3 forwards poised to break out of the zone. As the forwards move the puck between themselves and skate toward the red line, the defensemen move to the blue line to contain the offense. The forwards turn at the red line and come back 3 on 2. The play continues in the zone until they score or until the goalie freezes the puck or the defense takes control.

3. Players return to their original positions and the next units come out.

VARIATION

Start from one end only and utilize the full ice. In this variation, the forwards skate to the far blue line and the defense sets up at the red line. Units from each end alternate as the drill continues.

NOTE

See Drill 31 for Offensive and Defensive Maneuvers.

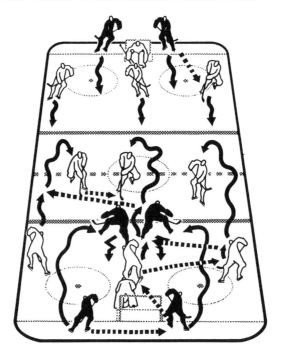

DRILL 33 (3 on 2 situation)

1. Divide the team into 2 units and group forwards, by line, and defense, in pairs, in opposite corners of the ice, as shown.
2. The drill starts at one end with a unit of 3 forwards and 2 defense skating to the far blue line. One of the forwards receives a pass from the corner as the line makes the swing to return. The defense is at center ice as the line comes back, moving the puck and attempting to set up a shot on the goal.
3. After the play is completed, skaters go to the end of the lines from which they started, while the next unit starts from the other end.

VARIATIONS

A. Instead of a pass from the corner, 1 of the forwards can pick up a loose puck at the blue line. Leave a quantity of pucks at both blue lines.
B. Form a line from the defense and have 2 forwards act as defense. Lines and defensemen can alternate.
C. The defensemen can execute the drill with their sticks turned upside down.

NOTE

See Drill 31 for Offensive and Defensive Maneuvers.

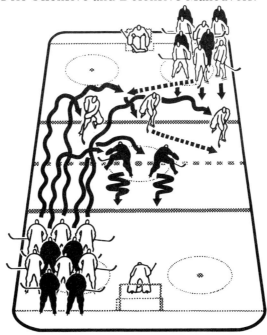

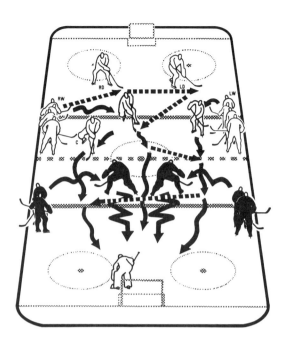

DRILL 34 (3 on 1 or 3 on 2 with breakout pass situation from the defensive zone)

1. Players are divided with a group situated on each side of the rink along the boards in the neutral zone. One defenseman is located at the top of each circle in 1 zone facing the lines in the neutral zone. The other 4 defenders are situated by the boards at the blue line.

2. The play begins when the wing on one side passes to the defense on his side in the defensive zone. As he makes a cut across the middle, the other winger starts out on his side and a centerman moves from the middle to the side vacated by the winger.

3. The defense who received the first pass passes to the other defenseman, who in turn returns the puck to the starting wing as he cuts to the middle. The 3 forwards then have a 3 on 1 or 3 on 2 and attempt to make a play for a shot on goal. As they come in to go against the defense, they move the puck back and forth between themselves.

4. The opening pass should come from one side and then the other on an alternating basis.

5. After the play is completed, forwards go to the ends of the lines from which they started.

DRILL 35 (drill to serve multipurpose situation)

1. Split the forwards into 4 groups and situate a group along the boards just inside the blue line on each side of the rink. The defensemen are divided and the units take up positions in center ice outside the blue lines. Put some pucks in each corner.

2. The drill starts at one end with a defenseman at the blue line skating into the corner, taking a puck and going behind the net, and then passing to the forward on that side near the blue line. When he receives the pass, he and the forward across the ice skate into the neutral zone, exchanging the puck, and go against a defenseman waiting for them at the blue line in a 2 on 1 situation. The play ends with a shot on goal or a turnover of the puck. The forwards join the lines in the end where they finished and where the next pair of skaters start from. The defense in that end again starts the play from behind the net. The defensemen remain in the middle, rotating passing and defending duties.

VARIATIONS

A. Put 1 defenseman at each blue line (2 on 1, 3 on 1 or 1 on 1).
B. Put 2 defensemen at each blue line for a 2 on 2, 3 on 2 or 1 on 2 exercise.
C. Put 3 defensemen at each blue line for any situation desired (1 on 1, 1 on 2, 2 on 1, 2 on 2, 3 on 1, 3 on 2, 3 on 3).

DRILL 36 (3 on 3 situation)

1. Forward lines are situated at each end of the ice, as diagramed. Defensemen are along the boards in either side of the neutral zone.

2. The drill begins in one end with a line against a checker and 2 defense. The center carries the puck from the corner behind the net and passes it to the uncovered forward. The line then moves down the ice trying to make a play against the defense for a shot on goal. The checker's job is to cover 1 of the players all the way through the play.

3. After the play is completed, players stay in that end of the ice as the next unit goes out. Each player will take a turn at checking duty. Ends alternate.

VARIATIONS

A. The drill may also go two ways. In this case, the coach has 2 options: (1) On the way back, 1 of the forwards can switch positions with the checker and the checker thus becomes an offensive player in the return exercise. (2) After gaining control of the puck in their defensive zone, one defenseman may rush the puck on the way back along with 2 of the

forwards. After the two-way drill, players return to their original groups; the defense alternate.

B. Defense may execute the drill without sticks or with sticks turned around, which forces them to play the body instead of the puck.

NOTES

A. OFFENSIVE MANEUVERS—Maneuvers are essentially the same as in a 2 on 2 situation unless the winger breaks loose from his checker, which changes the situation to 3 on 2.

B. DEFENSIVE MANEUVERS—Defense must operate as in a 2 on 2 situation, but must also watch to see that the checker has the other wing covered. Defense should make an effort to force the play at the blue line.

DRILL 37 (4 on 1 situation with breakout pass)

1. Forwards are grouped by lines in each end of the ice. Defensemen are situated along the boards on both sides of the neutral zone, with the exception of 2 defensemen, who are stationed in the corner of each zone (see diagram).

2. The drill starts at one end with the defense passing from the corner to either the center or a wing as the line goes out. All 4 players rush down the ice against 1 defense waiting at the blue line. Good crisp passing and good positioning are important in executing this drill properly. One of the players should also be prepared for a rebound if there is a shot on goal.

3. After the play is completed, forwards go to the ends of lines in the end where the play stopped. Defensemen go to center ice and another unit gets ready to come out of the same end.

VARIATIONS

A. Drill may be run two ways instead of one way. Here the defender who was on the defensive end of play will start the second rush with a pass to the offense and will become a part of that unit on the return. The

offensive defenseman will become the defender and attempt to contain the play on the way back.

B. Instead of splitting the lines, the entire team can be on one end of the rink.

C. The team can also be situated at center ice. The drill would be started by the coach or a player shooting the puck into the zone where a defense takes the puck for the breakout pass.

D. At any time, the coach can have the defense rushing the puck. Make certain there is someone to back him up in his position so that balance is maintained.

NOTE

See Drill 27 for Offensive and Defensive Maneuvers.

DRILL 38 (4 on 2 situation with breakout pass)

1. Divide the forwards by lines and situate units in both ends, as illustrated. The defense is located along the boards on both sides at center ice. One defenseman from each group goes to a corner to start the play in each end.

2. The drill begins at one end when the defense in the corner passes to the center or to a wing as the line comes out. All 4 players rush down the ice against 2 defensemen who come out to the blue line. The offensive unit will try to execute a scoring play against the defense. The defensive unit should treat this rush as a 3 on 2 situation since the attacking defense will be the fourth player coming in.

3. After the play is finished, players take up positions in the end opposite that from which they started. Defensive units switch at center ice. Ends alternate.

VARIATIONS

A. This can be a two-way drill. In this case, the defensive unit will start the play on the way back with a pass from the corner. The defenseman who was on the offensive unit during the initial rush will go on defense

on the way back along with a designated player from the offensive unit.

B. The entire team can be situated in one end for this drill.

C. The entire team can be situated at center ice. The coach or a player starts the play by shooting a puck into the corner for the defense.

D. At any time the coach can have the defense rushing the puck, but someone must be assigned to back him up in his position so that no positions are left open and so that balance is maintained.

NOTE

See Offensive and Defensive Maneuvers in Drill 31.

DRILL 39 (4 on 3 situation with breakout pass—game situation—power play and penalty killing)

1. Situate forward lines in both ends of the ice, as shown. Defensive pairs are split on either side of the neutral zone along the boards. Two defensemen go to a corner on each end to start the play and a player comes out as a checker.
2. The drill begins at one end with the defense making a pass from the corner to either the centerman or a wing. All 4 players make a rush against 2 defensemen, who come to the middle from the boards, and the checker. The checker picks up a wing in the starting zone and stays with him. The defense should treat the play as a 2 on 2 situation as long as the checker has his man since the offensive defenseman will normally be following the play.
3. After play is completed in the defensive zone, forwards stay with the lines in that end as the next unit goes out. The defensemen rotate. Play alternates from end to end.

VARIATIONS

A. The entire team can be situated at one end of the rink.

B. The entire team can be grouped at center ice, where the play is started by the coach or a player who shoots the puck into the corner for the defense.

C. The drill can also go two ways. In the two-way version, the defensive unit will start the return rush after the initial play is completed (by scoring or by the defense or goaltender in control of the puck). The defenseman who was on the offensive unit during the initial rush will go on defense on the way back along with a designated player from the offensive unit; checker may continue or may switch role on the way back with the skater he was playing against at his position.

D. The defense may rush the puck at any time provided he has someone to back him up in his position.

NOTE

See Drill 22 for Offensive and Defensive Maneuvers.

DRILL 40 (4 on 4 situation with breakout pass)

1. Situate forward lines in both ends of the ice, as shown. Defensive pairs are split on either side of the neutral zone along the boards. Two checkers are positioned at the blue line facing the defensive goal and 1 defenseman goes to a corner in each end to start the play.

2. The defenseman in the corner starts the drill with a pass to either the center or the wing and all 4 offensive players make a rush against the 2 checkers and 2 defensemen, who move to the center from the boards. The checkers will normally pick up their wings and the defense will start at the blue line and will try to contain the attack. The defense should approach the play as a possible 1 on 2 or 2 on 2 situation if the 2 wingers are covered by the checkers.

3. After play is completed in the defensive zone, forwards stay with the lines in that end as the next unit goes out. Defensemen rotate as play alternates from one end to the other.

VARIATIONS

A. The entire team can be situated in one end of the rink.
B. The entire team can be grouped at center ice, where the play is

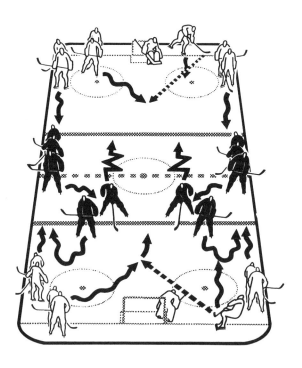

started by the coach or a player, who shoots the puck into the corner for the defense.

C. The drill can also go two ways. In this version, the defensive unit will start the play on the way back with a pass (after the offense has finished at the goal or the defense has control of the puck). The 2 checkers can remain at their positions or can switch roles with their opposition. The defenseman who was on the offensive unit during the initial rush will go on defense on the way back along with a designated player from the offensive unit. If the checkers are replaced, it will be by the players they were covering on the initial rush. The next play would come from the opposite end of the ice.

D. At any time, the defense may rush the puck provided he is backed up in his position.

NOTE

See drills 15 (Zone 1) and 22 for Offensive and Defensive Maneuvers, 2 on 1 and 2 on 2.

Team Checking Maneuvers

**DRILL 41 (5 on 1 situation with breakout pass: offensive team—
5 players—vs. checking team—1 player)**

1. Divide the forward lines and situate units in each half of the ice. A
pair of defensemen is behind each net and another pair is on each side
of the ice at the red line.
2. The drill starts at one end with the defense passing the puck between
themselves, then moving it to either the center or a wing as the line
breaks out. The 5 players start down the ice in a 5-man rush against 1
defenseman, who has moved to center ice from the boards. After the
play is completed at the net, the defenseman returns to center ice, while
the forwards and defense stay on that end as the next unit goes out. Play
alternates from one end to the other.

VARIATIONS

A. The whole team can be situated in one end of the ice for the drill.
B. The entire team can be at center ice. Play is started by the coach or a
player, who shoots the puck into the zone for the defense.

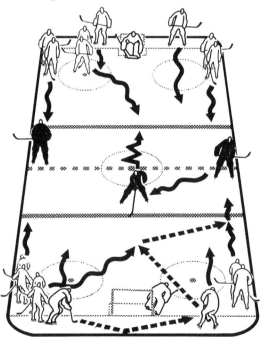

C. The drill can go one way or two ways. Play is stopped after the initial rush when a goal is scored or when the defense or the goaltender have control of the puck. On the return, the defensive defenseman switches roles with 1 of the offensive defensemen.

D. The defense may rush the puck as long as there is someone ready as backup.

NOTE

The purpose of this drill is to check proper functioning of the offensive team on the attack in all 3 zones. Checking points include good position in each zone, pass execution, shooting and positioning for rebounds. All players should have a turn as part of the offensive and defensive units.

**DRILL 42 (5 on 2 situation with breakout pass; offensive team—
5 players—vs. checking team—2 players)**

1. Situate forward lines in both ends of the ice, as illustrated. Defensive
pairs are situated behind each goal and on either side of the boards at
center ice.
2. The drill starts at one end as 1 defenseman passes behind the net to
his partner who, in turn, headmans to either the center or to the wing as
the line starts out. All 5 players go as a unit against the 2 defensemen at
center ice, who are waiting at the blue line. The offensive team will
attempt to execute a play for a shot on goal; the defensive pair should
approach the rush as a 3 on 2 situation, as the offensive defensemen will
be following the play.
3. After play is stopped in the offensive zone following a goal or by the
defense gaining control of the puck, players stay in that end as the next
unit starts out. Play alternates from one end to the other.

VARIATIONS

A. The whole team can be situated in one end of the ice for the drill.
B. The entire team can be at center ice. The coach or a player shoots the
puck into the zone to start the play.

C. The drill can go one way or two ways. In the two-way version, the defensive unit will start the return rush after the initial play is completed (by scoring or by the defense or goaltender gaining puck control). The defensive pairs should switch roles on the return.

NOTES

1. See Drill 31 for Offensive and Defensive Maneuvers (3 on 2 situation).
2. The purpose of the drill is to check proper functioning of the offensive team on the attack in all 3 zones. Watch for good positioning in each zone, pass execution, shooting and positioning for rebounds. All players should have a turn on the offensive and defensive units.

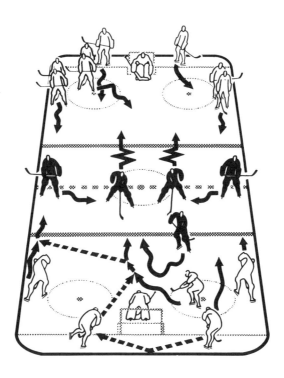

DRILL 43 (5 on 3 situation with breakout pass; offensive team—5 players—vs. checking team—3 players)

1. Situate forward lines at both ends of the ice. Defensive pairs are located behind each goal and along the boards on each side of center ice. One checker is at the blue line.

2. The drill starts at one end. One defense passes to his partner, who gives the puck to either the center or a wing as the line moves out. The 5-man unit goes against the checker and the defense and tries to set up a shot on goal. The checker should pick up a wing in the defensive zone and stay with him throughout the play. The defense may approach the play as a 2 on 2 situation, assuming the checker is covering his man, as the defense will be following the play.

3. After play is completed at the goal, the defensive pairs change positions; the forwards stay on that end as the next unit goes out. Ends rotate throughout the drill, and all players should have a turn on the offense and defense.

VARIATIONS

A. The entire team can be situated in one end of the ice for the drill.

B. The entire team can be at center ice. The coach or a player shoots the puck into the zone to start the play.

C. The drill can also go two ways. In this version, the defensive unit will start the return rush after the initial play is finished (by scoring or by the defense or goaltender gaining control of the puck). The same checker may continue, or may change positions with the player he was checking. The offensive and defensive defensemen switch roles.

D. At any time, the defense may rush the puck providing that a player is ready to back up his position.

NOTES

1. See Drill 22 for Offensive and Defensive Maneuvers (2 on 2 situation).

2. The purpose of the drill is to check proper functioning of the offensive team on the attack in all 3 zones. It is also effective in working with power play and penalty killing units.

DRILL 44 (5 on 4 situation with breakout pass; offensive team— 5 players—vs. checking team—4 players)

1. Situate the forward lines at one end of the ice. One pair of defensemen is behind the net; the remaining defensemen are along the boards on either side of the central zone. Two backcheckers are at the blue line in the defensive zone.
2. The defense behind the net start the drill by exchanging the puck and passing ahead to the center or wing as the line breaks out. All 5 players go as a unit against the 2 checkers and 2 defensemen. The checkers should pick up their wings in the defensive zone; the defensemen start at the red line to break up the attack. The defense should treat the play as a 1 on 2 or possible 2 on 2 situation, assuming the wingers are covered. All players should take a turn on the defensive and offensive teams.
3. After completing the play at the goal, the players return to the end from which they started and the next unit goes out.

VARIATIONS

A. The drill may go one or two ways. In the two-way variation, the defensive unit starts the play on the way back once play in the initial rush is stopped. The checkers can remain the same, or can switch positions with the wingers they covered. Defensive pairs should switch role,

so that the players who were on defense start the play on the return.

B. The defense may rush the puck at any time, providing that there is someone to back him up in his position.

C. The entire team can be at center ice. The coach or a player starts the drill by shooting the puck into the zone for the defense.

NOTES

1. For Offensive and Defensive Maneuvers see Drill 15 (Zone 1) for 1 on 2 situation and Drill 22 for 2 on 2 situation.

2. The purpose of the drill is to check proper functioning and positioning of the offensive team on the attack in all 3 zones. It can also be used in working with the power play and penalty killing units.

DRILL 45 (5 on 5 situation with breakout pass—game situation—offensive team—5 players—vs. checking team—5 players)

1. The forward lines are situated at one end of the ice, as diagramed. The defensive partners are split on either side of the rink at the red line; one pair is behind the net to start the play. Two checkers (wingers) are located at the top of the circles. The third checker (centerman) is in the slot area.

2. The defensemen set up behind the goal and then either (1) pass to the centerman or (2) carry the puck out themselves, as the 2 wingers should be covered by their checkers. (This situation is more difficult, so good positioning and proper execution of passes is essential to getting the puck moving out of the zone.) The first checker (centerman) should force the defense to make a play while the other checkers (wingers) cover the wings. The 2 defense will handle the puck carrier as in a 1 on 2 situation. It could become a 2 on 2 situation if a winger breaks loose. The offensive unit will attempt to make a play for a shot on goal and the defensive unit will try to thwart the play.

3. After the play is stopped at the goal (by scoring or by the defense or goaltender gaining control of the puck), players return to the end from which they started. Players should switch positions (offense/defense/checking) as the drill continues so that everyone has a turn as part of the offensive and defensive units.

VARIATIONS

A. The drill may also go two ways. In this case, the offensive team becomes the defensive unit (and vice versa) for the return rush. The defense again starts the play.

B. The entire team can be situated at center ice. Play is started by the coach or a player who shoots the puck into the zone.

C. A defenseman may rush the puck, providing that there is someone to back him up in his position and that no position is left open.

NOTES

1. See Offensive and Defensive Maneuvers in Drill 15 (Zone 1) for 1 on 2 situation and Drill 22 for 2 on 2 situation.

2. Check proper functioning in all 3 zones.

DRILL 46 (1 on 5 situation; checking team—5 players—vs. offensive team—1 player)

1. Forwards are situated at one end of the rink along the boards. Defensive pairs are split on each side of the rink along the boards at center ice. Three forwards are designated as checkers (see diagram).
2. The drill begins when a defense comes around the net and passes to the offensive player (usually the center), who is breaking down the ice alone. (The offensive player should be given a head start of about 30 feet on the checkers so that he has a chance to make a play on the defense.) The offensive player goes against the defensive pair waiting at the red line; checkers are trailing, which makes a 1 on 5 situation overall.
3. The defensive team must try to stop the offensive player in the neutral zone, gain control of the puck, and return on the attack, and possibly set up a 3 on 0 against the goaltender in the end where the play began.
4. After the unit scores or the goaltender has frozen the puck, a new unit comes out. Every player should have a turn as a part of the offensive and defensive teams.

VARIATIONS

A. After the defensive team has gained puck control at center ice and the checkers are preparing to attack, the player who started the play by

passing from the goal line to the centerman may come out as a single defense against the rush, making it a 5 on 2 situation.

B. Any defense may rush the puck provided that his position is covered.

NOTES

1. See Drills 13 and 15 (Zone 1) for 1 on 2 situation Offensive and Defensive Maneuvers.

2. The purpose of the drill is to check the proper functioning of the checking (defensive) team when the team is not in control of the puck and is trying to gain possession in the neutral or defensive zones, and when the team goes to the offensive formation after gaining puck control. Each player should understand clearly who is to force the puck carrier, who is to back up the defense, and what is done after regaining possession of the puck.

DRILL 47 (2 on 5 situation; checking team—5 players—vs. offensive team—2 players)

1. The forwards are situated at one end of the rink along the boards. Defensive partners are split on each side of the rink along the boards at center ice. Three forwards are checkers (see diagram).
2. The play starts in the zone with 2 offensive players receiving a pass from a defense behind the goal line (usually wingers), who pass the puck between each other and attempt to make a play on the defensive pair waiting for them at the red line while the checkers close in to back up the defense. The defensemen must try to stop the 2 offensive players, if necessary, with the help of the checkers, and then kick off the offensive attack once they have control of the puck. Whoever has control of the puck on the checking or defensive team should move it ahead to set up the 3 on 0 rush against the goaltender.
3. After the unit scores, or the puck is controlled by the goaltender, a new unit comes out. Every player should take a turn as a part of the offensive and defensive teams.

VARIATIONS

A. After the defensive team has gained control of the puck at center ice and the checkers are preparing to go on the attack, a defenseman may

come out to play against them, which could create a 5 on 3 situation.

B. Any defenseman may rush the puck as long as someone covers his position.

NOTES

1. See Drill 22 for 2 on 2 situation Offensive and Defensive Maneuvers.

2. Purpose of the drill is to check the proper functioning of the checking (defensive) team when it does not have control of the puck, when it is trying to gain control, and when it has taken possession and goes on the attack.

3. The offensive players receiving the pass that starts the play should be given a head start of about 30 feet so that the offensive has an opportunity to make a play on the defense.

DRILL 48 (3 on 5 situation; checking team—5 players—vs. offensive team—3 players)

1. Situate the forwards at one end of the ice along the boards. Defensive partners are split on each side of the rink along the boards at center ice. Three forwards are checkers.

2. The drill starts with 3 offensive players or a line receiving a pass from a defense behind the goal line and coming out and moving the puck between them as they go against the defensive pair waiting at the red line. The 3 checkers follow after giving the 3 offensive players a head start of about 30 feet.

3. At the start, the defensive team is at a disadvantage (see Drill 31 for Offensive and Defensive Maneuvers) with the 3 checkers coming in to back them up. The checking team is charged with halting the offense in the neutral zone and with taking over puck control for an offensive attack on the goal.

4. After the unit scores or the goaltender or defense has frozen the puck, a new unit comes out. Every player should have a turn as a part of the offensive and defensive teams.

VARIATION

Any defense may rush the puck provided that his position is covered.

NOTES

1. See Drill 31 for 3 on 2 situation Offensive and Defensive Maneuvers.
2. The purpose of the drill is to check the proper functioning of the checking (defensive) team when it does not have control of the puck, when it is trying to gain control and when it has taken possession and goes on the offensive.

DRILL 49 (4 on 5 situation; checking team—5 players—vs. offensive team—4 players)

1. The forwards are situated at one end of the rink along the boards. Defensive partners are split on either side of the rink along the boards at center ice. Three forwards are checkers.

2. The play begins at one end with 4 offensive players (a line composed of 3 players and 1 defense). They take the offense as a unit, moving the puck around, and going against the defensive pair for a shot on goal. (The 3 checkers follow the offensive unit of 4 players after giving it a head start of about 30 feet.) Until the 3 checkers come in to back up the defensive pair, the defenders are at a disadvantage and have at least a 3 on 2 situation (see Drill 31 for Offensive and Defensive Maneuvers), then it becomes a 4 on 5 situation.

3. The procedure is for the checking team to stop the offense, regain puck control and return immediately on the offensive attack.

4. Play is completed when someone scores or when the defense or goaltender freeze the puck. A new unit comes out at that time. Every line should have a turn as part of the defensive and offensive teams. Defensemen rotate.

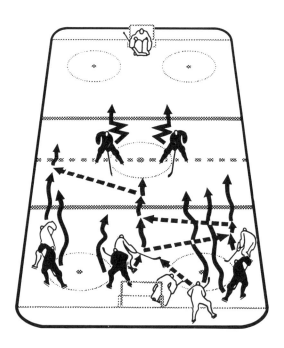

NOTES

1. Any defenseman can rush the puck, however someone must be prepared to cover for him in his position.

2. See Drill 31 for Offensive and Defensive Maneuvers in a 3 on 2 situation.

3. The purpose of the drill is to check the proper functioning of the defensive team when it does not control the puck, but is attempting to regain possession, and when it goes on the attack.

DRILL 50 (5 on 5 situation—game situation—checking team— 5 players—vs. offensive team—5 players)

1. Forward lines are situated along the boards at one end of the rink. Defensive partners are on either side of the rink along the boards at center ice. Three forwards are checkers.

2. The drill starts at one end when a 5-man offensive unit comes out. The 3 checkers give the offensive team a 30-foot head start before they move to help their defensive pair.

3. At the start, the 3 forwards of the offensive unit go against the defensive pair waiting at the red line 3 on 2 (the 3 checkers and the 2 offensive defense are trailing which then becomes 5 on 5) and attempts to make a play for a shot on goal.

4. If the defensive pair with the assistance of the 3 checkers, is successful in taking over control of the puck, the entire 5-man checking unit quickly moves to the attack in the end from which play began. If the offense retains control, play will conclude in the opposite end. Every line should take a turn as part of the offensive and defensive teams.

NOTES

1. See Drill 31 for 3 on 2 Offensive and Defensive Maneuvers.

2. At any time, a defenseman may rush the puck, providing that his position is covered.

3. The purpose of the drill is to check the proper positioning of the defensive team when it is trying to gain control of the puck and when it goes on the offensive attack.

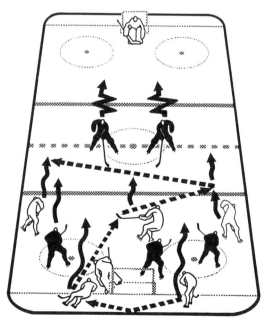

DRILL 51 (half ice scrimmage drills) (3 on 3 and 4 on 4 situations)

1. Half ice scrimmage drills offer another means of working on game situation strategy and the proper functioning of the offensive and defensive units. The objectives are puck control and the execution of plays and passes resulting in a shot on goal.

2. After the teams are set up in each end, the drills are run like scrimmages. After every goal, the team scored upon has to bring the puck outside the blue line before going on the offensive. If the goaltender freezes the puck, there will be a faceoff to the side of the net. If the defensive unit gains control of the puck after a shot on goal, it may not score off a rebound but must regroup—either in the corner, on the side or at the blue line—for a new attack on the net.

    Zone 1: 3 on 3 situation.
    Zone 2: 4 on 4 situation.

VARIATIONS

A. If there are an equal number of players working in each end, the coach can put a time limit on the drill (e.g., 5 minutes) and then have the winning and losing teams in each end play each other.

B. Have the defensive team play without sticks or with sticks turned around, then switch the teams around.

NOTE

    Players may rotate zones and situations.

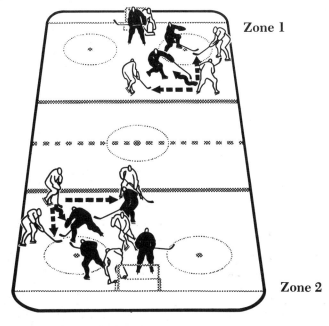

Zone 1

Zone 2

DRILL 52 (half ice scrimmage drills for power play and penalty killing situations)

1. These half ice scrimmage drills are exercises in game situation strategy where the objective is puck control by the offensive and defensive teams.
2. The drills are executed like scrimmages. The play goes on until a unit scores, or until the puck is driven out of the zone or frozen. After a stoppage of play, play resumes with a faceoff to the side of the net.
3. Both drills are effective in working on proper functioning of the power play unit (execution of plays and passes for good shots on the net) and of penalty killers in a shorthanded situation (positioning and defensive coverage).

Zone 1: 4 on 3 situation.
Zone 2: 5 on 4 situation.

VARIATION

In either or both zones, the defensive team can play without sticks or with their sticks turned around.

NOTE

Players may rotate zones and game situations.

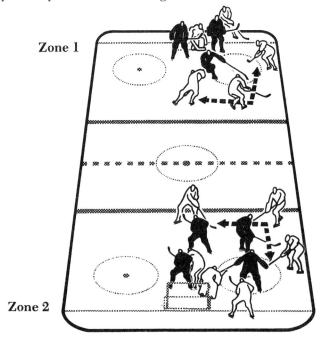

DRILL 53 (half ice scrimmage drills—6 on 5 and 5 on 3 situations)

Half ice scrimmage drills offer players an opportunity to work on positioning and game strategy in 6 on 5 and 5 on 3 situations. The objectives in both drills are puck control and proper functioning of the offensive and defensive units.

Zone 1: 5 on 3 situation. The offensive team is on the power play, while the defensive team is 2 men short. The scrimmage starts with a faceoff to the side of the net. Play stops when 1 team scores, when the defensive team gets the puck out of the zone or when the goalie freezes the puck. Play resumes with a faceoff to the side of the goal.

Zone 2: 6 on 5 situation. This scrimmage is effective for working out special strategy when the offensive team has pulled out the goal tender for an extra player. The play goes on until a unit scores, or until the puck is driven out of the zone or frozen. After a stoppage of play, play resumes with a faceoff to the side of the net.

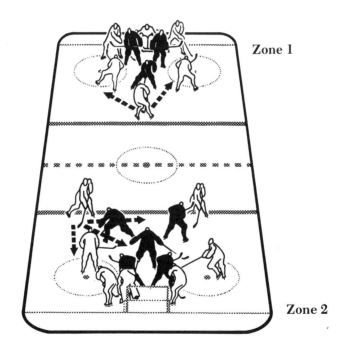

Zone 1

Zone 2

In the 5 on 3 situation, the defensive team may play without sticks or with sticks turned around.

NOTE

Players may rotate ends and game situations after a designated length of time.

DRILL 54 (blocking shots—2 zones)

Split the team into 2 groups and situate the defensemen in Zone 2 and the forwards in Zone 1.

Zone 1: Four players are at the blue line, as diagramed. The remaining players line up in the corners along the boards.

The first player in line on each side takes a puck, passes it to the first player at the blue line and then skates over quickly to block or deflect the shot from the point.

This drill develops quickness and precision in blocking or deflecting shots from the point. When the puck goes to the point, the forward should move in the direction of the line of fire toward the net, then advance on the shooter.

Zone 2: Four players are situated on each side at the blue line, while 2 defensemen are located in front of the net (see diagram).

The players at the blue line alternate in taking a variety of shots from the point; the defensemen on either side try to deflect or block the shots by using their sticks, bodies, skates or hands.

NOTES

A. Players should rotate positions and zones at specified times.
B. In these drills, sponge pucks or tennis balls may be used instead of regulation pucks as the purpose is to give players experience in blocking pucks and to teach proper positioning of the body, skates, sticks and hands.

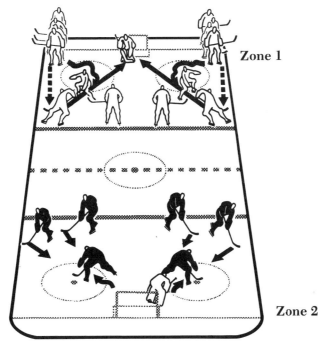

Zone 1

Zone 2

Thought Provokers

1. How much free time do you allow your players for practice of individual skills?

2. Have your defensemen move to forward positions from time to time in practice and have forwards take over for the defense. This not only helps them to become aware of the overall positional game, but improves skating skills.

3. Do you have a system of special maneuvers for different situations, such as 1 on 1, 2 on 2 and so forth?

4. Consider using sponge rubber pucks when your defensemen work on the technique of blocking shots.

5. How much time do you spend on positional play in practice?

6. Do you always work from one end of the rink or do you utilize both ends?

7. Have you considered having your players play their offside positions in practice?

CHAPTER 5 Team Strategy—The Offensive Game

In hockey, the object of the offensive game is to control the puck well enough and long enough to score goals and, hopefully, more goals than you allow the opposition. Before a team can attempt to score, it must establish an organized pattern of attack, that is, a plan or system. In the defensive zone, the offensive game is that of breaking out. The team moves the puck out of its defensive end into the neutral zone, where the players commit themselves to the system that leads to an assault on the enemy goal.

This chapter, like the defensive strategy chapter that follows it, is divided into two parts. Part 1 illustrates seven systems that may be employed by a team. Part 2 consists of a number of ideas employing offensive systems in each zone under varying conditions.

Each offensive system is identified numerically, for example, 2-1-2, 1-2-2, or 2-2-1, indicating the positioning of the attacking players. Under the 2-1-2 system in the offensive zone, 2 players roam deep around the net while 1 player is positioned in the slot. The 2 defensemen cover the blue line. On the breakout in the defensive zone, the 1-2-2 system will have the 2 defensemen behind the goal, the 2 wings along the side boards and the centerman high in the slot area in the middle.

The most challenging systems, and in a sense the most dangerous ones, are 2-1-2, 2-2-1, 1-2-1-1, 1-3-1 and 3-2. Because they are less conservative than say, 2-3 or 1-2-2, there is more room for player error. These systems call for quick, aggressive and speedy skaters.

There is a basic drill that can be used for work on any system. The players are situated either (1) along the boards at center ice or (2) at one end of the rink. If the players are at center ice, the coach or a player shoots the puck into the zone. If the team is at one end, the defense or centerman starts the play. The offense goes into its formation to break out of the zone against no defenders or 1, 2, 3, 4 or 5 defenders, at the coach's option. Each offensive unit makes one rush down the ice, executing properly in all three zones. Play ceases when the defensive unit, if any, gains control of the puck, clears the puck from the zone, or until the offensive team scores, the goaltender freezes the puck or the coach stops play with a whistle.

The drill gives the coach an opportunity to watch the functioning of the offense in each zone, including the execution of plays and passes, puck control and adaptation to defensive play. It is a team exercise and an important one, because each player has a responsibility to make it work, whether on the offensive or defensive end. It works the players on offensive and defensive strategy at the same time and fits all systems and all types of players. When the coach is teaching a system, run the drill without defense. Add defenders as the offense understands execution. For a variation, the defense can play without sticks or with their sticks turned upside down.

Because of the interlocking relationship between offense and defense, the chapters on these aspects of the game should be considered together and put into practice simultaneously. Because the material dovetails, some options of play given in one chapter are omitted in the other chapter. Further, while working on the defensive approach, for example, the coach may come up with his own ideas on how to stop or counteract attack formations and systems outlined earlier. By looking objectively at his team's attack and defense, the coach can pinpoint his team's strengths and weaknesses, select his systems and plan his practices accordingly. As you coach your players on your system(s), remind them to back each other up, keep the puck moving, keep in position and let the puck do the work.

Any system has advantages and disadvantages. It is up to the coach to decide which system or systems would be most effective for his team.

To make any system work, however, the players must be thoroughly acquainted with the plan and well conditioned as to its execution. Once a system is implemented, repetition in practice and in games should eventually make execution almost automatic.

Unity and responsibility are the keys to success. Each player must understand his responsibility to the overall effort, which of course depends on unified teamwork. There is no selfishness among players on an effective team. There is communication, trust and discipline.

Systems

SYSTEM I—1-2-1-1

INTRODUCTION

This diagram shows the same offensive system in both ends of the rink. The broken lines indicate the areas of responsibility for each player, whether the team is in the offensive, neutral or defensive zone. In other words, the same pattern and positioning is used when the team is on the attack as when it is in defensive zone coverage; and whether or not the team has control of the puck doesn't affect pattern and positioning.

If a player leaves his designated territory in order to make a play or to check a player in an attempt to regain puck control, it is imperative that one of his teammates backs him up in his position so that the team stays in balance. This rule holds true in each of the systems discussed in this chapter.

THE SYSTEM

As shown on the diagram, the defense is behind the net in the break-out formation in the defensive zone while his partner is in front of the net. The wingers are up high on the boards (lined up with the top of

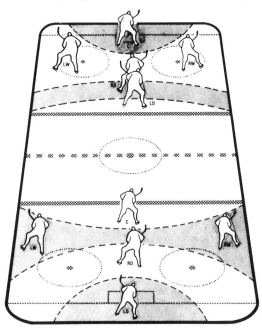

the faceoff circles), while the centerman is high inside the blue line in the middle. Behind the net, the defense has 4 options to pass the puck.

In the offensive zone, the center is in front of the net with the 2 wingers covering the side boards and corners, and the 2 defenders stagger each other inside the blue line. One defense covers the top of the slot area while his partner patrols the blue line.

SYSTEM II—1-3-1

INTRODUCTION

The diagram shows a full view of the hockey rink with an identical offensive system used at both ends of the ice. The broken lines show areas of positioning for each player under this system. The same pattern and same positioning are used whether the play is in the offensive, neutral or defensive zone.

THE SYSTEM

In the breakout formation in the defensive zone, 1 defense is behind the net while his partner is positioned in the slot area. The wingers are by the side boards and the centerman is high inside the blue line in the middle. The defender behind the net has 4 options to pass the puck in this pattern.

In the offensive zone, the centerman covers the net and the corners. The wingers handle the side boards and sometimes the corners, while the defensemen cover the blue line and slot area. The defense in the slot usually will be the man from the side opposite the corner where the puck is. For example, if the puck is in the right corner, the left defense goes into the slot area while the right defender covers the blue line. The defensemen switch as the situation in the zone changes.

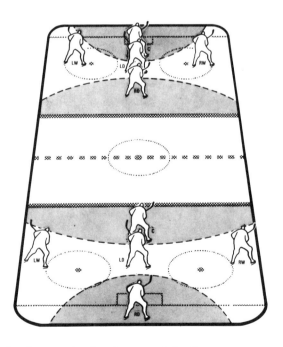

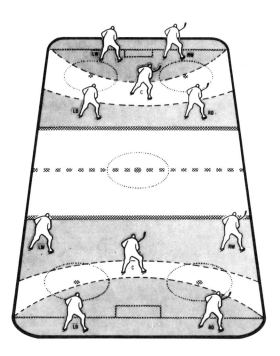

SYSTEM III—2-1-2

INTRODUCTION

Identical systems are shown in the offensive and defensive zones of the full rink illustrated. The same system would also be employed in the neutral zone (not shown). The broken lines divide areas of responsibility for each of the players. This territorial responsibility holds whether the team is on the offensive attack or in defensive zone coverage, and is the same in each zone.

THE SYSTEM

In the breakout formation in the defensive zone, the 2 defensemen are behind the net and the wingers are high along the side boards, as illustrated. The center is in the slot area. In this pattern, the defense has 3 options for passing the puck to begin breaking out.

In the offensive zone, the center remains in the slot area and also covers the side boards. The 2 wingers cover in front of the net and handle the corners. The defensemen cover the right and left halves of the rink at the blue line.

SYSTEM IV—1-2-2

INTRODUCTION

This diagram shows a full view of the hockey rink with an identical offensive system used at either end. The same pattern is used in the neutral zone, although it is not diagramed. The broken lines in the rink indicate positioning for each player, whether in the offensive, defensive or neutral zone and whether the team controls the puck or is attempting to regain control.

THE SYSTEM

As illustrated, in the 1-2-2 system the breakout has the 2 defensemen behind the net with the wingers near the side boards in line with the top of the faceoff circles. The centerman is up high in the slot area in the middle. This formation gives the defense 3 options for passing the puck.

In the offensive zone, the centerman covers the front of the net and the corners while the wingers cover the side boards. The defensemen handle their half of the ice at the blue line.

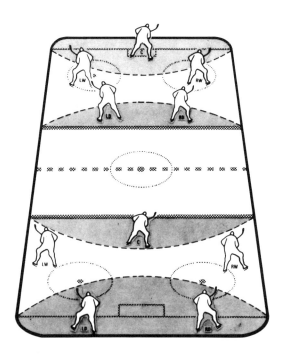

SYSTEM V—2-2-1

INTRODUCTION

This full-rink diagram shows the 2-2-1 system in effect at both ends of the rink. The same pattern should be used in the neutral zone, although this is not illustrated. The broken lines dividing the rink show the area assigned to each player under this system. The areas of responsibility remain the same in each zone and in both offensive and defensive situations (from attack to defensive coverage).

THE SYSTEM

In the breakout formation, 1 defense is behind the net and his partner is situated in the corner or along the boards. The centerman is on the opposite side of the rink, in the corner or along the boards. The wingers are high along the boards, as illustrated. In this pattern, the defenseman behind the goal has 4 options to pass.

In the offensive zone, the wingers cover the net and the corners, while 1 defenseman and the center cover the side boards. One defenseman covers the entire blue line.

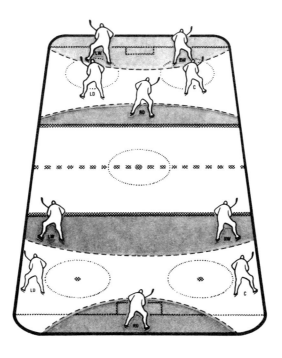

SYSTEM VI—3-2

INTRODUCTION

The 3-2 offensive system is shown in this full-rink diagram as it is employed on the breakout in the defensive zone and on the attack. The same system would also be used in the neutral zone, although this is not illustrated. The broken lines show each player's positioning in the defensive and offensive ends. The coverage areas remain the same from breakout to the attack and in defensive zone coverage and regardless of whether or not the team controls the puck.

THE SYSTEM

As illustrated, the 3-2 system on the breakout offers a couple of options on deployment of the defense. Two defenders may go behind the net, or they may operate with 1 defense in front of the net and 1 behind it. The 3 forwards overload one side of the zone in this system, forming a triangle. One player is along the boards, 1 in the middle or slot area and the third is positioned between the opposing defensemen to form the triangle. The forwards will be on that side of the rink where the puck will

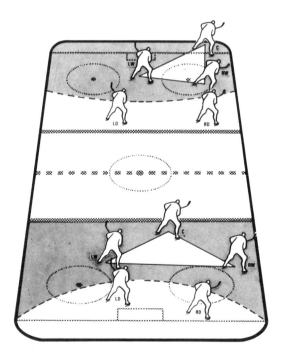

come out of the zone, left or right. The triangle pattern should be kept while the team has control of the puck and moves to the offensive zone.

In the offensive end, the forwards operate again in the triangular setup. The triangle covers half of the ice, depending on which side the puck is on, with 1 player on the puck, 1 covering the side boards and 1 covering the goal mouth. The player in front of the goal must be prepared to move behind the net when necessary. The defensemen control their own half of the zone at the blue line.

SYSTEM VII—2-3

INTRODUCTION

The 2-3 offensive system, as it is utilized on the breakout and attack, is illustrated in this full-rink diagram. The broken lines indicate each player's area of responsibility under the system, in both the defensive and offensive zones. The same system would be in effect in the neutral, but this is not illustrated.

THE SYSTEM

The 2-3 system on the breakout offers a couple of options on deployment of the defense. Two defenders may go behind the net, or they may operate with 1 defense in front of the net and 1 behind it. The centerman is in the slot area, or may also be in a corner opposite 1 of the defensemen. The 2 wingers stay on each side of the boards toward the points, thus giving the defense and centerman more room in which to maneuver.

In the offensive end, the wingers cover their own half-ice territories deep in the zone, while the 2 defensemen and center hang around the blue line, poised to move deeper into the zone for scoring opportunities or checking duties.

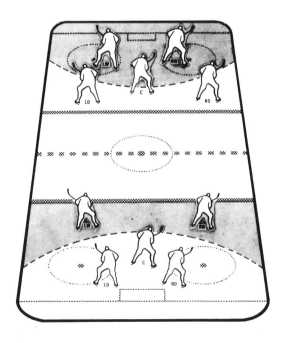

186 • *Hockey for the Coach, the Player and the Fan*

DEFENSIVE ZONE PLAY—BREAKING OUT

INTRODUCTION

Breaking out of your own end is the backbone of your offense, thus it is most important to spend enough time during practice in reviewing your breakout system. Everyone becomes more familiar with it and under any circumstances your players will be ready to execute properly.

Zone 1: 3-2 system. Two defensemen are behind the goal line in this formation. They may be positioned as illustrated, where 1 defense can be behind the goal with his partner in the corner. The player with the puck passes to the other defenseman, who turns and proceeds to skate out of the zone. He has the option of passing to the center, or passing it back to his partner, who is moving out from behind the goal line.

Zone 2: 1-3-1 system. In this formation, 1 defender is behind the net, with the second man in front of the goal. The defense behind the net with the puck may pass around the boards or directly to his wingers, or he may pass to the center.

DRILL

All of the players are positioned outside the zone at center ice along the boards. The coach shoots the puck into the zone, and a 5-man unit goes in to retrieve the puck and break out according to the coach's system. Drill may end in the neutral zone, or the coach may have each unit go the full length of the ice for a shot on goal after breaking out.

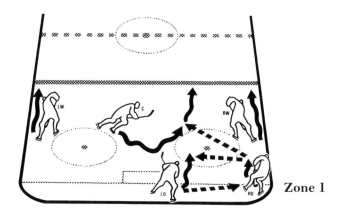

Zone 1

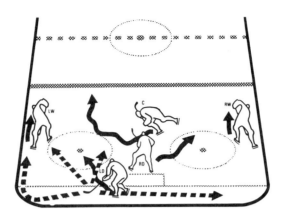

Zone 2

NOTE

Constant practice and careful attention to execution are necessary to install an effective breakout system. All of the players must know where to be and what to do—under pressure from the opposing team—and must be able to recognize and follow the options that go with the system.

DEFENSIVE ZONE PLAY: BREAKING OUT

Zone 1: 3-2 system. Breakout system has 2 defense behind the goal line. One defense has the puck in a corner and passes it behind the net to his partner in the opposite corner. He, in turn, can pass to either his wing or the center, or he can carry the puck himself, as shown in the diagram.

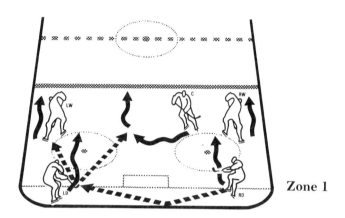

Zone 1

Zone 2: 2-2-1 system. The single defense behind the net has the puck, while his partner is situated in front of the net. The centerman makes a swing behind the net and may or may not pick up the puck. As the center swings wide to the boards, as diagramed, the winger on that side moves out or cuts toward the middle. If the center does not take the puck, the defense starts out and passes off to the centerman along the boards, to the winger, or to his partner, who moves out from in front of the net.

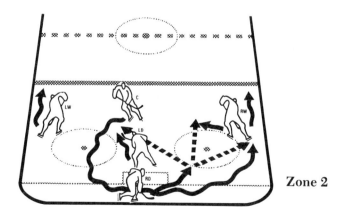

Zone 2

DEFENSIVE ZONE PLAY: BREAKING OUT

Zone 1: 1-2-2 system. In this formation, the winger has the puck in the corner. He passes the puck behind the net to the defense in the opposite corner, who in turn passes either to the winger on his side by the boards or to the wing who had the puck and is now breaking in the slot. Another option is for the defense to carry the puck out and pass off to his defensive partner, who is moving out from in front of the net.

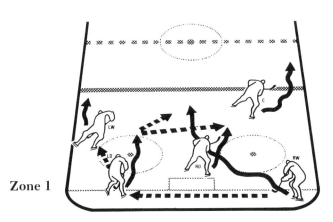

Zone 1

Zone 2: 1-2-2 system. Here again, a wing and a defenseman are behind the goal line. In this case, however, the defenseman has the puck, which he passes to the wing in the corner. The wing will attempt to skate the puck out, but may pass to either the centerman, who is making a swing to his side, or to the defenseman who was in front of the net, but is now taking over the center's position in the slot, as illustrated.

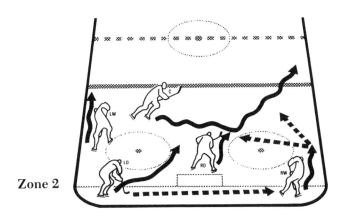

Zone 2

DEFENSIVE ZONE PLAY: BREAKING OUT

Zone 1: 2-2-1 system. One defense is behind the net with the puck; the other defenseman is in front of the goal. The centerman makes a swing to the corner on the same side as the defenseman behind the goal, as diagramed. As the center makes the swing, the wing on that side moves to the middle. The defense who controls the puck may pass either to the centerman or to the wing to start the breakout.

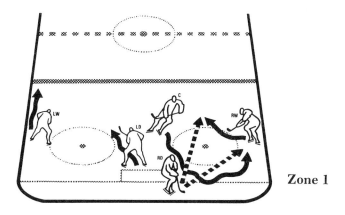

Zone 1

Zone 2: 3-2 system. Both defensemen are behind the goal line, as shown. Either one would have 3 options in this situation: a pass to his defensive partner, a pass to the centerman, or a pass to the winger on his side. In this case, the center usually is stationary in the slot area until he receives the pass from the defense and the breakout gets underway.

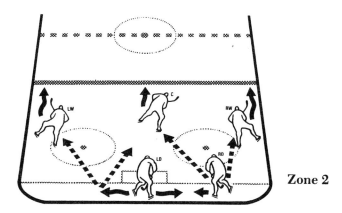

Zone 2

DEFENSIVE ZONE PLAY: BREAKING OUT

Zone 1: 2-3 system. One defenseman is behind the net and his partner is in the corner. The centerman makes a swing from the middle to the corner opposite that one where the defenseman is located. The defenseman with the puck behind the net will attempt to make a play or pass to the center who is making the swing. If he is unable to pass to the center because of pressure from the opposition, he will pass to his partner on the other side. In this situation, the defense in the corner passes to the center, who is coming back in the area or to the wing by the boards.

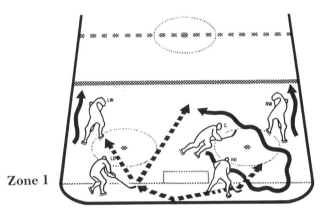

Zone 1

Zone 2: 2-3 system. One defenseman is behind the net, while the other defender is in front of the goal. Here the option is for the defense in front of the net to make a swing in his corner, while the centerman swings to the opposite corner. The defenseman with the puck can use either of these players to start the breakout. If he passes, for example, to the defenseman, the defenseman in the corner can, in turn, pass to the winger who is coming into the middle to replace the center, or he can return the puck to his partner, who is moving out front behind the net.

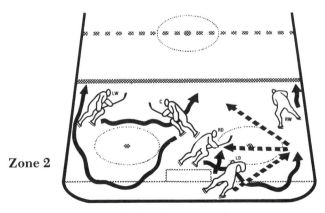

Zone 2

DEFENSIVE ZONE PLAY: BREAKING OUT

Zone 1: 1-2-1-1 or 1-3-1 system. One defense is behind the net; his partner is in front of the goal. The defenseman behind the net has the puck and has 2 options for passing. He may start out carrying the puck himself and pass off to his defensive partner, who is moving out from in front of the goal, or he may pass to the right wing, who is coming off the boards and cutting into the middle.

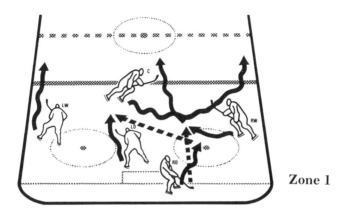

Zone 1

Zone 2: 1-2-1-1 or 1-3-1 system. One defense is in front of the net, while his partner has the puck behind the goal. He passes to the wing on his side, who in turn has 4 choices. The winger can drop a back pass to the defense, pass to the defenseman who is moving out from in front of the net, pass to the center swinging across the middle, carry the puck out himself, or make a long pass across the ice to his other winger, who is breaking along the boards.

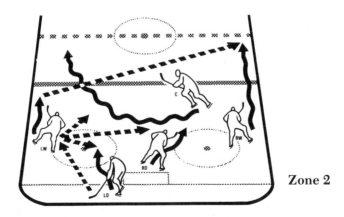

Zone 2

DEFENSIVE ZONE PLAY: BREAKING OUT

Zone 1: 1-2-1-1 or 1-3-1 system. One defense is in front of the net, while the other defender has the puck behind the net. The defense passes to the wing on his side as he starts out. The wing returns the puck with a drop pass and then the defense passes to the defenseman who was in front of the net, but is moving down the ice. He in turn may pass to the wing on his side, pass to the wing on the other side, who is now breaking into the middle after dropping the puck, or he may carry the puck himself.

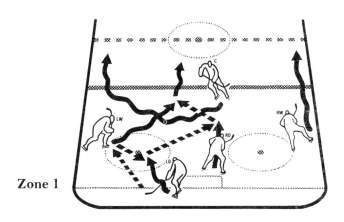

Zone 1

Zone 2: 2-2-1 system. In this formation, 1 defense has the puck behind the net, and his partner is situated in front. The defenseman with the puck pauses while the centerman makes a swing in the corner, then passes to the center and moves out. The center returns the puck to the defense, who then passes off to his partner, who is starting out from in front of the net. He, in turn, should be open to pass to the center as he returns to the middle.

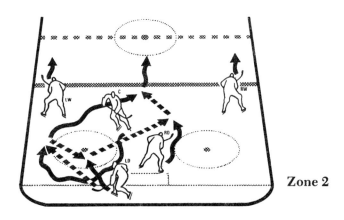

Zone 2

DEFENSIVE ZONE PLAY: BREAKING OUT

Zone 1: 1-2-1-1 or 1-3-1 system. One defense is in front of the net, while his partner is behind the net with the puck. The defenseman with the puck passes to the winger on his side and starts out. The wing may return the puck to the defenseman who started to the play, pass it to the other defense, who is moving out from in front of the net, or start down the boards and then pass off to the other winger, who has cut across to the middle and is moving up the ice. The center swings to the side to replace the wing, as diagramed.

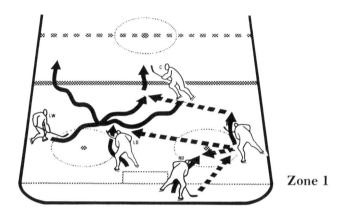

Zone 1

Zone 2: 2-3 system. This formation has 1 defense in front of the net and the other defenseman behind the goal with the puck. The centerman makes a swing to the corner, as shown, and is prepared to take a pass from the defenseman behind the net. Other options for the defense include passing to the wing, who is situated farther up on the same side, carrying the puck himself, or giving the puck to his partner as he skates forward and the partner moves to the right side, as shown on the diagram.

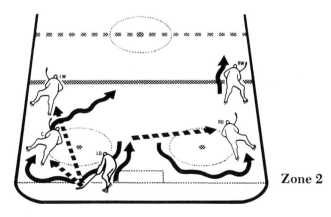

Zone 2

DEFENSIVE ZONE PLAY: BREAKING OUT

Zone 1: 2-2-1 system. The play starts with a winger, who controls the puck in the corner. He passes around the boards to the defenseman who is in the wing's position on the side. The defense has the alternatives of passing to his partner, who is moving out from in front of the net, to the winger who started the play and is moving down the ice, or to the centerman swinging into the middle.

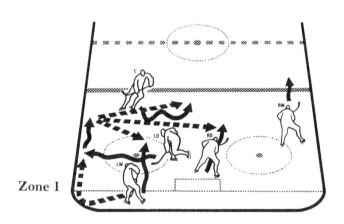

Zone 1

Zone 2: 3-2 system. One defenseman has the puck behind the net and his partner goes in front of the goal. The defense with the puck starts carrying it toward the side, where he has 4 options for passing. He can pass to his defensive partner in front of the net, pass to the wing on his side, who is making a large swing to the other side, to the opposite wing moving into the middle, or to the centerman, who is swinging to replace the wing on the overloaded side.

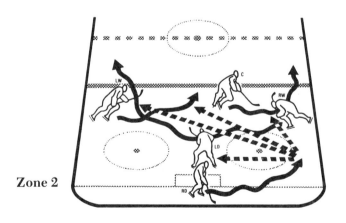

Zone 2

DEFENSIVE ZONE PLAY: BREAKING OUT

Zone 1: 3-2 system. In this instance, the right wing gets the puck at the blue line. Under pressure from the opposition, he moves the puck back to his right defense, who in turn passes to the left defense. At the point, the defenseman has 2 alternatives: a pass to the left wing or to the right wing who is coming across the middle. The purpose of having the center and right wing switch positions in the neutral zone is to give them the opportunity to shake off their checkers and get into the open to receive a pass and make a play.

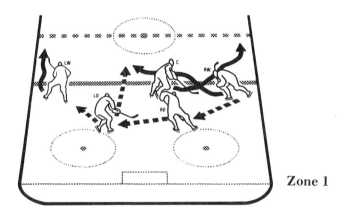

Zone 1

Zone 2: 2-2-1 system. If the puck is shot into the zone, or at the goalie, the defense picks up the puck and goes behind the net as the other defenseman covers the front of the net. The centerman will come in deep and make a swing toward the corner of the rink on the same side as the defense behind the net. The left wing comes off the boards and cuts across the middle, changing positions with the centerman, while the right wing skates on his side past the blue line. At that point he either cuts across the middle or stays on his side, depending on who is carrying the puck. The defenseman, with the puck behind the goal line, has 3 options to move the puck out of the zone following the diagram.

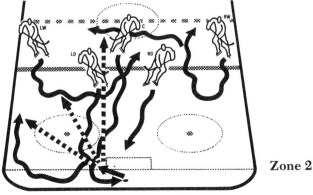

197

Zone 2

DEFENSIVE ZONE PLAY: BREAKING OUT (breakaway pass from faceoff)

Zone 1: From the faceoff, the centerman draws·the puck to the left defense, who is situated behind the center. The defenseman caroms a pass off the side boards, as illustrated, as the left wing races down the ice into the neutral zone in an attempt to get to the puck first and break in on the net.

NOTE

This type of play should be thoroughly discussed with the players before execution so that everyone knows what to do to make the play work and how to recover should the play fail to come off.

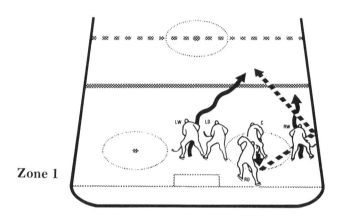

Zone 1

Zone 2: The center takes the faceoff and attempts to draw the puck to the left defense behind him. In this play, the defense passes off the boards on the opposite side of the rink and the right wing dashes for the puck in the neutral zone. If he succeeds in getting to the puck first there is a good chance he will be able to break in on the goal.

Zone 2

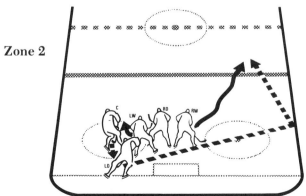

DEFENSIVE ZONE PLAY: BREAKING OUT

Zone 1: 1-2-1-1 system. In this case, 1 defense positions himself in front of the net as the other defense controls the puck behind the goal. The player with the puck has 2 options for passing; he can hit either the center or the right wing as they turn on side in the direction of the puck. A last option is for the defense to carry the puck out himself.

NOTE

All of the forwards must keep their eyes on the puck and be ready to move out of the zone as a unit.

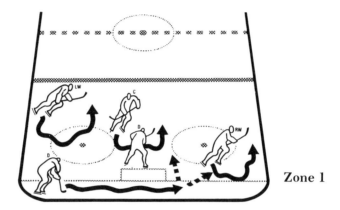

Zone 1

Zone 2: 3-2 system. One defenseman goes behind the net with the puck and stalls while his partner in front of the net swings in his corner and gets set to receive a pass. (The right defense in front of the net goes to the right, while a left defense would go to the left.) After the defenseman receives the pass from behind the goal, he can, in turn, pass to his center or carry the puck himself. If he elects to carry, the winger on his side should move out of the zone quickly to give the defenseman room to maneuver.

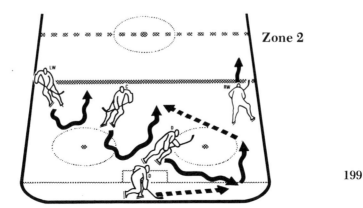

Zone 2

199

NEUTRAL ZONE PLAY—FORMATION OF ATTACKS

INTRODUCTION

Drills for offensive play in the neutral zone start in the defensive zone, either from a faceoff or as a continuation of the breakout play. In working with the team in neutral zone strategy, the coach may drop the puck for a faceoff to start play, or he may have the players work from the breakout and go the full length of the ice before stopping play.

In the neutral zone, it is important to maintain control of the puck through team effort. An individual player can't be allowed to give the puck away by trying to be fancy with the puck. If no play can be made in the neutral zone, the final choice is to shoot the puck deep in the offensive corner, where there is a possibility of recovering control. This is a better choice than shooting at the goal. In this case, the goalie will control the puck, turn it over to his team and thereby end your offensive hope.

The following thirteen examples of neutral zone play are based on the same situation: the offensive team has control of the puck while the defensive team puts a forechecker on the defenseman in possession of the puck in attempt to force the play and regain puck control. Seven start in the defensive zone, while six start in the neutral zone.

Zone 1: 3-2 system. In this situation, the defensive team sends in 2

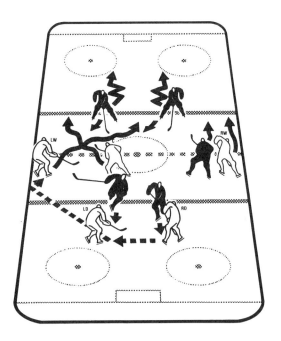

forecheckers deep on the defense. The offensive team should end up with 2 forward players open in the neutral zone. If the defense passes to one of them, the attackers have a chance at a 3 on 3, 3 on 2 or 2 on 2 situation against the defensive team. In a 2 on 2 situation, the 2 offensive players who control the puck can often catch the defense off guard by crossing lanes at the offensive blue line. This has proven effective on every level of hockey.

VARIATION

The coach may have the defensive unit play with sticks turned upside down or play without sticks.

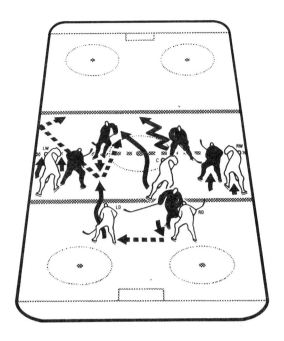

NEUTRAL ZONE PLAY (starting in the defensive zone)

Zone 1: 1-2-1-1 system. Here the defensive team puts the forechecker on the right defense, who has the puck. The defense can pass to his partner, who in turn can carry the puck out of the zone. Assuming the 2 wingers are covered by their checkers, the defense passes to his centerman. This could be a straight-ahead pass or could be a banked pass off the boards, which would likely catch the defense off balance. The play could lead to a 1 on 1 or 2 on 1 situation, or to a breakaway if the center anticipates the play correctly.

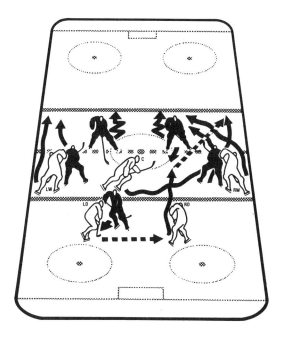

NEUTRAL ZONE PLAY (starting in the defensive zone)

Zone 1: 1-2-1-1 system. In this situation, a defenseman, who is being forechecked, passes to his partner, who has a chance to carry the puck out of the zone. If his wingers are covered, the defenseman with the puck must look for his centerman to take the pass. A play that can be employed here is to have 1 of the wings come off his side and cut across the offensive blue line, taking his checker with him. He can create interference with their defense and give the center an opportunity to sneak on his side along the boards where he is open for a pass from the defense. This catches the opposition's defense off guard, since he should be putting pressure on the puck carrier, and could result in a breakaway or in a 1 on 1 or 2 on 1 situation in the offensive zone.

NEUTRAL ZONE PLAY (starting from the defensive zone)

Zone 1: 2-1-2 system. In this example, the defense passes to his partner, who passes to the wing on his side, as illustrated. The winger cuts across center ice as the centerman swings to the side, avoiding the checker who is covering that side, and makes a rush down the ice. An option here is for the winger carrying the puck to pass ahead to either one of his line mates, who are speeding up on either side, catching the defense or the checker by surprise. This could end up with a 1 on 1, 2 on 1 or a breakaway.

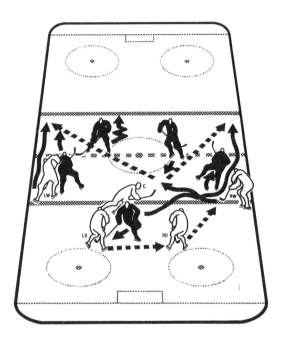

NEUTRAL ZONE PLAY (starting in the defensive zone)

Zone 1: 2-1-2 system. The defense who is being forechecked keeps the play going by passing to his defensive partner, who in turn passes to the center, who is making a swing at center ice (see diagram). As soon as the wing sees the play develop and sees the centerman coming toward his side, he comes off the boards and cuts to the middle, taking his checker with him, and tries to interfere with the opposing defense, who should be coming in to pressure the puck carrier. This play could give the center room to get free along the boards and set up a 1 on 1 or 2 on 1 break in the offensive zone.

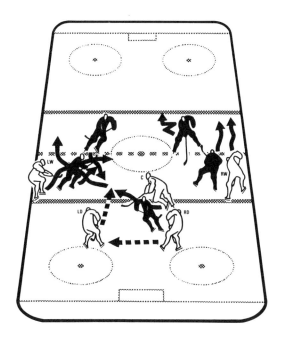

NEUTRAL ZONE PLAY (starting from the defensive zone)

Zone 1: 2-2-1 system. In the diagram for instance, the defense with the puck passes to his partner, who skates forward and out of the defensive zone. He looks for either his center or opposite wing, who cross paths in the zone (see illustration), and sends the puck to one of them. The wing comes off the boards and cuts across to get clear of his checker; the center swings to the wing's position in order to keep the team in balance. This play could develop into a 3 on 3, 3 on 2 or 2 on 2 situation against the defensive team.

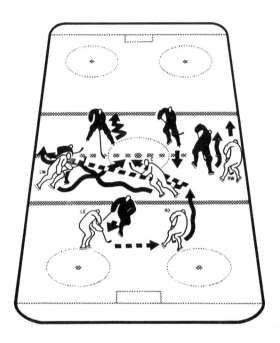

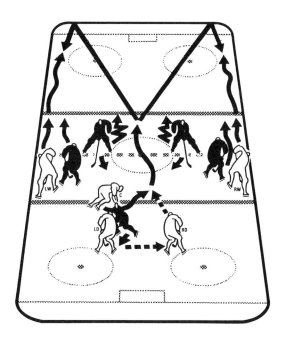

NEUTRAL ZONE PLAY (starting in the defensive zone)

Zone 1: 3-2 or 2-3 system. Using this system, the defense passes to his partner, who passes off to the centerman, as indicated. If the 2 wingers are covered by their checkers, the center finds himself up against 2 defensemen. His best choice is to shoot the puck into either corner, where a wing has a chance to regain control of the puck and to make a play from the corner in the offensive zone.

NOTE

If the centerman is a right-handed shot he will usually shoot to the left-hand corner (and vice versa). This will be a clue as to which wing breaking up the side should head to the corner to try to get possession of the puck.

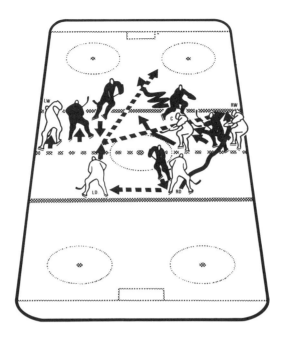

NEUTRAL ZONE PLAY (starting from the neutral zone)

Zone 1: 4-1 or 2-2-1 system. The defenseman who has the puck on the attack and who is under pressure, passes to his defensive partner, who carries across the red line as the other defense goes wide to his winger's side. The winger and center both cut to the middle, and the defense can receive a pass and take the puck into the defensive end. The key to this strategy is to catch the defensive team off guard and out of position by moving the centerman between the 2 defensemen and by having the opposite wing move toward their defense. The wing draws his checker and may be able to interfere with the opponent's defense; the center is open for a pass, as is the defenseman. A last resort, if the play does not work, is to shoot the puck deep into the corner.

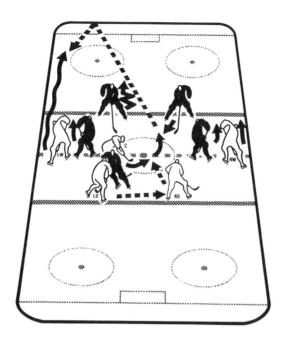

NEUTRAL ZONE PLAY (starts from the neutral zone)

Zone 1: 2-1-2 or 2-3 system. The defense who has the puck and is being checked passes to his partner, as illustrated, who passes forward to the centerman, who is making a swing at the red line. If the wings are being covered by their checkers, the center shoots the puck deep in the corner. One of the wings will break for the corner and try to regain control of the puck in order for the offensive team to make a play.

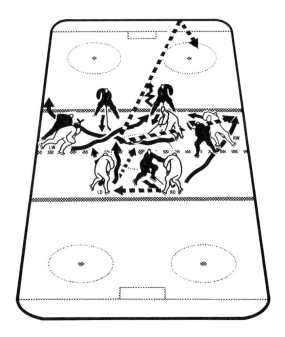

NEUTRAL ZONE PLAY (starting in the neutral zone)

Zone 1: 4-1 or 2-2-1 system. The defenseman with the puck passes to his partner, who skates ahead while the first defense goes wide to the winger's position to receive a return pass and try to bring the puck deep into the zone for an offensive play. Surprise is the tactic here. The members of the offensive team switch positions, making it difficult for the checker and the defense on the defensive team to control and contain the attack. This play gives a number of alternatives. One winger is cutting across, while the centerman swings to his side for balance. The other wing also cuts across, but toward their defense, taking his checker with him and tries to interfere with the defense on that side. This gives the puck carrier 3 options to pass: to the wing cutting in the middle; to the centerman swinging to the side, to his partner on defense going wide on his respective side. A last option would be to shoot the puck into the zone for the wing or center to go after.

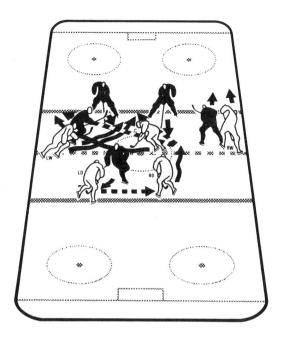

NEUTRAL ZONE PLAY (starting from the neutral zone)

Zone 1: 1-2-1-1 or 2-2-1 system. The defenseman with the puck, who is being checked, passes to his partner, who skates toward the red line. He has the options of passing to his winger, who has come off the side boards to cut across the middle, or to the center, who swings to the wing's position to keep the team in balance. If neither of these choices appears workable, he can cross the red line and shoot the puck into the corner in the offensive zone, where the wing or centerman will have a chance to retrieve it and make a play.

NEUTRAL ZONE PLAY (starting from the neutral zone)

Zone 1: 1-2-1-1 system. As shown in this example, the defenseman who is being forechecked passes to his partner, who carries the puck past the red line. If both wings are tied up by their checkers, the only alternative for the defenseman is to shoot the puck deep in one corner. He goes for the side where the centerman, after making his swing in the neutral zone, is headed. The center has some speed and momentum at this point, and should have a good chance to get to the puck first and get off a play in the offensive zone.

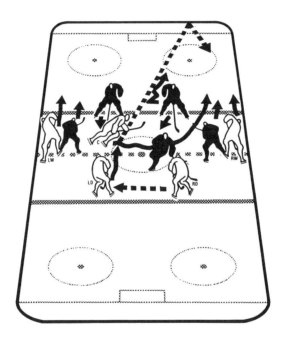

NEUTRAL ZONE PLAY (starting from the neutral zone)

Zone 1: 3-1-1 system. Under pressure from the forechecker, the defense with the puck passes to his partner. As he skates across the red line, the winger from the other side cuts across the middle and the centerman swings to the winger's side to keep the team in balance. The defense with the puck could pass to the winger, or he could shoot the puck deep in the opposite corner (see diagram). As the centerman is already moving in this direction, he may be able to reach the puck before the defensive team, regain control and make a play in the offensive zone.

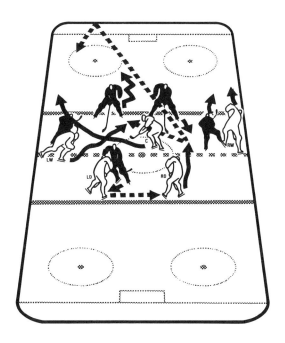

OFFENSIVE ZONE PLAY—COMPLETION OF ATTACKS

INTRODUCTION

Start the offensive zone drill from the breakout formation in the defensive end. The attack continues until play ends with a goal or until the goalie freezes the puck or the defensive team takes over puck control. As a variation, the coach may start the drill in the neutral zone from a faceoff, moving the puck into the offensive zone. To make maximum use of the ice, split the team into 2 units and work toward both goals from the neutral zone. All plays on offensive zone strategy are 3 on 2, but may be broken down to 2 on 1.

Zone 1: The winger carrying the puck in on his side has 2 options for passing the puck in the offensive zone if the centerman makes a rush toward the net. This example has the center skating in on the net as the other wing crosses the line and cuts to the middle. If the center keeps skating, the winger can pass to him behind the defense who is forcing him, or the wing can keep the puck and try a drop pass to his other winger, who is skating into the slot area for a possible shot on goal.

Zone 1

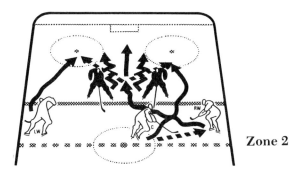

Zone 2

Zone 2: Here the winger has the puck at center ice, and cuts across the middle to enter the offensive zone. The center follows behind him and swings over to the side to keep the team in balance. In the middle, the wing can pass to either of his line mates, who are cutting around the defenseman, or he can take a shot at the net while the center and wing go in for the rebound.

NOTE

In any play, the important thing is to retain control of the puck. The basic rule in any offensive play is that the second man in should always go to the net for the rebound. Depending on who is carrying the puck, 1 of the 2 players should rush the net, thus forcing 1 of the defensemen to check him, leaving the other man open to make a play.

VARIATION

The coach may have the defense with or without sticks, or may have them turn their sticks upside down.

OFFENSIVE ZONE PLAY

Zone 1: In this offensive situation, the wing carries the puck deep into the zone in his own corner. There is nothing he can do except make a swing toward the boards and come back on his side looking for help from his line mates. The center should go deep into the same corner to possibly receive a pass, while the other winger should move into the slot area. This gives the puck carrier 2 options to pass, either to the center in the corner or to his wing in the slot.

.Zone 1

Zone 2: The right winger, who has the puck, carries into the offensive zone on his side. The centerman is the trailer and the other winger makes a rush toward the net. The puck carrier makes a drop pass to his center, then cuts around the defense giving the centerman an opportunity for an excellent shot on the net or a return pass to the winger cutting in on the right.

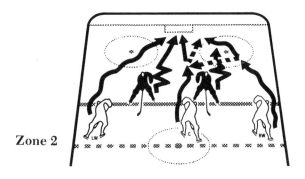

Zone 2

OFFENSIVE ZONE PLAY

Zone 1: The diagram illustrates a situation where the winger carries the puck deep into the zone and is about to go behind the net. The centerman, reading the play, skates to the faceoff circle to receive a pass and takes a shot on the net. This is the most logical location for the center for such a play. Normally this area is not covered because the defenseman is putting pressure on the puck carrier (the wing). The other defense has to cover the net. The second offensive wing skates to the opposite faceoff circle. From that position, he is ready to pick up a loose puck coming to his side and to check his man in case his team loses possession of the puck.

Zone 2: This is a similar situation: the wing has the puck on the attack, carries it deep into the offensive zone and goes behind the net with the puck. At this point, the other wing should be skating into the faceoff circle on his side, looking for a pass and a possible shot on the goal. The centerman should be around the opposite faceoff circle, especially when the puck carrier is behind the goal line, because that puts him in good position to capture a loose puck or to check the defensive wing on that side if the offense gives up possession of the puck.

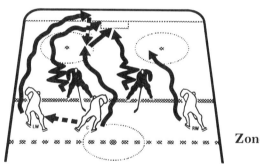

Zone 1

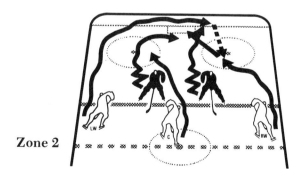

Zone 2

OFFENSIVE ZONE PLAY

Zone 1: The centerman controls the puck at center ice in this example and commits himself toward one side, faking a pass to his winger. He holds onto the puck and cuts to the middle of the slot area as both wings come down their sides. The center has 3 options: he can pass to either one of his wingers or take a shot at the net himself as the wings cut around the defense and go in for the rebound or for a loose puck.

Zone 2: The offensive play begins when the centerman, who controls the puck at center ice, carries it into the offensive zone on one side. The winger on that side trails the center, then cuts into the middle to retain line balance and prepare to take a pass from the centerman. The center should cut around the defense after passing and be ready for either a return pass or for a rebound. The other wing goes for the net on the other side.

NOTE

In any offensive play, the puck carrier has the right-away in bringing the puck into the zone. His partners should break in for an open spot and should always attempt to force 1 defenseman toward the net.

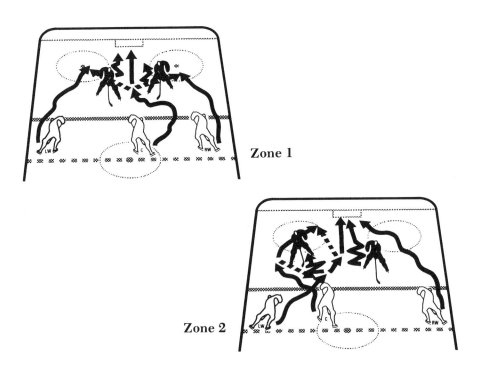

Zone 1

Zone 2

OFFENSIVE ZONE PLAY

Zone 1: In this situation, the wings work together behind the goal line after 1 winger has carried the puck in deep in his corner. His partner also goes in deep on his side, while the centerman heads into the slot area. This play gives the puck carrier 2 alternatives. He can pass to the center, if he is open, or he can pass to his other wing behind the goal line. They can exchange the puck again, or get it to the centerman in front of the goal.

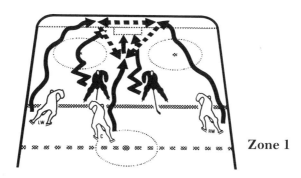

Zone 1

Zone 2: In this illustration, the attacking wing who controls the puck at center ice, shoots the puck into the opposite corner of the offensive zone as his other wing breaks in. The centerman should swing to the side where the puck will come off the boards and act as the trailer for a drop pass from the wing who gains control of the puck. He may return the puck to the wing as he cuts toward the goal, or he may take a shot on goal. The second wing breaks in on the net for the rebound.

Zone 2

OFFENSIVE ZONE PLAY

POSITIONING

Zone 1: This diagram illustrates proper positioning of the 5 offensive players when the puck is in the corner. One wing is in the corner with the puck. The centerman should be in the slot area near the side where the puck is located, while the other wing stations himself in front of the net, poised to move behind the net or into his corner if the puck gets loose or if the puck carrier needs help. In this position, he also screens the goal if the puck goes into the slot area or to the defense. The defensemen are located on the side and in the middle (not more than 40 feet apart), as illustrated.

Zone 2: Offensive zone positioning when the puck is controlled by a defenseman at the point as the other defenseman in the middle, in line with the far goalpost. The centerman is in the slot area for a possible pass or for a tip or deflection of a shot from the point. One wing goes in deep in the zone, on the same side as the puck carrier, to take a pass from the defense if called on, and the second wing sets up in front of the net. From his spot he can move into the corner or behind the goal if the puck gets loose, and he can also screen the goalie or take care of a rebound.

NOTE

With proper positioning, the puck carrier should have at least 4 options for moving the puck and setting up a shot on goal.

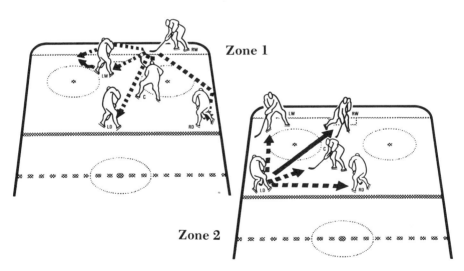

Zone 1

Zone 2

OFFENSIVE ZONE PLAY

POSITIONING

Zone 1: This example of proper positioning in the offensive zone has the puck in the possession of a wing by the side boards midway in the zone. One defense is by the boards on the same side at the blue line; the second defender is in the middle, in line with the pipe on the far side of the goal. The centerman should be in the slot area toward the side where the puck is being held, while the other wing is in front of the net to screen the goalie, look for a rebound, or go into the corner or behind the goal for a loose puck.

Zone 2: Here the situation is the same, i.e., the puck is controlled by a wing at the boards halfway into the zone, but positioning is somewhat different. His centerman is in the corner on the same side, and the opposite winger is in front of the goal. One defense is on or near the boards on the same side as the puck, and his partner is no more than 40 feet away at the blue line, usually in line with the far goalpost.

NOTE

Both of these formations give the wing with the puck at least 4 alternatives for passing before taking a shot on the net.

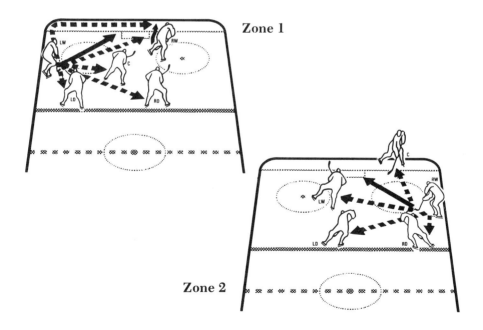

Zone 1

Zone 2

OFFENSIVE ZONE PLAY

"Give and Go"

Zone 1: "Give and go" play from the defense with a player located along the side boards. One side of the zone is overloaded with 3 players, as illustrated. The point man starts out by passing to his winger or to the center, who is by the boards. As he passes, he breaks in on the goal, receives a return pass from the centerman along the boards, and takes a shot on the net. This play is basically a 2 on 1 situation against the player who is covering the formation.

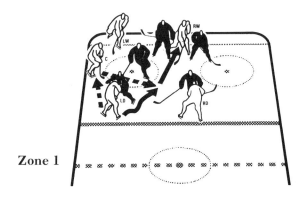

Zone 1

Zone 2: "Give and go" play from the corner to the point man. The player in the corner has control of the puck and passes to his point man. After passing, he moves along the side toward the point and takes a return pass from the man on the point, who in turn breaks for the goal. As he moves in on the net, he gets a pass from the player along the boards and goes in for a shot. Worked this way, the play is a 2 on 1 situation against the player who is covering the formation.

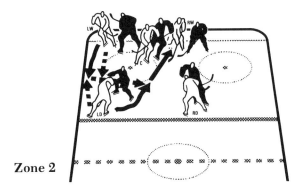

Zone 2

OFFENSIVE ZONE PLAY

"GIVE AND GO"

Zone 1: Double "give and go" play from the defense, or point man. The play is initiated by the point man in the offensive zone. He starts out by passing to the player located along the side boards and breaking in on the net. As he moves in, he gets a return pass from the side boards and quickly passes to the player in the corner. Still moving in, he receives a pass from the cornerman and takes a shot on goal. This setup, based on overloading one side of the offensive zone with 3 players, breaks the play down to consecutive 2 on 1 situations.

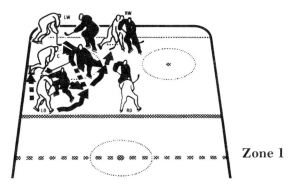

Zone 1

Zone 2: "Give and go" play from the player situated along the boards to a player in the corner. One side of the offensive zone is overloaded with 3 players. The player in control of the puck along the side boards starts the play out by making a pass to the cornerman and breaking in toward the net. He receives a return pass from the corner and takes a shot on the net. This again is a 2 on 1 situation against the checker coming at them.

Zone 2

OFFENSIVE ZONE PLAY

"Give and Go"

Zone 1: "Give and go" play from the corner. In this situation, usually the 3 forwards are involved and will rotate positions in a circular manner, as diagramed. The basic formation has 1 player in the corner, 1 in front of the net and 1 along the side boards. The forwards move in a circle in the corner while the player with the puck looks for an opportunity to pass to one of his teammates. The rotation allows the puck carrier to wait for a receiver to get open or to keep the puck until he can take a shot on the net, while keeping the checkers off balance.

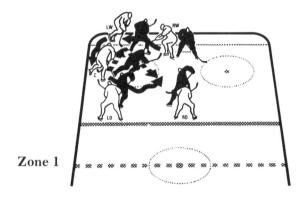

Zone 1

Zone 2: "Give and go" play from the side of the net. In this pattern, the 3 forwards are set up behind the goal line, at the faceoff circle and slightly in front of the far goalpost, as illustrated. The players circle the goal to keep away from their checkers, while the puck carrier looks for either a chance to pass to a line mate or to take a good shot on the net himself.

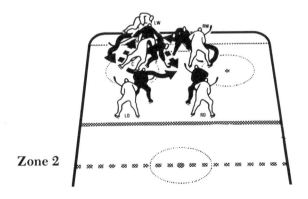

Zone 2

OFFENSIVE ZONE PLAY

TAKE-OUT PLAY PATTERNS

Zone 1: In this situation, the wing in the corner is passing to the man at the point on his side. In order to give him more time and room in which to operate, the centerman in the middle moves toward the opposing player who is covering the point. By obstructing his movement, the center gives the puck handler an opportunity to make 1 of 3 possible plays (see diagram).

Zone 1

Zone 2: In the offensive zone, the center and right wing overload one side in the corner. The wing passes to the centerman, as shown, and quickly moves in on the defense who is checking him. This move prevents the checker from covering the center, who is able to go around the net in control of the puck and look for an opening. There are at least 2 options open to the center in making a play.

Zone 2

OFFENSIVE ZONE PLAY

TAKE-OUT PLAY PATTERNS

Zone 1: In this pattern, the point man has control of the puck and passes to the winger along the boards on his side. After passing, he moves in front of the player who is checking him to give the wing time and space to make a play without interference from the checker. The wing can go behind his defense and go for one of several alternatives open to him for making a play.

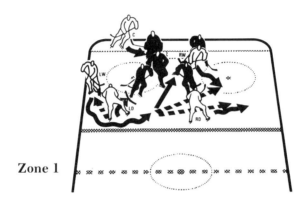

Zone 1

Zone 2: This situation has 3 players overloading one side, with the centerman and right wing in the same corner. The right winger makes a pass to the center and then moves in front of the opposite defense, who is trying to check the centerman. This gives the center time to circle toward the slot and make a play—either a shot on the net or a pass to the left wing or left defense.

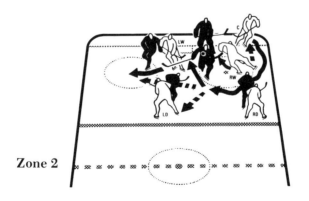

Zone 2

Thought Provokers

1. What is your offensive system in each zone?
2. Does your practice include offensive patterns?
3. Are your forwards able to break away from their checks and hit open areas so that the puck carrier can make a play?
4. How much time do you spend on offensive team strategy in practice? In off-ice sessions?
5. Do you establish firm rules your players must follow in implementing a system in the offensive, neutral and defensive zones?
6. When their defense is standing up at their blue line, have the wingers breaking so that the offense can either make a pass or throw the puck in.
7. In the neutral zone, players have a chance to read which side is sluggish or slacking off and to press on that side.
8. If their defense is backing in their zone, the centerman should be able to carry the puck in across the blue line.
9. The entire offense begins with an effective breakout.

CHAPTER **6** *Team Strategy—The Defensive Game*

It is impossible to create a powerful hockey team without a strong, efficient defense. In any sport, hockey included, it is the biggest and toughest part of the game. Defense isn't a glamour job; it's plain hard work. Discipline is at the heart of a good defense, and time spent on your checking game will pay dividends. What it takes is a system and dogged work at the system. Results won't happen overnight, but constant drilling will bring steady improvement, as well as more wins than losses.

In addition to the more tangible benefits of a good defense seen in the win–loss column, there is a decided psychological benefit. When players are satisfied with the defensive system behind them they can play a better game, strategically and technically, with confidence.

In a defensive system, every player knows his responsibility and each player can assume a responsibility best suited to his ability and skill. The system should fit the players, which in turns means that the players will suit the system. There is a system that will work for your team, whether it's an aggressive team, slow, hitting, skating, strong or small team.

When using a system, whether it is defensive or offensive, allow for some flexibility and some variations to suit the situation. Sometimes you cannot stay with the same formation, such as 1-2-2, the length of the ice. You may start with this formation in their offensive zone, but might have to break it from 1-2-2 into 1-3-1 or 1-2-1-1 in the neutral zone in order to force the puck carrier. The 1-2-2 pattern can be resumed back in your defensive zone, or on the offensive attack. Players should be aware of these variations, and given guidelines on what to do and when to do it as the situation on the ice changes.

There is a basic drill that may be used by the coach, with several variations, to work the team effectively on defense. The players are grouped either at one end of the rink or at center ice along the boards on either side. If the players are at the end of the rink, either the defense or the centerman starts the play. If the players are at center ice, a player or the coach will shoot the puck into the zone to start the play. The drill begins with the offensive and defensive teams in formation against each other. Since this chapter is devoted to the defensive game, the coach should start the drill with at least 1 checker and 2 defensemen, adding another checker and then a third one. This will add a checking line and complete the defensive team.

Each offensive unit will go against 1 defensive unit, and after 1, 2, 3 or 4 rushes, the units will switch assignments. The play isn't considered finished until the defensive team gets control of the puck, the goalie freezes the puck, or the offensive team scores. At that point, each unit returns to center ice (or the end) to start a new play. To give practice in playing the body, the coach may have the defensive team work without sticks or with the sticks turned upside down.

The drill will give the coach the opportunity to watch the offensive team and the defensive team and to check play execution in each zone, as well as proper checking in zone coverage. This is an important team drill because each player, whether on the defense or offense, has a responsibility to make it work. In the defensive game, this responsibility means not only proper execution of the player's assigned role but also total unselfishness. When a team goes on defense, it's dirty work time: checking, digging in the corners, backchecking and a lot of hard skating.

Hockey is a game of wits and determination, and every defenseman should remember this. It's also a game of guts and muscle, and nowhere is this better exemplified than in a strong defense. Your top defensive players are smart, quick, strong and aggressive in forcing the play or the puck carrier shift after shift. But most of all, an effective defense is a united effort by a group of well disciplined players ready and able to back each other up. This chapter deals with different systems of zone coverage, starting in the offensive end (forechecking), into the neutral zone (checking or backchecking) and ending in the defensive zone (checking and proper positioning). Defensive systems are identified by numbers, such as 1-2-2, 2-1-2, or 2-2-1. A 1-2-2 system has 1 forechecker in with the 2 wings covering their checks and the defense minding the blue line in the offensive zone. In the defensive zone, if you are using a 2-1-2 system, you will have 2 wingers covering the points, the centerman in the slot area, and the defensemen in front of the net and in a corner.

In all systems it is important to see that each player is skating about the same distance from one end of the rink to the other. For example, the defense should be skating from behind the goal line to the far blue line. If the centerman is the forechecker in the offensive zone, he will cover the blue line in his own defensive end. The skating distance should be about two-thirds of full ice for everyone. The coach can't expect a player to dig the puck out in the corner of the offensive zone and do the same thing in the defensive zone in the same shift. If this happens, the coach knows the workload isn't being properly distributed, and he isn't utilizing his manpower most efficiently. In addition, the player doing two jobs will tire rapidly and lose his effectiveness.

There are 3 ways to forecheck: (1) zone coverage, where each player is responsible for a certain area of the zone, (2) man-to-man coverage, where checking is by position, and (3) double-teaming the puck carrier with 2 checkers. All of these can be employed in all 3 zones, depending upon the system you are using.

In forechecking and neutral zone checking, the key is to be able to check as many offensive players as possible. The offensive has the advantage of knowing where it is going and what it is going to do and when, while the defense has to guess the play. If your checking system is working well, the team should be able to contain at least 3 or 4 of their offensive players, leaving 1 or 2 players, at most, open. This narrows their options against your defense to 1 on 1, 1 on 2 or 2 on 2, which the defense should be able to handle. It's not possible to stop a team every time it breaks out of the end. But by effectively checking most of the offensive unit, the defense has at least an even break. An important point in the checking team play is that the 2 defensemen must not give up their blue line. They have to force the play or pressure the puck carrier in the neutral zone as much as possible, using common sense. For example, you don't force the play or the puck carrier in a 3 on 2, 3 on 1 or 2 on 1 at your blue line.

As emphasized in the previous chapter, every system has advantages and disadvantages. It's up to the coach to decide which system or systems would benefit his team and fit his players. It is also permissible, and often advisable, to establish one pattern in the offensive forecheck-ing zone and a different pattern in the defensive zone and call it the team's system. What is most important is that all the players be well-acquainted with their responsibilities under the system and disciplined to execute it properly.

Systems

SYSTEM I—1-2-1-1

INTRODUCTION

Identical defensive systems are diagramed in the offensive and defensive zones. The same system would be used in the neutral zone,
although this is not illustrated. The broken lines define areas of responsibility for the players in each zone. The territories remain the same
whether the team is on the offensive attack or in defensive zone coverage trying to regain control of the puck.

There is nothing wrong with a player moving out of his area of responsibility; sometimes this becomes necessary in order to check an opposing player or make a play. When a player does leave his assigned area, a
teammate should come in to back him up and keep the team in balance.

THE SYSTEM

As shown on the diagram, the centerman puts pressure on the puck
carrier around the net and in the corners in the offensive zone. The

center should stay in front of the net until the puck carrier makes his move. The wingers handle the sides and help out in the corners, while the defensemen are staggered inside the blue line. One covers the high slot, and occasionally the sides, with his partner set to back him up as he covers the entire blue line.

In the defensive zone, the center is responsible for covering the point men and the blue line. The wings are on either side midway in the zone, with 1 defense covering the slot and the sides and the other defense in the immediate vicinity of the net.

NOTE

It is extremely important to forecheck or check the puck carrier at all times so as to give him the least possible time and space in which to make decisions and make a play. Consider double-teaming the puck handler, especially in your own zone, before any damage can be done.

SYSTEM II—1-3-1

INTRODUCTION

The diagram shows a full view of the rink with the same 1-3-1 system in operation in the defensive and offensive zones. The broken lines show areas of positioning for each player in this system. The same pattern and same positioning are used whether the play is in the offensive, defensive or neutral zone.

THE SYSTEM

In the offensive zone, the pattern has the centerman pressing the puck carrier around the goal and in the corners. The forechecker should stay out in front of the net initially and wait until the offense makes its move before going behind the goal. The wingers with a defenseman would be covering the middle of the zone. The defense, who is generally the player from the side opposite the side where the puck is located, handles the slot. His defensive partner backs him up and covers the blue line.

The centerman checks the point men and patrols the blue line in the defensive zone, while the 2 wingers cover the sides and corners. One defense is in the slot area ready to go into the corner when necessary, and the other defense works around the net.

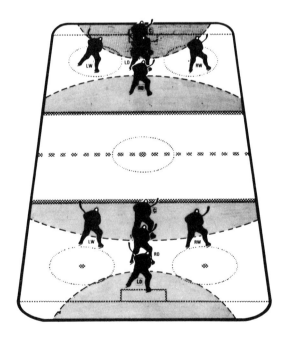

SYSTEM III—2-1-2

INTRODUCTION

Identical systems are shown in the offensive and defensive zones of the full rink diagram. The same system would also be used in the neutral zone (not shown). The broken lines divide areas of responsibility for each of the players. This territorial responsibility holds whether the team is on the attack or in defensive zone coverage and is the same in each zone.

THE SYSTEM

As illustrated, the 2 wingers are charged with keeping pressure on the puck carrier around the net and in the corners in the offensive end. The centerman has the slot area and the sides and the defensemen cover their own half-ice areas at the blue line.

In the defensive zone, the wings check the point men and cover the blue line. The center again covers the slot and the sides, while the defense move into the area around the net and in the corners.

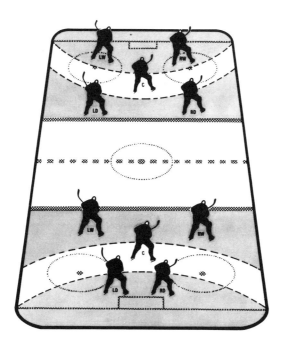

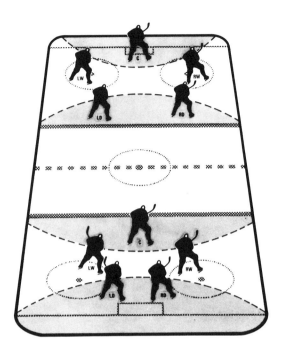

SYSTEM IV—1-2-2

INTRODUCTION

The diagram shows a full view of the hockey rink with an identical 1-2-2 system in operation in either end. The same pattern would also be employed in the neutral zone. The broken lines in the illustration indicate positioning for each player, whether in the offensive, defensive or neutral zone, and whether or not the team controls the puck.

THE SYSTEM

In offensive zone coverage, the centerman puts pressure on the puck carrier around the net and in the corners. His best play is to wait until the offense makes a move before he goes behind the net. The 2 wingers cover the sides and overload the center in the corners, as needed, and the defensemen cover their own halves of the blue line.

In the defensive zone, the centerman covers the point men and/or the blue line. The wings take care of the sides and the defense roam in front of the net and in the corners on their sides.

SYSTEM V—2-2-1

INTRODUCTION

The full-rink diagram shows the 2-2-1 system in effect at both ends of the rink. The same pattern should be used in the neutral zone, although this is not shown. The broken lines dividing the rink show the area assigned to each player under this system. The areas of responsibility remain the same in each zone and in both offensive and defensive situations (from attack to defensive zone coverage).

THE SYSTEM

In the offensive zone the wingers put pressure on the puck carrier, whether the puck is behind the net or in the corners. The centerman will back up the wing who is forechecking the puck carrier on his side and will cover the side where the puck is situated. The defenseman from the side opposite the side where the puck is being played moves in to back up the winger forechecking deep in the zone and the other defense covers the blue line.

In the defensive end, the 2 wingers cover the point men on the blue line while the centerman covers one side and the corner, leaving the other side and corner to the defenseman from the side opposite that where the puck is in the play. The second defense works in front of and around the goal.

SYSTEM VI—3-2

INTRODUCTION

The 3-2 defensive pattern is shown in this full-rink layout as it is employed in the offensive and defensive zones. The same system would be used in the neutral zone, although this is not illustrated. Player positioning is shown by the broken lines. The coverage areas remain the same on offense and defense and whether or not the team controls the puck.

THE SYSTEM

As illustrated, the 3 forwards set up a triangular pattern, which they maintain in all zones. Usually, the triangle covers half of the zone. The players continuously force the puck carrier to one side of the rink or the other, putting great pressure on the team controlling the puck. The pattern in effect gives the defensive team a man advantage because they do not cover the wing farthest off the play as they limit coverage to half ice. The triangle based on 1 forward covering the puck carrier, 1 forward covering the side boards and the third forward in the slot area ready to

move in deeper in the zone. The defensemen cover the blue line on their sides.

The triangle is set up in the defensive zone in much the same manner. Depending upon where the puck is in play, 1 forward covers the side boards, 1 forward is in the slot area and the third man covers the point. The idea is to cover about half of the ice in the zone and keep the offense from penetrating the triangle. The defensemen work on their sides, in the corners and around the net.

SYSTEM VII—2-3

INTRODUCTION

The 2-3 defensive system is diagramed in this full-rink layout as it is employed in the offensive and defensive zones. The same system would be used in the neutral zone, although this is not shown. Player positioning is indicated by the broken lines. Areas of coverage for each player remain the same on offense and defense and whether or not the team has control of the puck.

THE SYSTEM

The 2 wingers cover their own half, deep in the offensive zone, as illustrated, while the center and the 2 defensemen are spread out at the blue line. With this system, the team will always have 3 men coming back, thereby making most of the offensive threats against them 3 on 3 situations. In the defensive zone, the 2 wingers will cover the points, while the centerman will be responsible for the slot area and the defensemen handle the net area and the corners.

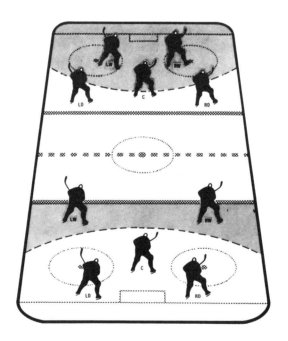

OFFENSIVE ZONE PLAY—FORECHECKING

INTRODUCTION

Forechecking is the backbone of any defensive system just as "the breakout" is to any offensive system. You need teamwork and self-discipline on the part of every player if you are going to be effective. A good drill is to have the players positioned outside the zone at center ice along the boards. The coach shoots the puck into the zone, and a defensive unit goes in to forecheck the offensive unit already there and trying to break out of the zone. In this manner, the coach can implement his forechecking system and supervise its execution.

Zone 1: 2-2-1 or 2-1-2 system with double teaming. In this example, the offensive centerman swings to the corner to take a pass from his defense to start the breakout. The defensive center and right wing move in to double team the puck carrier, while the right defense checks their left wing, who is open for a pass if he stays on the side. If the left wing should come across the middle, it is up to the left defense to move in as checker. The defensive left wing should stay with his check (their right wing). The 2 defensive defensemen stagger each other at the blue line, with 1 man always backing his partner up. (Note: In this, and all other defensive plays, communication between the defensemen is not only very helpful, but essential.)

Zone 2: 2-1-2, 2-2-1, 2-3 or 3-2 plan with double team approach. The right defense is shown taking a pass from behind the net to begin the zone breakout. The defense responds by moving in to check the attacking players who may be open for passes. In this case, the centerman and left wing will try to double team the puck carrier (their right defense) in the corner. Then the left defense should move in on their right wing, who is a possible receiver, while the right defense goes into the slot area to check the opposing center. The right wing stays with his check, their left wing.

Zone 1   **Zone 2**

OFFENSIVE ZONE PLAY: FORECHECKING

Zone 1: 2-1-2 or 2-2-1 system double teaming the puck carrier. This variation shows the puck up for grabs in the corner. The defensive right wing goes up against their left defense to fight for control of the puck and the left wing moves behind the net to cut off any offensive player in this area. The wings work together to contain their defense, who are trying to recapture the puck. The center, meantime, is covering the slot area and their centerman, and the defense move in on their wings to check them off a possible pass, should the attacking team get control of the puck.

Zone 2: 2-2-1, 2-1-2 or 3-2 system of double teaming. Another double teaming approach to offensive zone forechecking is seen in this diagram, which shows a loose puck in the corner. Here the left winger goes in to battle for the puck, while the right wing comes in from the slot area to challenge their defense and go after the puck. The centerman covers their center, who is a possible pass receiver, and the defense stay with the offensive wings to head off a possible pass play there.

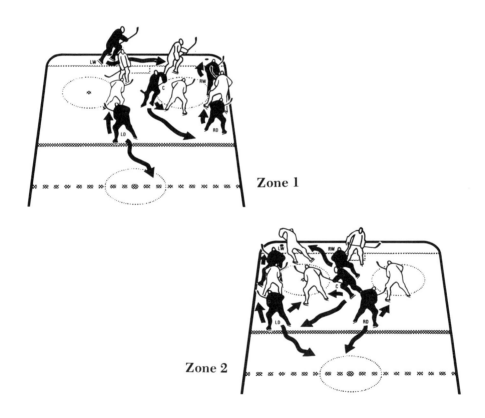

Zone 1

Zone 2

OFFENSIVE ZONE PLAY: FORECHECKING

Zone 1: 1-2-2 or 1-3-1 system. A man-to-man checking system is employed in this system of offensive zone forechecking. Your center puts pressure on the puck carrier by staying in front of the net and forcing him to go behind the goal to make a play. The wings stay with their checks, and the 2 defensemen stagger each other as they work to check the opposing center, who could be a pass receiver.

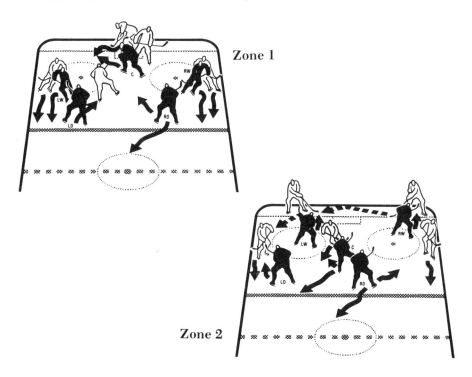

Zone 1

Zone 2

Zone 2: 2-1-2 or 2-2-1 system. In this forechecking system, the 2 wingers skate in deep to force their defensemen to give up the puck in their own end. The right wing should go for the puck carrier in this pattern, while the left wing attempts to cut off their defense from any pass options. Your centerman covers the slot area and his offensive counterpart, who is also a choice for a possible pass. The center is also a backup for the defenseman who is pressing their right wing (the puck carrier). Their 2 wingers should be covered by the defense at the blue line. As 1 defense moves in to check the puck carrier, he is backed up by the centerman and by his partner, who watches out for the other opposing wing and for the puck.

OFFENSIVE ZONE PLAY: FORECHECKING

Zone 1: 2-1-2 or 2-3 system with double team approach. Going into a breakout play, the opposing center skates behind the net to pick up the puck from his defense and prepares to carry the puck out or to make a pass. Your centerman will try to lead the puck carrier into the corner as the left winger moves in on him from the side. If the puck carrier gets off a pass to his defense in the slot, a defenseman should move in quickly from the blue line to back up the winger who is caught deep in the zone. The other defenseman moves to help the center check the winger coming down the side. Your other wing, who is not involved in the play, stays with his check.

Zone 2: 1-2-2 system with man-to-man checking. In the situation shown, the centerman forces the puck carrier behind the net by staying in front of the goal and waiting for him to make a move. Thus contained, the center will probably pass. Your wings should be with their checks, the centerman and a defenseman, to make them unavailable to receive a pass, and the defensemen cover their wingers, who are high in their zone by the blue line.

NOTE

The 1-2-2 is a conservative system, but a highly effective one. In most situations, this pattern leaves only 1 offensive player open to attempt to control the puck against your 2 defensemen. If you use this system offensively, you are well prepared to check the opposition in case of a turnover.

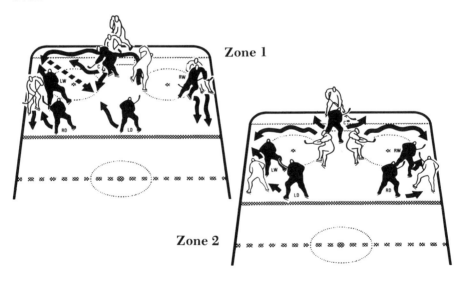

Zone 1

Zone 2

OFFENSIVE ZONE PLAY: FORECHECKING

Zone 1: 2-3, 3-2 or 2-1-2 system with double-team approach. The puck carrier in this setup is the left defense, who moves to pass ahead to his centerman. The 2 wingers should go in deep, 1 on either side of the net, to put pressure on the puck carrier and force him to make a play. The centerman covers the slot and the defensemen are deployed in the zone so that they can check the wings and/or the offensive center.

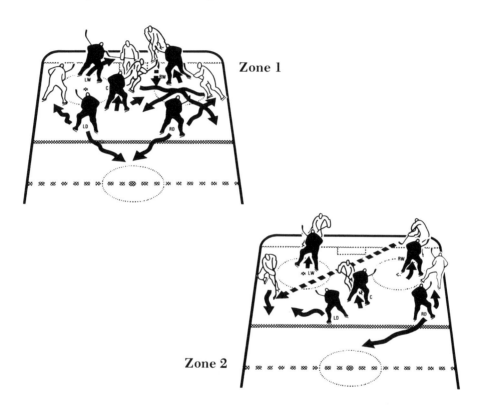

Zone 1

Zone 2

Zone 2: 2-3 or 2-1-2 system. The offensive defensemen, who are behind the goal line in control of the puck, are forechecked by your wingers. The right wing should go to the puck carrier (their left defense) and the left wing should move in on their right defenseman to cut him out of any passing play. In the diagram, the forechecker on the puck carrier was unable to forestall a pass off the wing. As a response to the play, your right defense, who has moved in earlier on their left wing, drop back to back up your left defense, who goes in and forces the puck carrier (wing) on his side.

OFFENSIVE ZONE PLAY: FORECHECKING

Zone 1: 2-2-1 or 2-3 system with man-to-man checking. The left defense, who has the puck, is checked by the defensive centerman, who tries to pin him in the corner with no out for escape behind the net. The left wing will keep moving in on the right defense to cut him out of a possible play, and the right wing checks their left winger. The 2 defensemen must move in on this play. The man on the left side checks their right wing and the right defense covers the player in the slot.

Zone 2: 1-3-1 or 1-2-1-1 system with man-to-man checking. With the defensemen deployed in front of and behind the goal, the defensive center forces the puck carrier (the left defense) to make a play while covering the territory in front of the goal. The wings are man-to-man on the attacking wings and a defense moves in to the top of the slot area to cover the opposing center. The second defenseman backs him up in the middle at the blue line inside the zone.

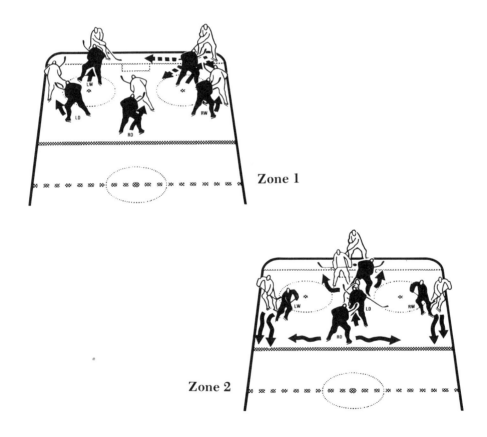

Zone 1

Zone 2

OFFENSIVE ZONE PLAY: FORECHECKING

Zone 1: 1-2-1-1 or 1-3-1 system with man-to-man checking. The defensive centerman forces the puck carrier in the corner (the left defense) then follows the puck if the defenseman gets off a pass. The wingers should stay with their wings on the sides. One defense should move into the slot area and check the opposing centerman, while his partner backs him up in the middle at the blue line.

Zone 2: 3-2 system with man-to-man checking. The defensive centerman forces the puck carrier in the corner (left defense), then goes back to the slot area, if the puck goes to the other side, or to the corner of the rink. The right winger stays with his man, while the left wing mans the slot ready to move in on either the other defender or on his checker on the other side. Your 2 defensemen are ready at the blue line and can, if necessary, move in on either offensive winger in order to keep pressure on the offensive zone.

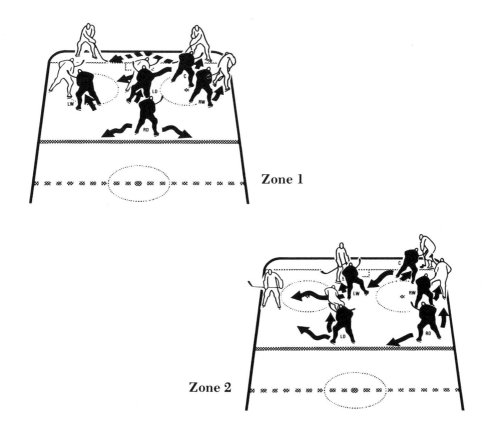

Zone 1

Zone 2

NEUTRAL ZONE CHECKING (starting from the offensive zone)

INTRODUCTION

Neutral zone checking is the area of the rink where man-to-man coverage is very important under any system. For one thing, it facilitates the task for your defensemen to contain the puck carrier, that is, if your wingers are good checkers and take care of their respective area and man. This is also the area where most teams play conservatively, since the opposition has control of the puck, therefore, gambling by throwing 2 players on the puck might put you in deeper trouble than you think. So, the job of everyone on the defensive team is to cover and check the proper area and the man he is responsible for.

The best policy in neutral zone checking is to keep your checkers wide and let your defense handle the middle of the ice. If your defense stand up as they should, your checkers should be ready to back up your defense under any circumstances.

Zone 1: 1-2-2 system. In this pattern, the wing is the first checker on the puck carrier deep in the offensive zone. Your right wing forces the puck carrier to pass, in this case to the left wing, who starts out of the zone. Your centerman picks up the opposing center; the left wing picks up his man on his side. They stay with their checks and look for the defensemen to contain or control the puck carrier. The forechecking wing comes back on his side and tries to pick up and check any player who might be open for a possible pass.

NEUTRAL ZONE CHECKING (starting from the offensive zone)

Zone 1: 1-2-2 system. This diagram illustrates defensive play where the centerman is the only checker on the puck carrier in the offensive zone. The center attempts to force the puck carrier (right defense) to pass. The wings pick up the offensive wings, which leaves their centerman open to receive a pass and carry it into the neutral zone against your defense. The defensemen should be able to contain him and regain control of the puck.

NEUTRAL ZONE CHECKING (starting in the offensive zone)

Zone 1: 1-3-1 or 1-2-2 system. Here the offensive team controls the puck halfway out of their zone. The defensive centerman forechecks the puck carrier and forces him to pass. The play is contained as the left defenseman anticipates the move and is in good position to challenge the playmaker and regain control of the puck. The wings should cover their opposition on the side; the centerman comes back to check the offensive center and the right defense is the backup in the zone.

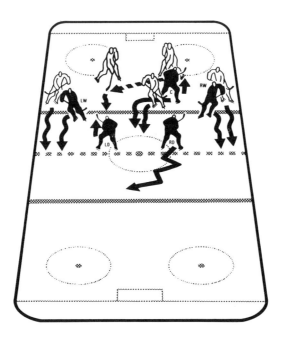

NEUTRAL ZONE CHECKING (starting in the offensive zone)

Zone 1: 1-2-2 or 1-3-1 system. By sending the centerman in as fore-checker, the defensive team can limit the puck carrier's options by more or less directing the flow of play. In the diagram, the puck-carrying defenseman has to pass, under pressure, to his partner, who in turn attempts to pass to the wing coming across the middle. Your defense should be able to anticipate this move and be in position to check their playmakers as the other defense backs him up. Your 2 wings should pick up their men and stay with them. The defensive center, after forcing the play, will be ready to pick up a loose puck or to check any player who finds an opening in the coverage.

NEUTRAL ZONE CHECKING (starting in the offensive zone)

Zone 1: 1-2-1-1 or 1-3-1 system. Halfway out of the offensive zone, the centerman forechecks the puck carrier and forces him to pass to his partner. As he passes, the defenseman on that side reads the play and moves in to check the playmaker and then his partner backs him up in the middle. With the opposing wings covered on the sides, your center can trail and be ready to grab a loose puck or check a player who is left open.

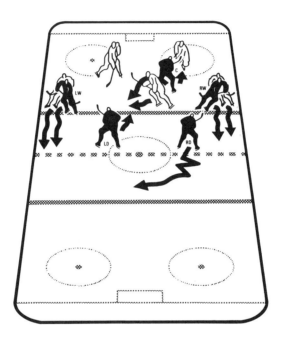

NEUTRAL ZONE CHECKING (starting in the offensive zone)

Zone 1: 2-2-1 and 1-2-1-1 or 2-3 combination. Two forecheckers go in, the centerman covering the puck carrier (the right defense) and the right wing covering the left defenseman. The left wing picks up the opposing wing on his side and takes him out of the play. Under pressure by your centerman, the puck carrier is forced to pass to his partner, who is also being checked. Whether he passes to his center or left wing, your right defense is in good position to contain the play. The forecheckers come back looking for a loose puck and checking any offensive player who might break clear of his checker.

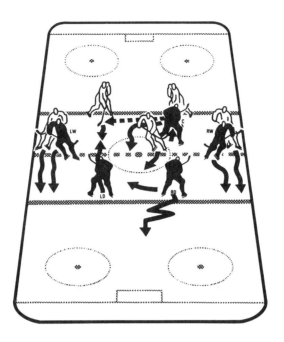

NEUTRAL ZONE CHECKING (starting from neutral zone play or faceoff)

    Zone 1: 1-3-1, 2-2-1 or 2-3 combination system. With play continuing, or resuming after a faceoff, in the neutral zone, the defensive center forechecks the puck carrier (the left defense), who passes to his partner on the right. Because his center is now covered by the defensive center-man (see diagram), the right defense starts to carry the puck. Your defensive player on that side should be able to read the situation and move in on the puck carrier and try to contain him. Your right defense should back his partner up as the wingers check the attacking wings on each side.

NEUTRAL ZONE CHECKING (starting from neutral zone play or faceoff)

Zone 1: 1-2-1-1 and 1-3-1 combination system. In this diagram, play is in the neutral zone, with the offensive team in control of the puck. The defense sends in the centerman as forechecker on the puck carrier (the right defense), forcing him to pass. Your wings should cover the attacking wings on the sides and stay with them all the way back, or until the defense regains the puck. One of the defense goes to the side where the play will be made by the offensive team, while his partner backs him up and looks for a loose puck. The defense should be able to anticipate where the play will go and move in on the logical receiver, who in this case is the center. Your center's role is to come back and to try to check any offensive player who might be left open for a play.

NOTE

If you have good checking in the neutral zone, especially by the wingers covering their checks, chances are that your defense will face a 1 on 2 situation, with their playmaker open against your defenders. This is an example of how strong, persistent checking can turn a play to your advantage by increasing the odds of a turnover and giving the defensive team an opportunity to dominate the game and get the greater scoring chances.

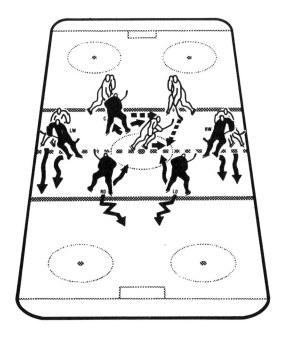

NEUTRAL ZONE CHECKING (starting from neutral zone play or faceoff)

Zone 1: 2-2-1 or 2-3 system. This plan of checking in order to regain possession of the puck in the neutral zone employs 2 forecheckers. In this play, the puck carrier is the left defense, who responds to forechecking by the defensive center by passing to his partner on the right side. This brings in your second forechecker, the wing on the side where the puck is in play, who forces the puck carrier. The puck handler has 2 options: he can pass to either his wing or his centerman. Your defense on that side should be able to anticipate the pass and move in quickly on the playmaker. The other defenseman must back him up in case the other offensive player gets clear of the check, or in the event that the puck comes loose. The right winger, who is not involved in the play, stays with his man, and the forecheckers come back to pick up and check any offensive players open for possible plays.

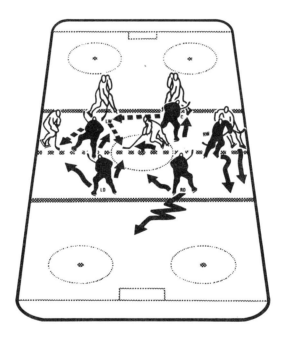

NEUTRAL ZONE CHECKING (starting from neutral zone play or faceoff)

Zone 1: 2-2-1, 2-1-2 or 3-2 combination. With the offensive team in control of the puck in the neutral zone, the defensive unit sends in 2 forecheckers. The right wing is the first forechecker, and goes in to put pressure on the left defenseman, who has the puck. He gets off a pass to his right defense, and your left wing, the second forechecker, moves in, as illustrated. Your centerman ties up his opposing number at center ice. The only attacker open for a pass is the right wing, and either the defenseman on his side or the center should be able to anticipate the play and check him. If the defense gets to the puck carrier first, his partner drops back to cover, and also puts himself in position to check their center or pick up a loose puck. The first forechecker goes back to his side to pick up his man.

NEUTRAL ZONE CHECKING (from the red line into the defensive zone)

Zone 1: 1-3-1 system. In this diagram, play is at the red line, with the offensive right defense in control of the puck. Your centerman goes in to forecheck the puck carrier and forces him to pass to his left defense. As soon as the defense on the side where the play is made understands the situation, he should move in on the puck handler, whose only option is to give the puck up by shooting it into the zone. This system relies on effective work by your wingers in covering their checks on the side all the way down the ice, and by quick action on the part of the defense in going back after the puck (in this case, the left defense). The centerman should come back and cover the slot and be ready to start on the attack again.

NOTE

Your defense should never allow anyone to skate without resistance across the blue line to make a play. Their mission is to put on pressure and to force the play at the blue line. There is always a better alternative than just backing in on your goalie.

DEFENSIVE ZONE COVERAGE AND CHECKING

INTRODUCTION

With the attack in high gear in your defensive zone, positioning, determination and discipline are severely tested. This is the time when players must stick to the system and use their heads, as well as their bodies. There can be no letup in pressure on the offense. The defensive team must be aggressive in exerting pressure by forcing the play or by double-teaming the playmaker, so that he doesn't have time or room to make a play. Proper positioning cuts down the offensive team's options and gives the offense little opportunity to set up a play. Discipline keeps players operating effectively rather than running around aimlessly. Under any system, any player can move anywhere at any time, as long as the players back each other up. It is always possible to switch from man-to-man coverage to zone coverage (and vice versa) if everyone uses good judgment in adjusting to the attack as it develops. Remind the players to keep their sticks on the ice in readiness for an interception or deflection.

Zone 1: 2-2-1 system. This is a man-to-man checking approach in which 2 wingers cover the offensive point man. One defense and the center go into the circles to watch the slot man, sidemen or cornermen, while the other defense covers the area in front of, and around, the net.

Zone 2: 1-2-1-1 system. In this man-to-man system, the center is available to handle either point men, as play dictates, while the 2 wings are midway in the zone, watching the offensive players in the slot and corners and at the sides. One defense in the slot covers that area and the corners and his partner is situated immediately in front of the goal.

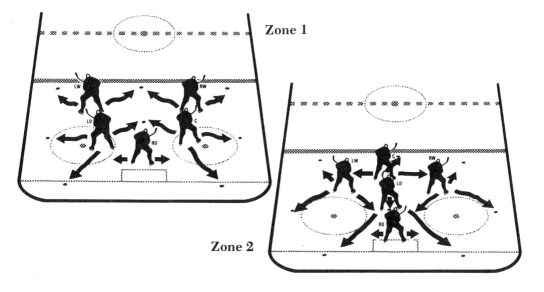

Zone 1

Zone 2

DEFENSIVE ZONE COVERAGE AND CHECKING

Zone 1: 2-3 system. The defensive wings cover the players on the point or in the slot in this man-to-man defense. Your defensemen are near the boards on either side, available to handle their man in front of the net, cornerman or slot man. The center is in front of the crease, covering the net, the slot man and the sides, depending on where the puck is and where it is going.

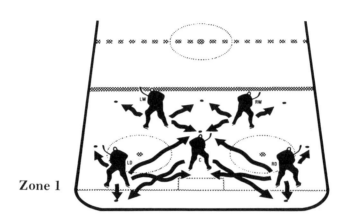

Zone 1

Zone 2: 2-1-2 system. Another man-to-man checking system has the center in the slot midway in the zone, where he can cover the man in the slot or the corners or sides. The defensemen are in front of the net on either side and available to move into the corners; the wings are high, covering the players at the points or in the slot.

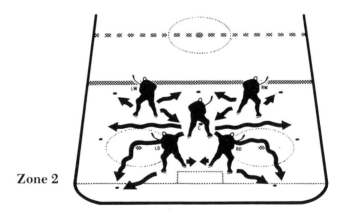

Zone 2

DEFENSIVE ZONE COVERAGE AND CHECKING

Zone 1: 1-2-2 or 3-2 system. In this pattern, the center covers the 2 point men, while the wings are in the middle of the zone in position to handle the points or players in the slot or on the sides. The defense are in front of the goal on either side, where they cover the corners, sides or slot area.

Zone 1

Zone 2: 1-3-1 system. The right defense is in front of the crease in this man-to-man coverage approach. His partner is in front of him in the slot, covering the offensive player in the area. The wings are in the circles and are responsible for the players at the sides, points (when needed), corners and slot area. Your centerman is alone inside the blue line covering the 2 point men.

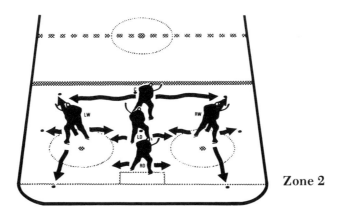

Zone 2

DEFENSIVE ZONE COVERAGE AND CHECKING (double-teaming the puck carrier)

Zone 1: 2-1-2 or 3-2 system. As the defenseman at the point controls the puck, he is double-teamed in this checking system by the left winger, who attempts to force him toward the boards, and the center-man, who will try to steal the puck or get a loose puck. The other wing leaves the man on the opposite point to cover the slot man, while the 2 defensemen stay in front of the net watching the offensive wings. This system leaves the left defense open, but he is, under this zone plan, the least dangerous offensive player in the end.

Zone 2: 2-1-2 or 3-2 system. In this version of zone checking, the puck is controlled by the right winger in the corner. Since this is a 2-1-2 system, the left defense should force the puck carrier into the corner with the help of the center, who moves from the slot. The right wing, who is covering the left point man, drops back into the slot area to cover their center and the left wing stays with his man at the other point. Your right defense stays in front of the net to check the opposing left wing. There is little the attacking left defense at the point can do to make a play, so he is left unprotected.

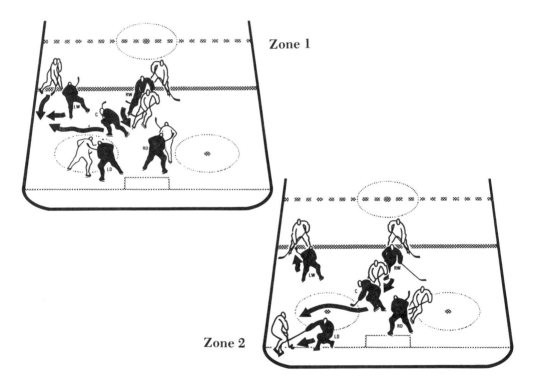

Zone 1

Zone 2

DEFENSIVE ZONE COVERAGE AND CHECKING

Zone 1: Double-teaming the shooter. This pattern goes into operation when the puck is controlled by the defense at the point, and involves a double-teaming effort on the shooter. The premise is that the defensive team has lost control of the puck deep in its own end and that the opposition is setting up its attack. With the point man looking for a passing or shooting opportunity, the 2 players closest to the point (in this case the defensive center and left wing) move in to double-team the shooter. The key to the play is for both of these players to get into the possible line of fire as interference. This is particularly important for the left wing, who should not go straight to the point, but cut across the shooter's shooting path, and then skate to the point. The other defensive players cover their areas and opposing players as shown on the diagram.

Zone 2: Single checker on the shooter. A turnover deep in the corner of the defensive zone results in a play to the left point. The defensive right wing, caught between the corner and the point, checks the shooter by cutting across his possible line of fire toward the middle and swinging to the point. Your left wing skates to block a possible play to the defense, and the other players maintain coverage of their opposition.

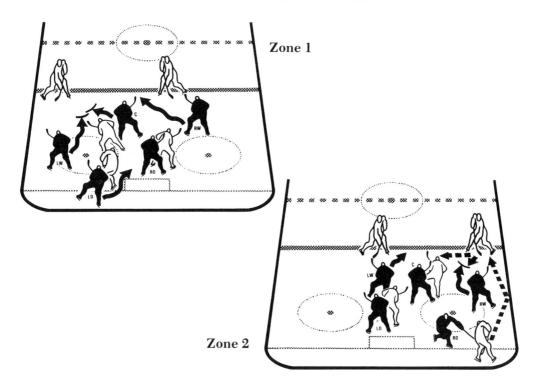

Zone 1

Zone 2

Thought Provokers

1. Keep a plus–minus record as a means of evaluating each player's defensive effectiveness.
2. Do you have a system that works?
3. Hockey games are won and lost in the defensive zone, where mistakes are disastrous. Consider the success of such teams as Montreal, Boston, New York Islanders and New York Rangers.
4. Have your defense always use a circling approach instead of rushing directly at an attacker.
5. How much time do you spend on defensive strategy in practice? In off-ice sessions?
6. Establish rules that become a part of your system when play is in the offensive, neutral and defensive zones, and make the rules stick.
7. Explain the effects of coasting while checking (illegal holding, hooking and slashing penalties).
8. Do you have your defense work without sticks on such drills as 5 on 3, 5 on 4 or 5 on 5?
9. Do you know that most teams enter the offensive zone (about 55 percent of the time) on the right side? About 15 percent of attacks are at center ice, and about 30 percent of offensive rushes come on the left side.
10. A study shows that 70 percent of body checks are made in the defensive zone, with 5 percent occurring in the neutral zone and 25 percent in the offensive zone.
11. "The best offense is a good defense."

CHAPTER 7 *The Power Play Game*

Hockey contests are often won on power plays because they can change or influence the course of the game. Any power play system is good if it works. Those that are successful are those that involve the right players at the right time in a very specific plan of action—the system.

Who are the right players? They are your best stickhandlers, strong quick skaters and smart playmakers. The power play calls for a strong player in front of the net and accurate shooters, especially with good low shots and quick release, at the points. Players can be either forwards or defense, or any combination thereof, depending on their abilities. What is essential, however, is that the unit be disciplined.

Control is the key to a successful power play. A goal is a goal, whether it takes 15 seconds or the full 2 minutes. So the best plan is not to rush, but to set up carefully and use your 2 minutes most effectively. Obviously, keeping control of the puck is a must.

Use the maximum ice available. Keep the wingers wide when they go on the offensive, because this makes the penalty killers' job more difficult. Let the puck do the work (nobody can outskate a pass). There are many systems for moving the puck from your own end to the neutral zone and into the offensive zone, and this chapter is devoted to these plans. For instance, the coach can use a basic formation, such as 2-2-1 or 1-2-2 or 1-3-1, and work the power play off of it. You can use 2 zones or 1 zone (defensive zone) for starting the power play. Once the puck is in the offensive end, the idea is to move the puck around, create interference with the penalty play unit and pick your shots. Remember, quality is more important than quantity of shots on goal.

Since the power play unit has a man advantage (or 2-man advantage), the players should be able to capitalize on tying up the penalty killers. This is the job of the forwards, and in particular, the wings, who should keep moving, creating interference and opening up holes in the defense. The centerman, as playmaker, is free to shoot or make a play and the point men are open to shoot. Getting the puck to the point is important in the power play, as they are in good position to see what is going on in the zone and make a play accordingly. If nobody moves and presses the defense to move out of position, the power play winds up passing the puck around the outside of the defensive box with little chance to score. Pulling the penalty killers out of position must be a definite objective of the power play. One method that is effective is overloading one side of the zone, meaning that 3 players are on one side of the zone and 2 are in the middle as they begin to set up for a scoring opportunity. This system, and others, are included in the material in this chapter.

Most of the formations are 5 on 4 situations, because this is the most frequent power play situation. Some of the ideas and options can be adapted for 5 on 3 and 4 on 3 situations.

There are 2 drills that can be used to work the team on the power play. One drill has all of the players at center along the boards. The coach shoots the puck into the zone, and 2 units go after it—the power play unit of 4 or 5 players and the penalty killing unit of 3 or 4 players. They play until the power play unit scores, or until the goalie freezes the puck or the shorthanded team gets control of the puck.

In the second drill, the team is divided into groups in each end of the ice. Players are split into a power play unit and a penalty killing unit in each end. They work against each other in the zone, continuing play until there is a goal, until the penalty killing team takes over possession of the puck, or until the goalie stops the play. The exercise begins from a faceoff in each zone. In either drill, the coach may have the penalty killing team work without sticks, or with their sticks turned upside down.

Drum it into the players: only 1 goal can be scored in the 2-minute penalty period. It's never a question of how fast they get the puck into

the end, but rather of how well organized they are and how well prepared they are to hang onto the puck and use their 120 seconds most
advantageously.

Zone Formations

DEFENSIVE AND NEUTRAL ZONES: BREAKOUT

4-1 system. This 5 on 4 situation begins in the defensive zone and moves
into the neutral zone with a 4-man rush (4-1).

The centerman goes behind the net to pick up the puck, but leaves it
for the defense, who passes off to the wing on the side where the centerman came from. The wing moves along the boards as the center picks up
momentum going into the neutral zone and passes to the center when
he crosses the blue line. The 2 wingers and the defense who was in front
of the net make the rush with the center, who has a good chance to make
a play and to get the puck into the offensive zone. At the offensive blue
line, this could be a 2 on 1 situation, involving the playmaker and the
left defense (see diagram).

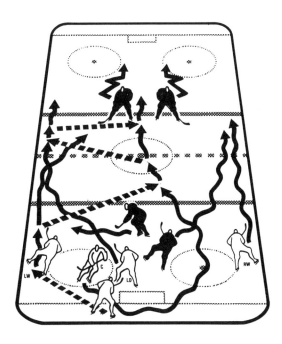

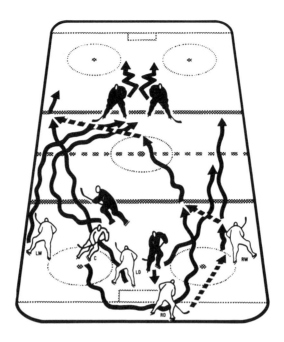

DEFENSIVE AND NEUTRAL ZONES: BREAKOUT

4-1 system. The diagram shows a power play formation starting in its defensive zone and moving into the neutral zone with a 4-man rush. The centerman goes behind the goal from the right side to pick up the puck, but leaves it to his defense, who passes to the right wing along the boards. (The centerman comes from the side where the play will be made.) As the center gains speed leaving the zone, the right winger tries to get the puck back to him soon enough so that he can make a play either to the wings or to the left defense making the rush. As illustrated, the left wing has drawn his checker toward the middle over the red line, leaving the side open for the left defense to move in, take a pass from the center and move the puck into the offensive zone.

DEFENSIVE AND NEUTRAL ZONES: BREAKOUT

4-1 system. In the defensive zone, the puck is controlled by the defense behind the net, who passes to the wing on his right. At the same time, the defense in front of the net goes to center ice to replace the centerman moving to the left boards. As the players leave the zone, the right wing passes to the defense in the middle. He should be able to make a play to the center in the neutral zone, providing the left wing has succeeded in pulling his checker toward the middle, leaving the left side to the centerman.

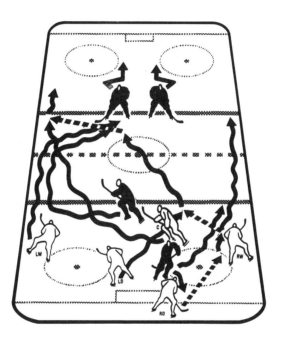

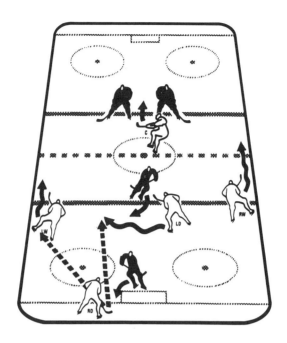

DEFENSIVE AND NEUTRAL ZONES: BREAKOUT

1-3-1 system. As illustrated, the power play spreads out over 2 zones in
the 1-3-1 system, giving the players plenty of open ice to work with and
forcing the penalty killing unit to open up. The defense behind the net
passes ahead to the wing on the side or defense in the middle, as the
center in the neutral zone keeps the opposing defense tied up at their
own blue line. The wings and defense should be able to break out in a 4
on 2 situation for 2 zones and keep control of the puck into the offensive
end. Puck control and passing are key factors in this, and any, 2-zone
formation.

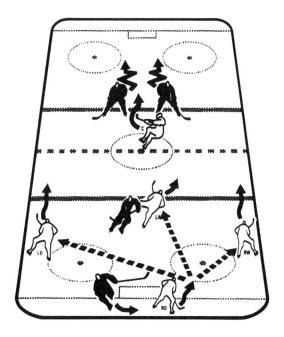

DEFENSIVE AND NEUTRAL ZONES: BREAKOUT

1-3-1 system. The 1-3-1 system utilizes 2 zones, giving the power play team ample ice to maneuver against the penalty killers. The center is in the neutral zone, thereby tying up the penalty killing team's defense at their blue line. The play starts with the defense, who stickhandles from behind his net and makes a play, as shown, to his left wing, left defense, or right wing. With the shorthanded team's defense stymied at their blue line, the power play will have a 4 on 2 advantage for 2 zones.

1-2-1-1 system. Another 2-zone breakout pattern has the offensive wings in their zone at the blue line, with the defenseman behind the net making the initial play. His options are to pass to the defense across the slot or a long lead pass to the right wing. As the centerman is keeping the penalty killing unit's defense busy at the blue line, the 4 players in the zone should be able to break out 4 on 2 for 2 zones.

DEFENSIVE ZONE: BREAKOUT

Zone 1: 4-1 system. The diagram illustrates a 4-man rush starting in the defensive zone with the puck carrier (left defense) behind the net. The defense in front of the net will be the fourth man in the rush, along with the forward line. The puck carrier behind the net passes to any open player as the unit starts up ice.

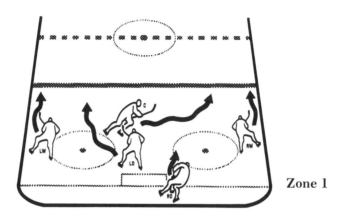

Zone 1

Zone 2: 3-2 system. The defense anchor this breakout formation, which has the forwards and center high in the zone. The puck carrier behind the net passes to his partner in the corner as the wings swing to their opposite sides and the centerman cuts across the middle. From the corner, the defense headmans the puck to the forwards, who are breaking into the neutral zone.

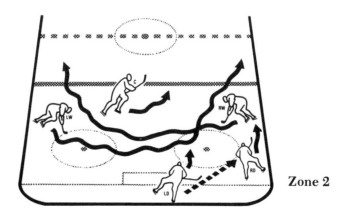

Zone 2

DEFENSIVE ZONE: BREAKOUT

Zone 1: 4-1 system. The puck is controlled behind the net by the defense, while the defenseman in front of the net is ready to join the forwards in a 4-1 rush into the neutral zone. The wings are on their sides; the centerman swings behind the net and into the middle from the left faceoff circle. As he makes the swing, the pass goes to the left wing. Another option in this play is for the center to take the puck with him when he skates behind the net.

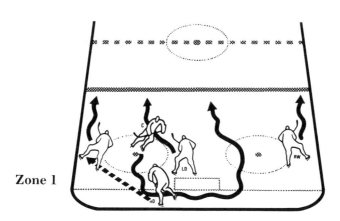

Zone 1

Zone 2: 1-2-2 system. In this case, the centerman is roaming the neutral zone inside the red line and the wings are high along the sides. The defenseman with the puck behind the goal passes to his partner in the corner, moves to the middle and stays in the middle of the ice all the way into the offensive zone.

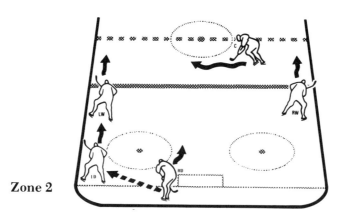

Zone 2

DEFENSIVE ZONE: BREAKOUT

Zone 1: 2-1-2 system. This diagram shows a power play formation starting from the defensive zone with the puck carrier (left defense) behind the net. The wings are in position near the red line, keeping the shorthanded team's defense tied up; the centerman is in the middle and the other defense is in along the boards, as shown. The puck carrier may pass to either the defense or the center, setting up a 3 on 2 situation going out of the zone.

Zone 1

Zone 2: 2-2-1 system. A balanced breakout formation, the 2-2-1 starts with the defense behind the net, the second defense and the center along the boards midway in the defensive zone and the wingers inside the red line with the opposing defense. The puck handler has the options of passing to either the centerman or to the defense to get the breakout going.

Zone 2

NEUTRAL ZONE

2-2-1 system. The power play unit is in the neutral zone, either as the result of a stoppage of play and faceoff, or in the process of reorganizing the unit to bring the puck into the offensive zone. By sending 2 forwards to their offensive blue line, the power play ties up the penalty killing unit's defense and gains the advantage of a 3 on 2 situation against their 2 checkers. If the left defense is the puck carrier, as shown, he can pass to his right defense along the side boards or to the left wing. Either receiver would have the option of passing to the player on the opposite boards, passing to the center, or carrying in the puck himself, making a play with the 3 forwards at the offensive blue line. The last option would be to shoot the puck into the zone.

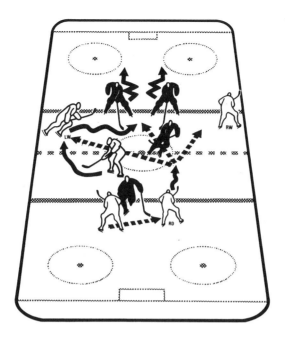

NEUTRAL ZONE

2-1-2 system. The diagram shows a power play formation starting in the neutral zone from a faceoff situation or as the result of an effort to re-group for the attack. The 2 wingers go up near their offensive blue line, forcing the defense to stay in position and giving your centerman and defense a 3 on 2 situation against their checkers. As all of the players are in the neutral zone, positioning, timing and good pass execution become critical with limited space and time to make a play. The left defense is the puck carrier. Under pressure from a checker, he passes to his partner on defense, who in turn starts out with the puck and looks for 1 of 3 options: a pass to either wing or to the centerman. To get in position for a pass, the left wing cuts across the middle while the center swings over to his side, possibly catching their defense off guard. As a last resort, the puck could be thrown into the zone.

NEUTRAL ZONE

1-2-2 system. This system calls for the centerman on the power play to move to his offensive blue line to tie up the shorthanded team's defense. This leaves 2 wings and 2 defensemen against their 2 checkers, or a 4-2 situation. If the puck carrier is the left defense, there are 3 alternatives available to him for making a play under pressure from a checker. He can pass to his defensive partner in the middle or to either wing on the sides to get the attack on the offensive zone going.

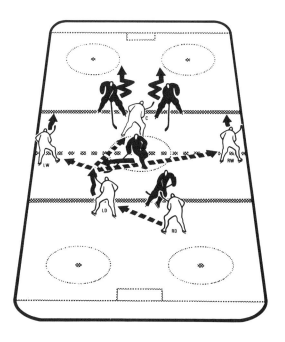

NEUTRAL ZONE

1-3-1 system. This formation for the power play in the neutral zone has the puck in the possession of the left defense, the centerman near the offensive blue line in the middle, and the wings and a defenseman inside the red line, as illustrated. The defense in this pattern acts as a center. The puck carrier, who is being pressed by a penalty killer, can pass to either of his wingers or to his defensive partner in the middle. This gives the power play a 4 on 3 situation going into the attack, which is easier than a 5 on 4 setup.

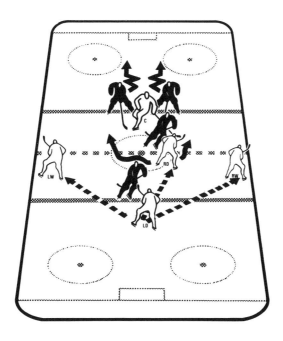

OFFENSIVE ZONE

Zone 1: 2-1-2 system. The diagram shows a power play system in the offensive zone with 3 players overloading the same side and play starting in one corner of the offensive zone. The wings and center overload the corner where the puck is in play in order to give the centerman the space and time necessary to make a play to one of the point men. The left wing at the side must take out their defense on that side, who is putting pressure on the puck carrier, and the defense should move behind their checkers, as shown.

Zone 2: 2-1-2 system. Another version of the power play in operation with the play starting in one corner and the side overloaded has the left point man breaking in between their 2 checkers to receive a pass and take a shot on goal. The left wing on the side takes out the penalty killing unit's defense in the corner to allow the centerman to make the play.

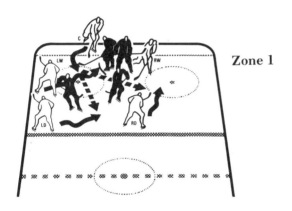

Zone 1

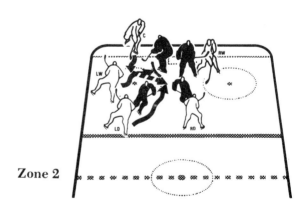

Zone 2

OFFENSIVE ZONE

Zone 1: 2-1-2 or 2-3 system. With the puck in play in the corner, 3 players overload the zone on the side—the right wing who controls the puck, the center and the right defense. The strategy here is to move the puck to the centerman, who in turn skates around his defenseman. The defense on the side is moving in from the point to interfere with the penalty killer covering the point, thereby giving the center time to either pass to his other defense or to take a shot on goal. In this play, the wing who started the play in the corner, goes to the front of the net and works with the other winger to tie up their 2 defense in front, giving the 3 offensive players space in which to maneuver and set up for a good shot on goal.

Zone 2: 2-1-2 or 3-2 system. Three players overload the side in which the puck is in play in the possession of the power play team. In this situation, the right wing in the corner is in control of the puck. He passes to the centerman, who is at the goal line, and skates in to check the opposing defenseman covering the corner. This allows the center to come into the slot area for a shot or for a pass to the point man, who is moving in deep. The left wing should be in front of the goal crease tying up the penalty killer positioned there.

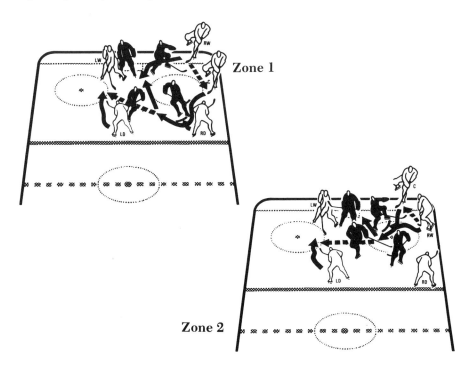

Zone 1

Zone 2

OFFENSIVE ZONE

Zone 1: 1-2-1-1 system. In this diagram, the power play unit is in control of the puck in the offensive zone. The puck is at the point, and 3 players overload the side. The play starts with the point man passing to the player by the boards, as illustrated. After making the pass, the player at the point sneaks to the middle as the player at the side passes to the wing in the corner. The wing takes the puck behind the net and attempts to set up a scoring opportunity by hitting the defenseman in the slot. The player on the side who received the first pass, in this case the center, moves to the front of the net to tie up 1 defenseman, while the other wing checks the second opponent in front of the crease. By keeping the defense in front of the goal busy, the puck carrier has an opportunity to get around behind and make his play.

Zone 2: 1-2-1 system. This 4 on 3 situation sets up from the corner, where the power play unit controls the puck. The wing in possession passes to the center in the corner or behind the goal line, and after making the pass, skates in and interferes with the defenseman covering the corner. The other winger is in front of the net tying up the third penalty killer. The puck carrier can swing into the slot area and either take a shot on goal or make a play to his open point man.

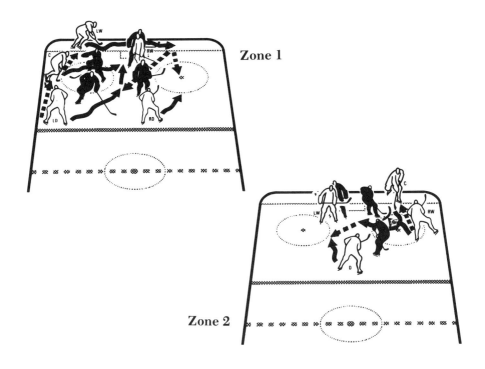

Zone 1

Zone 2

OFFENSIVE ZONE

Zone 1: 1-2-2 system. This idea for power play strategy in the offensive zone has one side overloaded with 3 players and the puck controlled by the offensive wing in the corner. The object is to neutralize 2 checkers and set up a play from the middle. The player in the corner can pass to his point man because the checker in this area is tying up the power play team's center. The puck handler at the point slides over toward the middle as the winger in the corner goes in front of the net and the right wing moves into the slot area to interfere with the checker there. The right defense skates to the top of the circle to replace the wing and to keep the team in balance. With the checkers in the middle covered, the player with the puck at the blue line has a choice of moving in for a shot on goal or passing to either his center or right defense.

Zone 2: 1-2-2 system. The power play unit has control of the puck at the right point in this diagram, and has overloaded the same side with 3 players. In this case, the centerman is on the side of the slot and the right winger is in the corner. The puck handler at the point passes to the wing in the corner, who takes the puck behind the net and attempts to make a play to his left defense. To make this work, the wing on the left side must take out their checker in the slot, while the centerman goes to the front of the net to tie up their defense and look for a rebound.

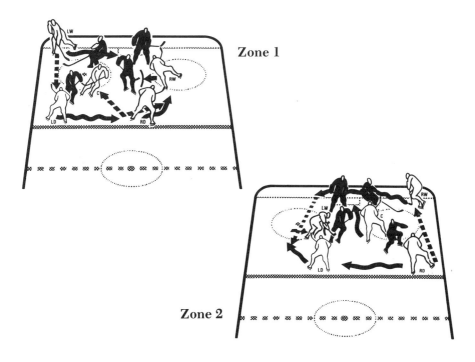

Zone 1

Zone 2

OFFENSIVE ZONE

Zone 1: 2-1-2 system. This is a quick passing play by the power play unit in the offensive zone. The puck is controlled in the left corner, and 3 players move to overload that side. The centerman in the corner passes to his wing, who gives the puck to the point man on his side. The player at the point sends the puck to his partner in the middle. After passing, the center moves from behind the goal line to the middle of the faceoff circle, while the wing swings into the slot area to be in position for a pass. The right point man sends the puck to his center, who passes to the player in the slot for a quick shot on the net.

Zone 2: 1-2-2 system. With the puck in the possession of the power play's centerman in the left corner, the left wing and point man overload the side. The cornerman passes to his wing near the boards, as diagramed, and skates to the front of the net, drawing his checker with him. The puck carrier moves into the slot and can either take a shot on the goal or make a play with the winger on the right side.

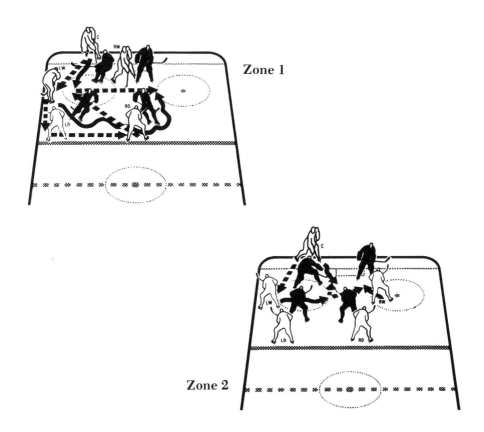

Zone 1

Zone 2

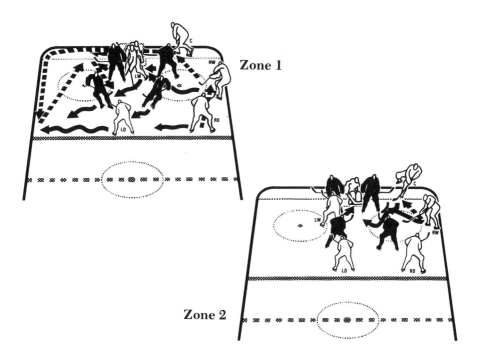

Zone 1

Zone 2

OFFENSIVE ZONE

Zone 1: 3-2 or 2-1-2 system. Passing the puck from player to player is the key to this power play pattern. The play starts at the right point and has the right side overloaded with players at the side and in the corner. The point man passes to the wing on the side, who gives the puck to his centerman in the corner. The center shoots around the boards to his left defense, who has moved to the boards from the middle. As the center skates behind the net to the left side, he takes a return pass from the left point and sets up his left wing, who has moved out from in front of the net to the side of the slot area. After the right wing has passed to the center, he goes to cover the crease and the right defense slides over to the middle.

Zone 2: 3-2 system. The forwards make the play in this power play formation, which shows the puck in the right corner and the side overloaded with 3 players. In this situation, the right wing has the puck in the corner. He passes to the center at the goal line, then quickly moves in on the defender in the corner, giving the centerman an opportunity to swing around them and go in for a shot on the net. A second alternative for the center would be a play with the left wing, who would move in and take out their other defense to get in scoring position in front of the net.

OFFENSIVE ZONE

Zone 1: 1-2-2 system. In this situation, the power play unit's center-man has the puck in the corner on the right. Three players overload the side in which the puck is in the play. The center moves the puck to his right wing and skates in front of the net, while the left wing comes across the slot toward the puck carrier, forcing the checker to pick him up and leaving the left point man open for a pass. Because the right defense would move to the middle to back up the position at the blue line, the right wing should drop back to keep team balance in the zone.

Zone 2: 2-2-1 system. A power play formation starts from behind the offensive goal line, where the center and right wing are located. The second wing and a defenseman are on top of the faceoff circles and the other defender is high in the middle by the blue line, ready to move into the slot area to receive a pass from either of the players behind the goal line. The key to this balanced pattern is to hold on to the puck behind the net and wait for 1 of the 3 players in front to break in on the goal for a pass and a quick shot on the net.

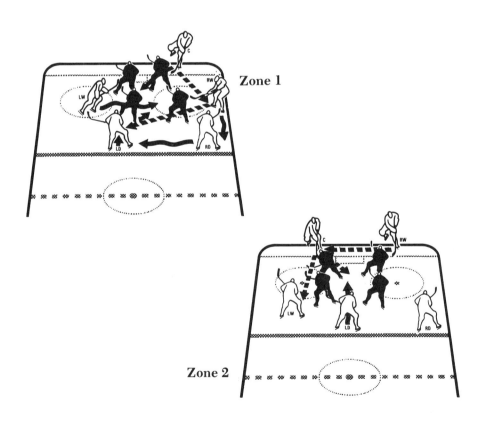

Zone 1

Zone 2

OFFENSIVE ZONE

Zone 1: 1-2-2 system. The puck is held by the right wing by the boards and the point man and center overload the zone. The idea in this offensive zone pattern is for the power play team's winger to pass the puck to his centerman and then to move to the front of the goal to become a possible pass receiver. If the center hangs on to the puck and makes a play to his right point man moving into the slot, the right wing would drop back to cover the point.

Zone 2: 1-2-2 system. This unbalanced power play formation has the puck in the possession of the right wing in the corner and four players overloading the zone: the left wing in the middle by the boards, the defense at the point and the center on the side of the slot. In this instance, the center is being checked, so the winger passes to his partner by the boards, who in turn passes the puck to the right point. The pointman could take a shot on goal, or could fake a shot and pass to the center near the slot. The right wing, after passing, should break for the front of the goal and watch for a deflection, tip-in or rebound opportunity.

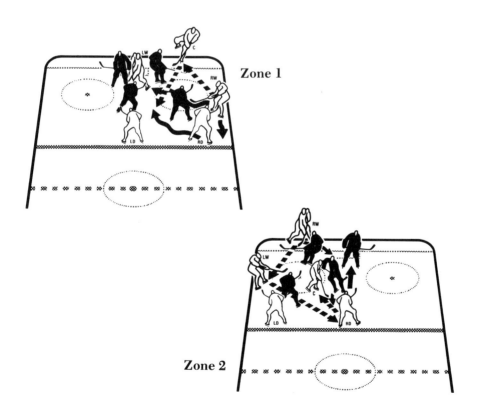

Zone 1

Zone 2

OFFENSIVE ZONE

Zone 1: 2-1-2 system. In the offensive zone, the power play unit controls the puck in the left corner and overloads the side with 3 players. The centerman in the corner passes to his wing by the boards and skates to the front of the goal to help his right winger tie up the defense. The right point man breaks in on the net behind his checker for a pass from the left side and a shot on goal. The passer moves to the point as the left defense goes to the middle in order to keep the team in balance.

Zone 2: 1-2-2 system. The power play team's centerman has control of the puck in the corner on the left in this pattern, and 3 players overload the side in the offensive zone. The center moves the puck to the wing at the side, who in turn, can make a play with either point man. The point man on his side breaks in on the net between 2 checkers to become available for a quick pass and a shot on the net. As he goes out of position, the right point man slides over to back up the position and be ready for a possible pass. The right winger must watch the play and be prepared to drop back in order to cover the blue line.

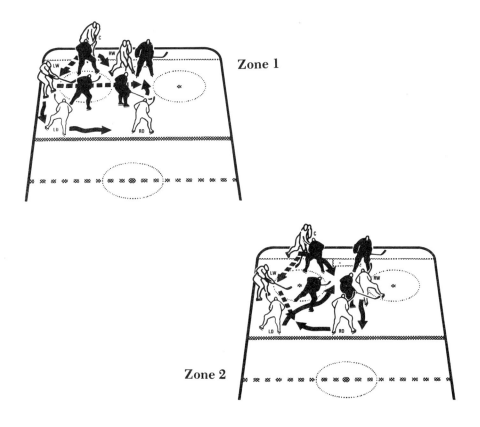

Zone 1

Zone 2

OFFENSIVE ZONE

Zone 1: 2-2-1 system. This suggestion for a power play pattern in the offensive zone starts with the defense in control of the puck at the blue line. The 2 wingers are near the net tying up the shorthanded team's defense, while the centerman and a defense are situated near the top of the faceoff circles. The puck carrier has 3 options for plays in what should be a 3 on 2 situation against their pair of checkers high in the zone, and could break down into a 2 on 1 situation for a shot on goal.

Zone 2: 1-2-2 system. The puck is controlled by the center in this power play formation, which has 3 players overloading the right side of the zone. The play hinges on the right wing's being able to move in on their defense on that side and tie him up long enough for the centerman to skate behind them and make a play to the left side. The possible receivers are the left wing, who could be open if the checker decides to cover the point man, or the player on the left point, who should move into the slot area for a possible pass.

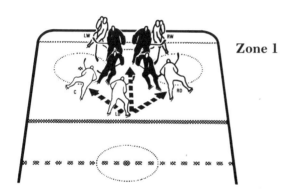

Zone 1

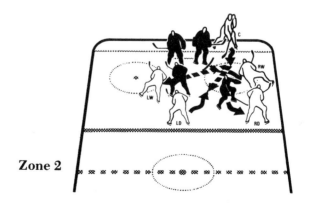

Zone 2

OFFENSIVE ZONE

Zone 1: 2-1-2 system. The puck is in play behind the goal line in this diagram, which has 3 players overloading the side in which the play will be made. The left winger passes to his right wing, who has 3 pass options. He can go to the centerman in the middle near the slot; he can pass to his right defense, who moves in from the blue line, or he can hit the left point man skating in for a pass and a shot on goal.

Zone 2: 1-2-1-1 system. This situation has the side in which the puck is in play in the offensive zone overloaded with 4 players. The power play team's center has the puck in the corner, and passes to his right wing at the boards. After passing, he breaks for the front of the net. Because a checker has been pulled out his normal position by the overloading formation, the left winger should be open to take a pass and get off a shot on the net.

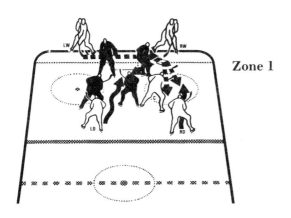

Zone 1

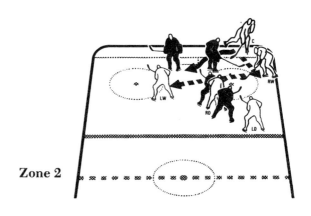

Zone 2

OFFENSIVE ZONE

Zone 1: 1-2-2 system. The diagram shows an evenly balanced power play pattern starting from the offensive blue line, where the puck is controlled by a point man. The setup has the centerman in front of the net, the wings inside the 2 faceoff circles and the defense in the middle of the zone at the blue line. To start the play, puck handler could pass to his opposite point, or to either wing. All would have a chance for a shot on goal, and the centerman is in good position for a deflection or to pick up a rebound.

Zone 2: 2-1-2 system. Another balanced pattern for the power play in the offensive zone has the centerman in the slot with the wingers flanking the front of the goal and tying up the defense. If the puck is controlled by the right point man, the play would go either to the other point or to the center in the slot. The wings would be in position for deflection, screening and picking up a rebound.

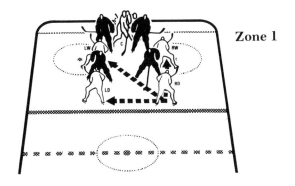

Zone 1

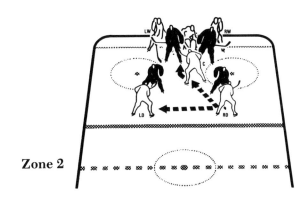

Zone 2

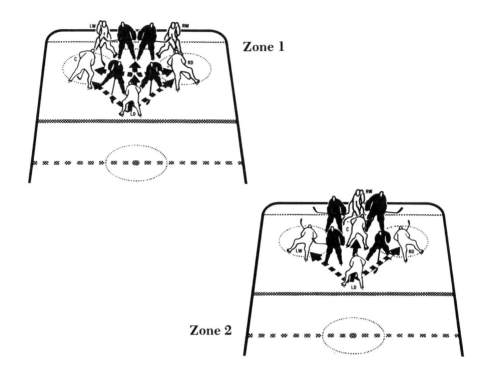

Zone 1

Zone 2

OFFENSIVE ZONE

Zone 1: 2-2-1 system. As illustrated, the puck is controlled by a point man at the blue line in the offensive zone. The power play team is balanced with the wings in front of the net and the centerman and a defense near the top of each faceoff circle. The wings are responsible for tying up the defense in front of the goal and watching for a deflection, rebound or a screening opportunity. The puck carrier has 3 options for making a play in what is essentially a 3 on 2 situation. He can skate the puck in himself or pass to either the center or defense.

Zone 2: 1-3-1 system. Another evenly balanced pattern which can be used on the power play when the puck is controlled by a point man at the blue line, has a wing in front of the net and 3 players midway in the zone. The centerman is in the slot area (in the shorthanded team's defensive box), and is flanked by a defense and a wing. The puck handler inside the blue line has the possibility of a 4 on 2 situation against their checkers, and could move the puck to any of the 3 players in the middle to set up a shot on goal.

OFFENSIVE ZONE

Zone 1: 1-2-2 system. In this illustration of a power play formation in the offensive zone, the offense has a 2-man advantage. With the puck in the possession of one of the point men, players go to a balanced pattern, sending the center to the front of the net, the wings in the faceoff circles and the point men inside the blue line in the middle. The puck carrier, as shown, could set up 4 players for a possible shot on goal.

Zone 2: 2-1-2 system. This is another balanced formation which could be employed when the power play team has a 2-man advantage and play is with a point man. The wings flank the front of the net, tying up the defenders, while the centerman is in the slot area with the third checker. The point men move the puck back and forth, waiting for an opportunity to take a shot on goal.

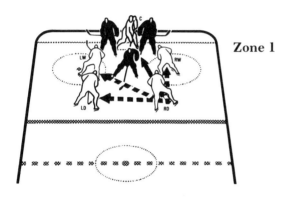

Zone 1

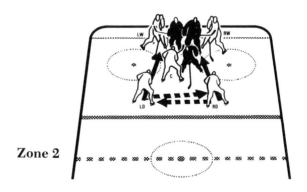

Zone 2

OFFENSIVE ZONE

Zone 1: 2-2-1 system. With the puck controlled by a point man in the offensive zone and the power play enjoying a 2-man advantage, players set up in a balanced attack. The wingers are in front of the net with their defense, while the centerman and 1 point man are positioned near the top of the faceoff circles, as diagramed. The puck carrier, who is in the middle near the blue line, has a 3 on 1 situation to work with in setting up the center or defense for a shot on goal.

Zone 2: 1-3-1 system. Another balanced formation that may be used when the opposition is 2 men short has the centerman in front of the goal tying up their defense, and the wingers and 1 defense spread out between the faceoff circles, as shown. The defense in the slot area interferes with their checker, which leaves the wings open and the point man with the puck controlling the middle. A pass to either wing should set up a good shot on goal.

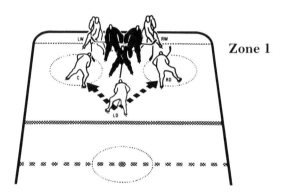 Zone 1

Zone 2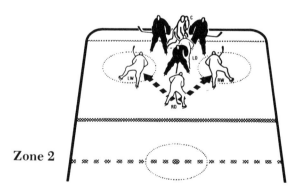

OFFENSIVE ZONE

Zone 1: 2-2 system. In a 4 on 3 power play situation, a balanced formation in the offensive zone would have a wing and a center in front of the goal and the point men in the middle, as diagramed. If the forwards have the defense tied up, the point men move the puck back and forth and proceed with the attack as in a 2 on 1 situation against their only checker.

Zone 2: 1-3-2 system. When the goaltender is pulled for a sixth skater at the end of a period or in the last minute of a game, the offense operates in the same manner as in a power play situation in the offensive zone. In this instance, an evenly balanced pattern has a wing in front of the net, 3 forwards spread from one faceoff circle to the other, and the point men in normal positioning inside the blue line. The right wing and center are responsible for tying up checkers in the slot area, giving the point man with the puck an opportunity to make a play to his partner or to the wings in the faceoff circles for a shot on goal.

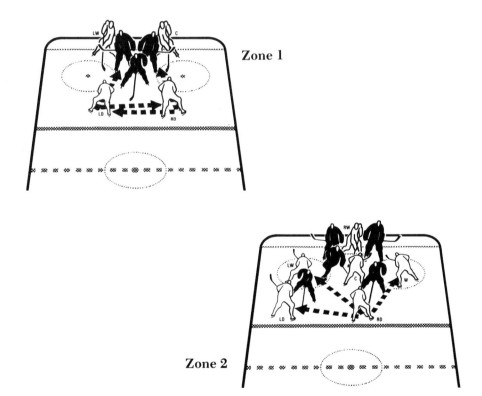

Zone 1

Zone 2

OFFENSIVE ZONE

Zone 1: 1-3-2 system. Another special power play situation is a 6 on 3, where an extra player replaces the goaltender at some critical point in the game. The team is balanced in the zone with the centerman in front of the net tying up their defense and a wing in the slot with the third checker. Wings are in the faceoff circles and the point men are in the middle of the zone at the blue line, controlling the puck. With the situation relatively stable, the point men should move the puck back and forth looking for a good shooting opportunity. The wings in the circles could move in to help the centerman and to be ready for a tip-in, deflection or rebound.

Zone 2: 1-3-2 system. When the power play team controls the puck in the offensive zone and a sixth skater is sent in to replace the goal tender, this pattern could be against a box formation by the shorthanded team. The right winger goes to the net to tie up the defense, while the centerman is inside the box in the slot area. Wings are in the faceoff circles and the puck is in play at the point. The puck carrier (left defense in this case) has 3 options for moving the puck in order to set up a shot on goal.

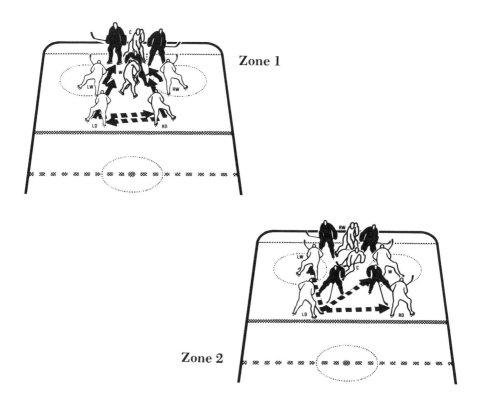

Zone 1

Zone 2

Thought Provokers

1. Have you ever considered switching your 2 wingers to their offside positions in the power play?
2. Everyone on the team should have work on the power play in practice, plus game experience.
3. Do you have a definite power play system? For each zone?
4. Try using a point man playing his offside position.
5. How much time do you spend on the power play in practice?
6. Do you keep statistics on power play opportunities (per game and per season) and power play goals (per game and per season)?
7. A power play goal is an excellent example of capitalizing on an opponent's mistake. Some successful teams count on the effectiveness of their power play for the winning edge.

CHAPTER 8 *The Penalty Killing Game*

The team that is unable to kill penalties effectively game after game is very likely to lose more of them than it wins. Close games are often decided on how well the penalty killing unit performs, and in a sense, penalty killing is a good indicator of overall team discipline.

Penalty killing requires more discipline from the players than any other aspect of the game. The best penalty killers are defense-minded players with good skating ability, superior puck control, sound hockey sense, quick reflexes and cool heads. (With one man already in the box, this is no time to go headhunting!) Anticipation and timing are particularly important in shorthanded situations. Being able to read the offense and react quickly and decisively in a disciplined manner is part of a successful effort. The other part of it is knowing where to go and what to do if and when you gain control of the puck when you are one or two men short.

This chapter gives ideas on different systems for containing the power play unit in each zone of the rink—offensive, neutral and defensive—and in one-man- and two-men-short situations.

The system you use will depend on the players you have to work with. Some different systems include the 2-2, or standard box zone coverage; the 1-2-1, or diamond box pattern; the 2-1-1, or *Y* formation; the 1-1-2, or *I* formation; and a combination of the standard and diamond box systems (when you are one man short). With two men short, you can use the 1-2 or 2-1 system.

In covering the defensive zone, be sure to emphasize zone, rather than man-to-man coverage. Because you are shorthanded, there is always one man who won't be covered, and if you play man-to-man, this could cost the team a goal. It's a good policy to see that both offensive wings are checked properly. This forces the power play unit to use at least one point man in order to gain a 2 on 1 advantage entering the offensive zone. Be strict in keeping your defensemen in position at all times: They can't afford to run around in a shorthanded situation.

Penalty killing is basically a matter of killing time. With an effective system, this is best accomplished by controlling the puck in your own end of the rink or better yet at center ice. Assuming that the attacking team has a good power play, it's quite likely that the shorthanded club will have to go on the offensive in its zone. The objective at this stage of the game should be to prevent shots from the slot. It's not possible or practical to expect to keep the power play team from getting any shots on goal.

Zone Formations

OFFENSIVE ZONE CHECKING

Zone 1: 1-1-2 system (*I* formation). One checker is deep on the puck carrier with the second checker lined up behind him midway in the zone. The idea is to force the puck carrier to make a play on one side only, giving your checkers and defense an opportunity to limit and contain the play. The checkers should work with the defense as they retreat from the zone.

Zone 2: 1-2 system. The checker tries to cover the middle and make the power play unit carry the puck to the outside. This gives the opposition only 1 possible play, whereas, if they stay in the middle, they have 2 choices, plays to either side of the rink.

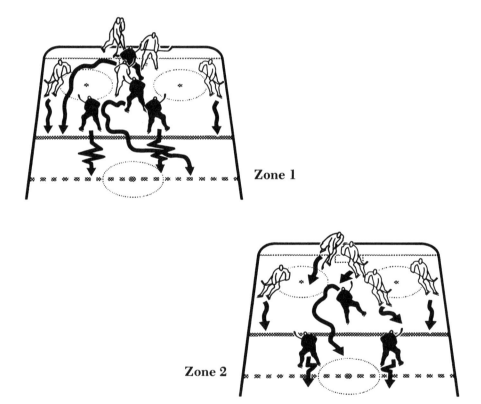

Zone 1

Zone 2

OFFENSIVE ZONE CHECKING

Zone 1: 2-2 system. The 2 checkers are side by side in this pattern. They pick up their wingers in the offensive zone and stay with them until the play goes into your defensive zone. The defense will try to force or contain the puck carrier, and in some situations, may also be able to check the extra attacker.

Zone 2: 1-1-2 system (*I* formation). One checker goes in deep on the puck carrier, while the second checker backs him up higher in the zone. The objective is to press the puck carrier to make a play on one side or the other, rather than to the middle. The checkers swing back to check the attacking wings on their side, and your defense will try to force or contain the puck carrier and check the extra attacker.

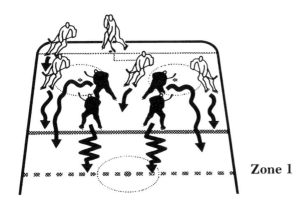

Zone 1

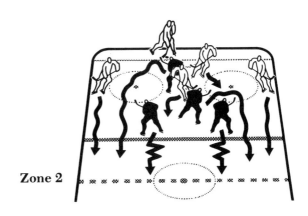

Zone 2

OFFENSIVE ZONE CHECKING

Zone 1: 2-2 system. In this formation, the 2 checkers go deep in the offensive zone. When they see the attacking centerman go behind the net to get the puck, 1 checker goes behind the goal from the opposite direction, while the other checker makes a swing in front of the net. The defense should stand up at the blue line and be ready for the possible attack and retreat.

Zone 2: 1-1-2 system (*I* formation). In this instance, one of the checkers goes deep and attempts to force the puck carrier behind the net to make a move. The other checker covers the winger on the side where the play is made. The defense stands up for a possible attack at the blue line and prepares to retreat.

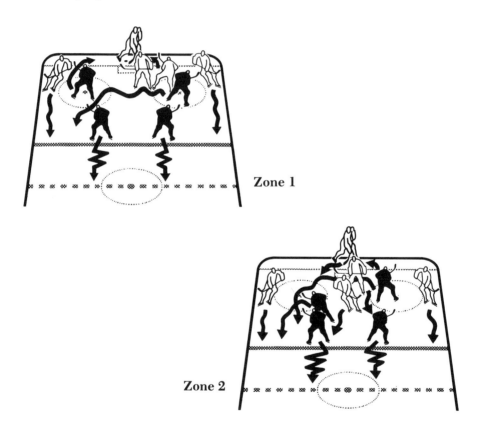

Zone 1

Zone 2

OFFENSIVE ZONE CHECKING

Zone 1: 2-2 system. The checkers pick up their wingers in the offensive zone. One of the defense moves into the play to force the puck carrier, while his partner backs him up at the blue line. Having the defense move in on the puck carrier sometimes catches him by surprise and throws him off balance.

Zone 2: 1-1-2 system (*I* formation). Your first checker will stay in front of the net in the offensive zone and press the puck carrier to make a play to the side. The other checker goes to the side where the puck goes, and forces the new puck carrier. The defense should be prepared for the attack at the blue line and should be ready to retreat.

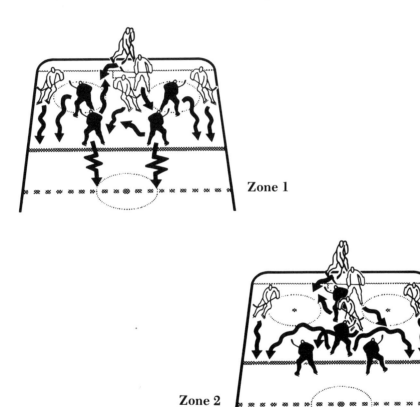

Zone 1

Zone 2

NEUTRAL ZONE CHECKING

Zone 1: 1-2 system. In this pattern, the checker covers the middle in the neutral zone and tries to force the power play team to carry the puck to the outside. At the defensive blue line, the checker will back up whichever defenseman attempts to force the play or the puck carrier.

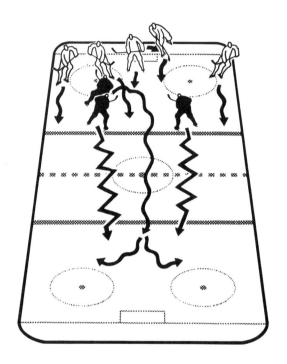

NEUTRAL ZONE CHECKING

Zone 1: 1-2 into a 2-1 system. In this system, the checker is covering the middle in order to make the power play team carry the puck to the side. As the puck carrier approaches your blue line, the defenseman on that side tries to force the play, which sets up a 1-2 situation. As he makes his move, the checker quickly goes to the side to shift the balance to a 2 on 2. The defense continues to put pressure on the puck carrier, leaving the checker to cover the other forward and act as a backup for the defense.

NEUTRAL ZONE CHECKING

Zone 1: 2-2 system. In most shorthanded situations, the best way to cover the neutral zone is to have the checkers covering the sides or the opposing wings. The defense has the responsibility of handling the puck carrier and the extra offensive player. The checkers should back up the defense and be on the alert in case one of the defensemen decides to challenge the puck carrier at your blue line, as illustrated. Unless the power play unit shoots the puck into the zone, the penalty killers have a good chance to contain the play at the blue line because usually at that point it becomes a 4 on 4 situation.

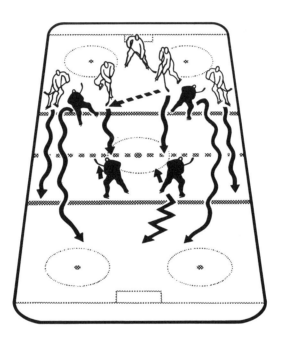

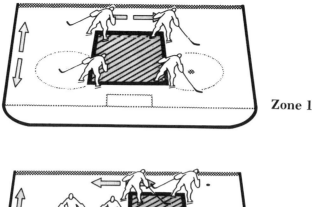

Zone 1

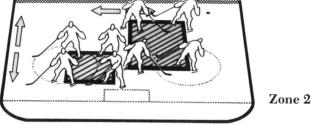

Zone 2

DEFENSIVE ZONE COVERAGE

Zone 1: 2-2 system (standard box). The diagram shows the basic box defense with the 4 checkers at right angles to each other. The objective in defensive zone coverage is to protect the area in front of the net. As much as possible the checkers should try to keep the puck to the outside of the boxed area. The standard box is effective in penalty killing only as long as the checkers stay in their positions. This is zone coverage, and if one of the defenders is lured away from his position, there is always an extra man on the offensive who can cause trouble.

Zone 2: 2-2 system (standard box). This diagram shows how the 4 checkers forming the box should react to movement of the puck by the power play team. If the puck is in the corner, for instance, the box should contract because the play is closer to the net. If the puck is at the point, the box should expand because the area of coverage is larger in front of the net.

NOTE

Movement of the checkers is indicated by the arrows. The cross-hatched area is the zone which should be protected from penetration by the offense and the puck.

DEFENSIVE ZONE COVERAGE

Zone 1: 1-2 system (triangle from standard box). With two men short, the penalty killing unit may employ a defensive triangle based on the box formation. The shape of the triangle formed by the 3 checkers is that of the box sliced in half diagonally. The formation shifts to keep the power play team to the side with the puck, and has 1 checker up front and 2 back on the side where the puck is located. This makes the more advantageous situation.

NOTE

If you allow the power play team to control the puck in the middle of the zone it will create the least advantageous situation up front against the lone checker. This is why it is important to keep the puck to the side and maintain the more advantageous situation.

Zone 2: 2-1 system (triangle from standard box). A different version of the triangle can also be used when your team is two men short. As shown, 2 checkers are up front with the third checker in back, creating a more advantageous situation wherever the puck may be in play in the zone.

NOTE

The triangle will be smaller or larger depending on the location of the puck in the zone. The triangle should be smaller when the puck is deep in your end and larger when the puck is on the point at the blue line. The puck should not be allowed in the crosshatched area. Movement of the formation in the zone is indicated by the arrows.

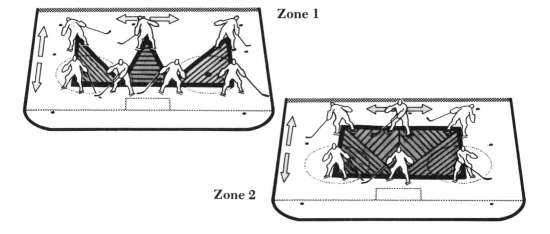

Zone 1

Zone 2

DEFENSIVE ZONE COVERAGE

Zone 1: 1-2-1 system (diamond box). Another system of zone coverage in a shorthanded situation is the diamond box formation shown here. Four checkers go into the box to protect the slot from penetration by the attackers and/or the puck. In order to be effective, the players must be disciplined to keep in position and not break away from the formation. The arrows indicate movement of the box in the zone.

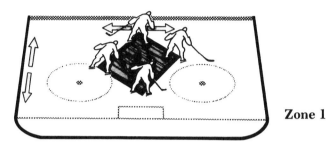

Zone 1

Zone 2: 1-2-1 system (diamond box). The drawing shows how the checkers react to offensive play in the diamond box system. When the puck is in the corner, the box should shift toward the corner and contract. When the puck is controlled by the man at the point, the box should move toward the point and expand to cover the increased territory available to the power play unit.

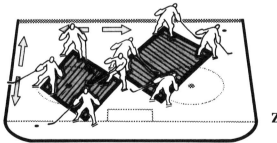

Zone 2

DEFENSIVE ZONE COVERAGE

Zone 1: 2-1 system (triangle from diamond box). With two men short, the penalty killers can create and maintain a 3 on 2 situation in the defensive zone with a triangle derived from the diamond box. Two checkers form the wide base in front of the net and the third checker is behind. The triangle should expand and contract according to the location of the puck in the zone. Player movement is shown by the arrows.

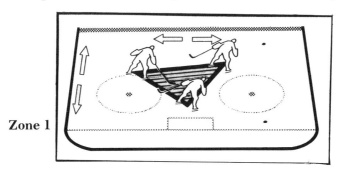

Zone 1

Zone 2: 1-2 system (triangle from diamond box). The triangle created from the halved diamond box is reversed in this system, which has 1 checker up front and 2 in back. If the checkers, by moving in formation, are able to keep the power play and the puck to the side, they have an opportunity to hold out in a more advantageous situation. If the attackers penetrate the middle, it becomes least advantageous against a single checker, which is definitely dangerous.

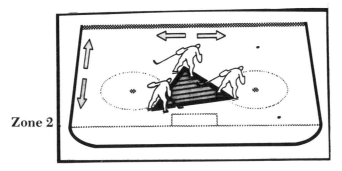

Zone 2

DEFENSIVE ZONE COVERAGE

Zones 1 and 2: 2-2 and 1-2-1 combination system. This system combines the standard box (2-2) and the diamond box (1-2-1) formations. It is simply a matter of going from the rectangle to the diamond and back as required by the offensive play. As in other penalty killing formations, the boxes get larger and smaller according to the location of the puck in the zone. While in the box, checkers have the responsibility of keeping the puck to the outside and not allowing any penetration into the protected area.

Zone 1

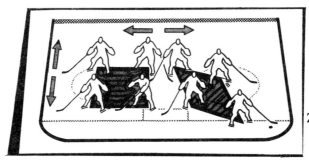

Zone 2

DEFENSIVE ZONE COVERAGE

Zone 1: 2-2 system. In this example, the team on the power play has overloaded one side of the zone with 3 players. The box formation put into play on that side creates a more advantageous situation against the checkers on that side. The object is to stay in the formation and force the offense to move the puck around the boxed area.

Zone 1

Zone 2: 2-2 system. The diagram illustrates the use of the 2-2 system against a power play unit employing a balanced formation in the zone. One of the offensive players is caught in the box, which creates an even situation with your checkers, but leaves an open man behind the front checkers. One of the penalty killers in the box will have to be responsible for the player inside the box.

Zone 2

DEFENSIVE ZONE COVERAGE

Zone 1: 2-1-1 system (*Y* formation). This system has 2 checkers up front to cover the point men in the opponent's power play. One of your defensemen moves in to cover the slot area, while his partner is directly in front of the net. The arrows indicate each player's responsibility in covering the zone according to the location of the puck at any given time.

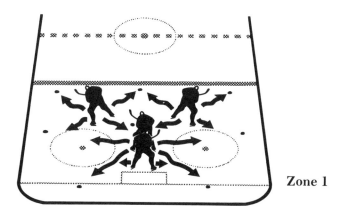

Zone 1

Zone 2: 1-2-1 system (diamond box). In this formation, 1 checker is in front of the goal, 2 checkers are by the circles in the middle of the zone, and the remaining checker is in front near the goal line. Each player's responsibility in maintaining coverage in the slot area is shown by arrows.

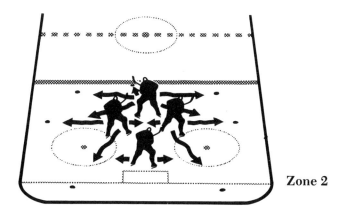

Zone 2

DEFENSIVE ZONE COVERAGE

Zone 1: 2-2 system (standard box). With one man short, 4 checkers form a box in the middle, as illustrated. Two checkers are in front and 2 are in back. The arrows indicate the responsibility of each player in zone coverage as the puck moves around the outside of the box.

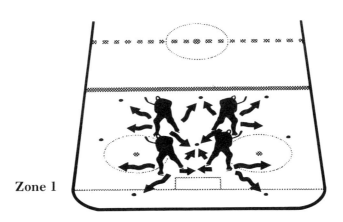

Zone 1

Zone 2: 1-2 system (triangle). In this shorthanded situation, zone coverage is maintained by 3 checkers in a triangular formation. One player is in front and 2 checkers are back. Each player's responsibility in responding to movement of the puck by the power play team is indicated by the arrows.

Zone 2

DEFENSIVE ZONE COVERAGE

Zone 1: 2-1 system (upside down triangle). Two checkers are up front and 1 checker is back covering the net in this defensive system. With this pattern, you have 2 checkers on the strong side (the side of the rink where the puck is in play), thus creating a more advantageous situation against the front checkers when the puck is on the point, as shown. The arrows show each player's responsibility, depending on where the puck carrier is situated in the zone.

Zone 2: 2-1 system (upside down triangle). The diagram shows another example of the upside down triangle in operation by a team which is two players short. In this case, the puck is in the corner and the side is overloaded by 3 offensive players. Two of the checkers stay on the strong side, with the third penalty killer covering the area in front of the net. The arrows indicate the checkers' responsibilities in maintaining zone coverage as the puck is moved by the offense.

Zone 1

Zone 2

DEFENSIVE ZONE COVERAGE

Zone 1: If the shorthanded team should gain control of the puck in their end, the best move is to play conservatively while playing out the clock and getting the puck out of the zone. This example has the defense, who has captured the puck following a shot on goal, with the puck behind his net. One of the front checkers should go to the boards on the side where the puck will be brought out, while the other checker attempts to break in between their defense. This forces the power play unit to back out of the zone, and gives the puck carrier 2 options to pass in order to clear the zone.

Zone 2: In this play, the defense has regained control of the puck in the corner. One checker should position himself between the point men, while the other checker breaks for the boards on the side opposite the side where the puck is in play. The defenseman with the puck has the 2 options illustrated. Because the opposite side would most likely be open, clearing around the boards behind the net might be the best choice.

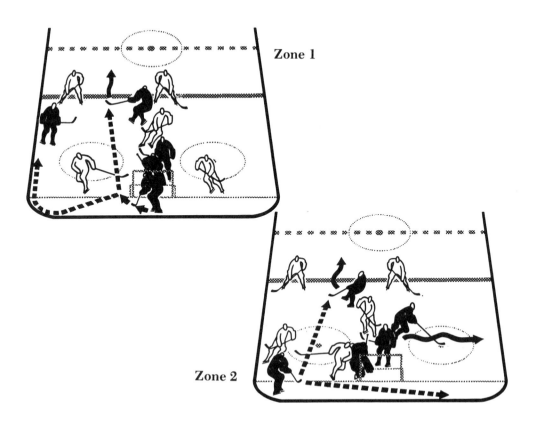

Zone 1

Zone 2

Thought Provokers

1. Have you ever used 3 defense when you are two men short?
2. How much time do you spend on penalty killing in practice?
3. Consider using 4 penalty killers playing their offside positions. That is, all 4 of them will carry their sticks toward the middle, blade faces into the slot, which can be advantageous.
4. Do you have a sound system that works?
5. Do you have basic rules for coverage in each zone?
6. Everyone on the team should learn how to kill penalties under your system.
7. Try using 4 defensemen as penalty killers.
8. If both attacking wings are checked, the power play will have to use a point man to gain a 2 on 1 advantage entering the offensive zone.
9. Don't let your players get so eager to get the occasional shorthanded goal that they get reckless.
10. Shooting the puck into the zone on the power play can be good news to the penalty killers. Do your players know what to do?

CHAPTER **9** *The Faceoff Game*

Many knowledgeable hockey people will say the game is won or lost on the percentage of faceoffs won or lost during the course of the game. A simple rule in hockey states that if you win the faceoff in the offensive zone, the team should get a shot on goal. A shot, of course, is a potential goal. If the team loses the faceoff in the offensive zone, the opponent controls the play and should break out of their end. The situation is reversed in the defensive end.

It figures that if the team wins more faceoffs than it loses, it is in control of the puck for longer periods of time and thereby is giving the opposing team fewer chances to score. By simple deduction, one concludes that practice time spent on faceoffs is well worth it.

This chapter will present some ideas on positioning players for faceoff situations in all 3 zones of the rink—offensive, neutral and defensive. This is not intended to be a full-blown discussion on team offensive and defensive strategy as chapters 5 and 6 cover what will transpire when the faceoff is won or lost. A number of alternatives for either system have already been put forth in these chapters, and anything added here would be repetitious. What you will find are diagrams on positioning, as well as a short explanation of offensive and defensive maneuvers if the faceoff is won or lost.

The illustrations show by solid lines where the puck could go if the faceoff is won. If the team loses the faceoff, defensive checking maneuvers go into operation in order to regain control of the puck. This is shown by the lines where the arrow is crossed with a *t*-line to indicate the approximate area where each player should go according to the team strategy—defensive or offensive—to be employed. The diagrams do not show the opposition. This was done to avoid cluttering the diagrams and to give a clearer picture of what can be done with different faceoff formations.

The centerman is the key man in faceoffs, in most cases. He should direct player positioning, especially that of the player who has the best chance to gain puck control in any zone, or who can start the play, whether it is a shot on goal or a breakout pattern, in your own end. Both centers are in an offensive position at the faceoff; both teams are prepared to go on the offense. When the puck is dropped, one team gains possession and it's back to offense and defense, just as in basketball after tip-up. The team must be prepared to execute different maneuvers in each zone.

OFFENSIVE ZONE FACEOFFS

Zone 1: 5-5, 5-4, 5-3 formation. Three forwards are in line in this formation. The right defense is on the top of the circle behind the centerman and the left defense stays in the middle.

The diagram shows 5 options for movement of the puck if the faceoff is won. Three of them would give potential shots on goal.

If the team loses the faceoff, the crossed arrows show where each player could go in order to set up their offensive zone coverage and to regain puck control.

Zone 2: 5-5, 5-4, 5-3 formation. Two forwards are positioned in front; the right wing is behind the center outside the top of the circle. The right defense moves in by the side boards and the left defense stays in the middle.

If the faceoff is won, there are 4 possible ways the puck can go, 3 of them resulting in shots on goal. If the faceoff is lost, players have a number of options in moving to positions for coverage of the offensive zone and recovery of the puck (see diagram).

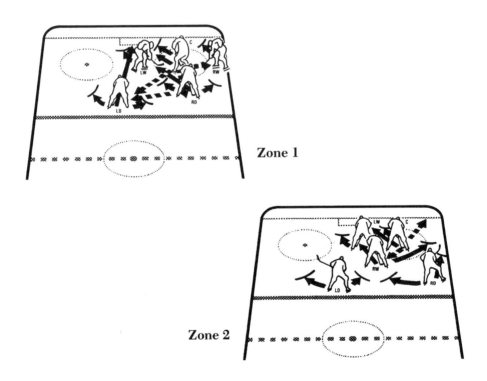

Zone 1

Zone 2

OFFENSIVE ZONE FACEOFFS

Zone 1: 6-5, 6-4, 6-3 formation. Diagram illustrates the formation to be used in the offensive zone when the goaltender has been pulled in favor of an extra player.

Four players are lined up in front, overloading the middle, with 2 players in back: 1 by the top of the circle behind the centerman and 1 in the middle.

If the faceoff is won, there are 5 places the puck can go. Three of the options are potential shots on goal. If the draw is lost, players move in the direction of the crossed arrows to establish offensive zone coverage in order to regain puck control.

Zone 2: 6-5, 6-4, 6-3 formation. Illustration shows a second formation, which can be used in the offensive zone when the goaltender has been pulled for an extra skater.

In this formation, 5 players are in line in the front, overloading the middle, with 1 player in back in the middle of the zone. The diagram indicates 4 directions the puck can take if the team wins the draw. Two of them are potential shots on goal. If the team does not win the faceoff, players can move in the areas indicated for offensive zone coverage.

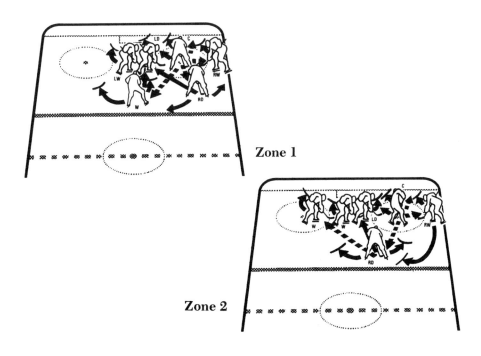

Zone 1

Zone 2

OFFENSIVE ZONE FACEOFFS

Zone 1: 5-5, 5-4, 5-3 formation. Three forwards are in a line overloading the middle with the wings. The right defense moves to the area near the top of the circle while the left defense stays in the middle.

The diagram shows 4 options for movement of the puck after the team gets the draw. Three would be potential shots on goal. Possibilities for each player to move into offensive zone coverage if the faceoff is not won are also diagramed.

Zone 2: 5-4, 5-3 formation. Four players are positioned in line up front with 3 players overloading the middle. This formation leaves the right defense back in the middle, and usually is used when the team has a one- or two-man advantage. The diagram shows 3 options in moving the puck after winning the faceoff; 2 of them could result in shots on goal. If the team does not get the draw, players can move in the directions indicated to take up offensive zone coverage and to regain puck control.

NOTE

Overloading the middle is done in order to screen the goalie and to be ready for possible rebounds.

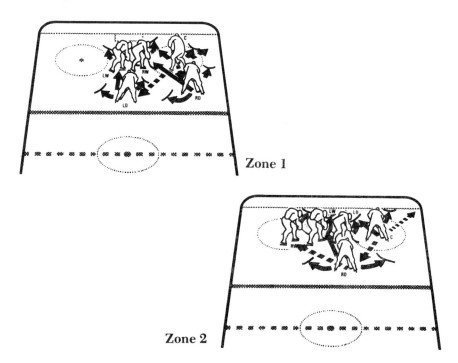

Zone 1

Zone 2

OFFENSIVE ZONE FACEOFFS

Zone 1: 3-3, 3-4, 3-5 formation. In a situation where the team is two men short, only 1 player is in front for the faceoff (see diagram), with the 2 defensemen located in back, 1 along the side boards and 1 in the middle.

The diagram shows 4 options for movement of the puck after the team wins the faceoff; 3 of the moves could result in a shot on goal. If the team does not win the draw, possible player movements for offensive zone coverage are indicated by the crossed arrows.

Zone 2: 4-4, 4-5 formation. When the team is one man short, the 2 forwards are up front with the 2 defensemen back—1 along the boards and 1 in the middle (see diagram). If the team wins the draw, the player has 4 options for movement of the puck, 3 of which could result in shots on goal. If the team loses the draw, players have a number of options for setting up offensive zone coverage, as indicated by the crossed arrows, and for regaining puck control.

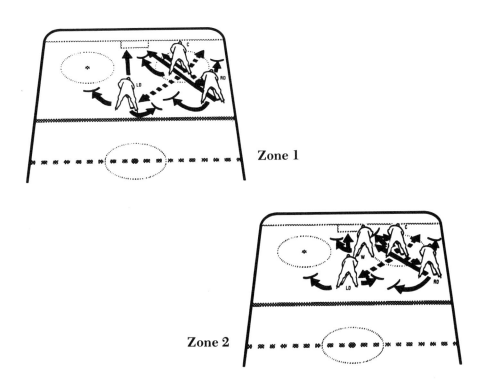

Zone 1

Zone 2

NEUTRAL ZONE FACEOFFS

Zone 1: 4-4, 4-5 formation. With one man short, line up 3 players in front with the right defense back in the zone behind the centerman. Normally, 1 defenseman is moved up front for the faceoff in the neutral zone in a shorthanded situation.

The diagram shows 5 options for movement of the puck after the team wins the draw. If the team does not win the faceoff, there are numerous options (indicated by the crossed arrows) for regaining puck control and/or setting up neutral zone coverage.

Zone 2: 3-3, 3-4, 3-5 formation. In this setup, the team is two men short. The center, flanked by right and left defense, line up parallel for the faceoff at the line of scrimmage.

Four options for puck movement if the faceoff is won are indicated by the broken lines; alternatives in player movement if the faceoff is lost are shown by the crossed arrows.

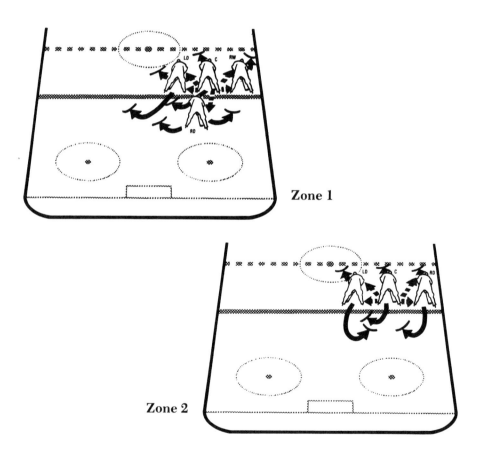

Zone 1

Zone 2

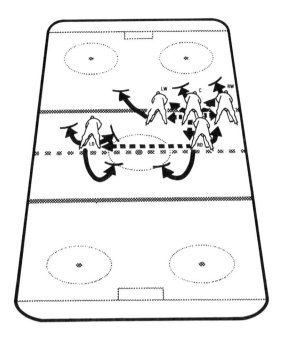

NEUTRAL ZONE FACEOFFS

Zone 1: 5-5, 5-4, 5-3 formation. As illustrated, the centerman and wings line up at the line of scrimmage. One defense is directly behind the centerman while the second defense is on the outside, making it an unbalanced formation. The idea is to give the defense the opportunity to take the puck if the faceoff is won and to carry it into the offensive zone.

The diagram shows 5 options for movement of the puck after the faceoff is won. If the team loses the draw, players have the options of movement illustrated by the crossed arrows.

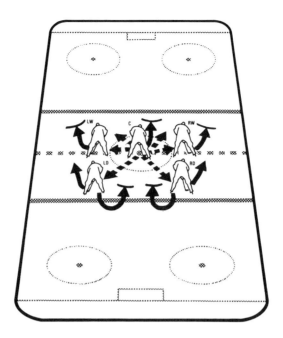

NEUTRAL ZONE FACEOFFS

Zone 1: 5-5, 5-4, 5-3 formation. This is the most commonly used formation for a faceoff in the neutral zone. The 3 forwards are in line at the faceoff circle with the 2 defensemen behind in a balanced formation.

The diagram shows 6 options for movement of the puck if the faceoff is won. If the team does not win the draw, players can move into neutral zone coverage by choosing from the alternatives shown by the crossed arrows.

DEFENSIVE ZONE FACEOFFS

Zone 1: 5-6, 5-5, 5-4 formation. The 3 forwards are at the line of scrimmage in this formation, with the 2 wingers overloading the middle. One defense is behind the centerman and the other defense is located next to the goaltender.

If the faceoff is won, there are 2 directions the puck can go as the players set up for breakout from the zone. If the team loses the draw, possibilities for player movement to establish defensive zone coverage are as illustrated by the crossed arrows.

Zone 2: 5-6, 5-5, 5-4, 5-3 formation. Here the center is flanked by his right and left wings at the point of faceoff. The left defender is behind the centerman and the right defense is next to the goaltender.

The diagram shows 3 options for movement of the puck and key players after the faceoff is won and the team prepares to break out. If the team loses the draw, the players can go into defensive zone coverage by skating to the positions shown by the crossed arrows.

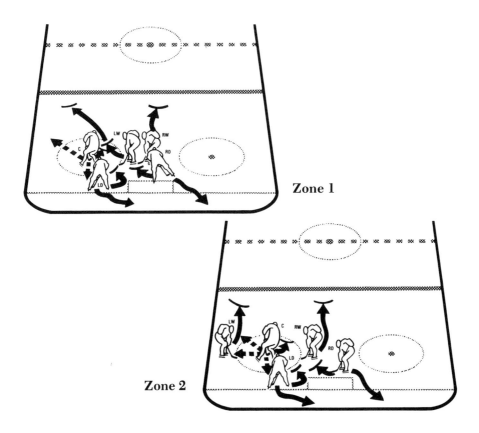

Zone 1

Zone 2

DEFENSIVE ZONE FACEOFFS

Zone 1: 5-6, 5-5, 5-4, 5-3 formation. Four players are at the line of scrimmage in this formation, overloading the middle for the faceoff. One defense is behind the line and slightly to the right of the goal. Note that the right wing is behind the left defense at the faceoff point.

The diagram shows 3 options for movement of the puck if the team wins the faceoff; the unbroken lines also indicate movement of key players when the draw is won and the players prepare to break out of their zone. Crossed arrows indicate where the players could go to set up defensive zone coverage if the faceoff is lost.

Zone 2: 5-6, 5-5, 5-4, 5-3 formation. All five players are lined in a row in this formation; the right wing is behind the centerman near the boards, while the right and left defense and left wing are one behind the other in the middle.

Three options for puck and/or player movement are available if the team wins the draw and prepares to break out. If the team fails to win the faceoff, the players can move to the positions indicated to set up defensive zone coverage and try to regain puck control.

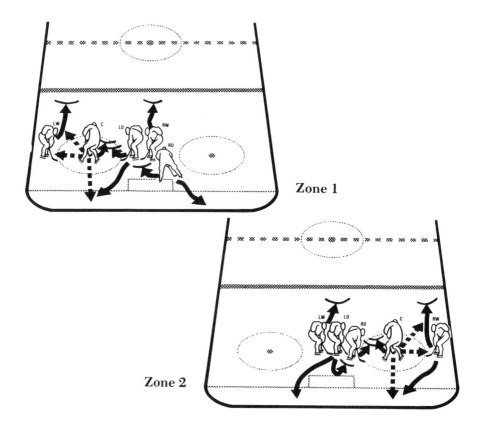

Zone 1

Zone 2

DEFENSIVE ZONE FACEOFFS

Zone 1: 5-6, 5-5, 5-4, 5-3 formation. Two players overload the middle and 3 skaters are located at the line of scrimmage: center, left wing and right defense. The right defense is placed just outside the circle in the middle and the right wing is next to him. The other defenseman is behind the centerman.

The diagram shows 3 options for movement of the puck and players should the team win the draw. From the positions indicated the players can set up their breakout pattern. If the team does not win the faceoff, defensive coverage is set up by the players, who move in the directions indicated.

Zone 2: 5-6, 5-5, 5-4, 5-3 formation. Here again, the players overload the middle as the faceoff occurs in the defensive zone. This variation has the center flanked by the left wing and right defense. The right wing is behind the right defense and the left defender is behind the centerman and outside the circle.

If the center wins the faceoff, there are 3 alternatives for puck and player movement in order to set up the breakout. If the team loses the draw, players may move in the directions indicated to establish their zone defense and try to regain control of the puck.

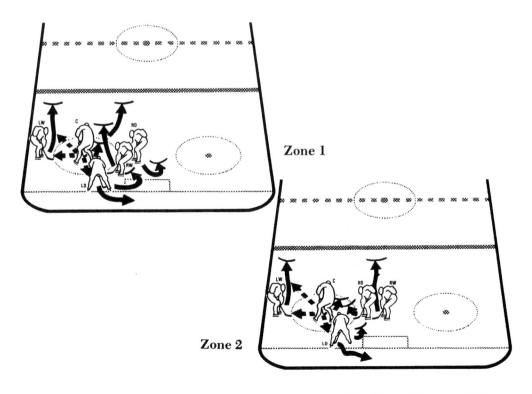

Zone 1

Zone 2

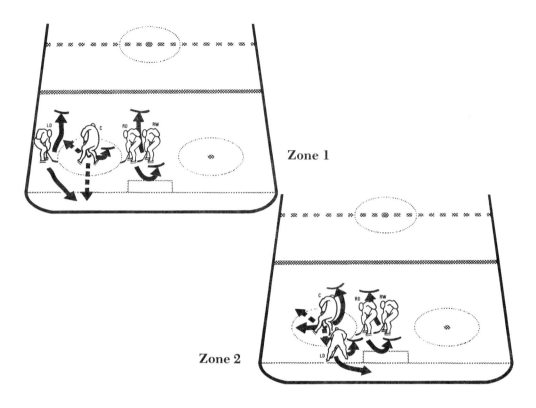

Zone 1

Zone 2

DEFENSIVE ZONE FACEOFFS

Zone 1: 4-3, 4-4, 4-5, 4-6 formation. With the team one man short, all 4 players on the ice are in a single line with 2 players overloading the middle of the ice. The centerman is flanked by the left and right defense, while the other wing is behind the right defense in the middle.

There are 2 directions the puck and the center could take if the faceoff is won and the players prepare to break out. If the team loses the draw, players may go in the direction of the crossed arrows to set up zone defense.

Zone 2: 4-4, 4-5, 4-6 formation. With one man short, three players—the center, right defense and right wing—take up positions indicated at the point of faceoff. The defense and wing are outside the circle, over-loading the middle. The left defense is behind the center.

The diagram shows 2 options for movement of the puck if the center wins the faceoff. He has the same 2 options as the players move to break out. If the team loses the faceoff, players may go in the directions indicated by the crossed arrowed lines to set up zone coverage in order to regain puck control.

DEFENSIVE ZONE FACEOFFS

Zone 1: 5-6, 5-5, 5-4, 5-3 formation. In this formation, the wings and defense are up front and the center is back. The left defense takes the faceoff; the other skaters are all outside the circle.

If the team wins the faceoff, there are 3 options for player and puck movement prior to starting the breakout. If the team does not win the faceoff, players go to any of the positions indicated in the diagram to establish zone coverage and hopefully gain puck control.

Zone 2: 4-3, 4-4, 4-5, 4-6 formation. When the team is one man short and the faceoff is in the defensive zone, line up the players with the right wing outside the circle near the boards and the left defense and center overloading the middle. The right defense takes the faceoff.

There are 3 alternatives for movement of the puck and the right defense should the team get the draw and set up to break out. The team loses the faceoff, players may establish zone defense by going in the directions indicated on the diagram.

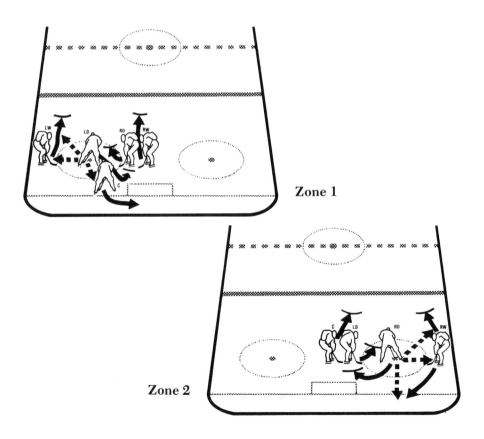

Zone 1

Zone 2

DEFENSIVE ZONE FACEOFFS

Zone 1: 3-3, 3-4, 3-5 formation. When the faceoff comes in the defensive zone and the team is two men short, situate the left defense outside the circle and behind the center and the right defense outside the circle on the line of scrimmage.

The diagram shows 2 options for movement of the puck and/or centerman if the team wins the faceoff and prepares to break out of the zone. The crossed arrows show options for player movement if the team does not get the draw and goes into defensive zone coverage.

Zone 2: 5-5, 5-4 formation. This formation is an unbalanced setup which can be used when the team is at full strength in its own end. The right defense is back behind the centerman and outside the circle. The left defense and wings are outside the circle and overloading the middle, as illustrated.

If the team gets the draw, there are 2 options for movement of the puck from the faceoff, along with directions the key players may take to start the breakout. If the team does not win the faceoff, each player may take the directions indicated to go for zone coverage in order to regain puck control.

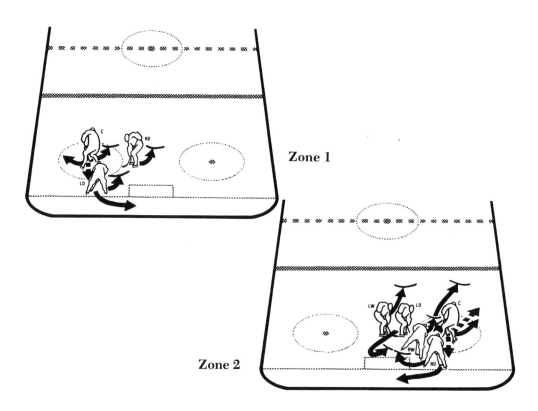

Zone 1

Zone 2

DEFENSIVE ZONE FACEOFFS

Zone 1: 5-6, 5-5, 5-4, 5-3 formation. This setup for a full-strength faceoff in the defensive zone has the right defenseman taking the draw. The right wing is outside the circle to his right and the left defense, left wing and center are positioned outside the circle to overload the middle (see diagram).

The drawing gives 4 options for puck movement from a winning faceoff, as well as alternatives for directions the key players may take to break out. If the team does not win the faceoff, players have several options for positioning themselves for defensive zone coverage.

Zone 2: 5-6, 5-5, 5-4, 5-3 formation. Four players are at the line of scrimmage in this zone formation. One defense is behind the line to the left of the goaltender, the second defenseman and a wing are outside the circle in the middle and the other wing is behind the centerman on the outside.

If the team wins the draw, the puck and the key players involved can take any one of the directions indicated as the players go into the breakout pattern. Suggested directions for player movement into zone defense are shown by the crossed arrows.

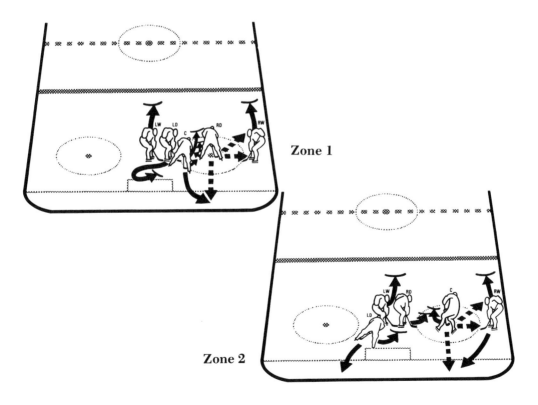

Zone 1

Zone 2

DEFENSIVE ZONE FACEOFFS

Zone 1: 5-6, 5-5, 5-4, 5-3 formation. As shown, 4 players are at the line of scrimmage in this setup, while the fifth player—the right defenseman —is next to the left defense, thereby overloading the middle with 3 players.

The diagram gives 4 options for movement of the puck and/or key players should the team win the faceoff and prepare to break out of the zone. The crossed arrows show the directions players may take to set up defensive zone coverage if the team does not get the draw.

Zone 2: 5-6, 5-5, 5-4, 5-3 formation. All 5 players are in line in this defensive formation. The centerman is positioned outside the circle near the boards and the right defenseman takes the faceoff. Backing him up outside the circle in the middle are the left defense and the wings.

Three options for movement of the puck after a winning faceoff are diagramed. Key players have the same options. If the team fails to win the faceoff, players move out in the directions indicated by the crossed arrows to set up defensive zone coverage.

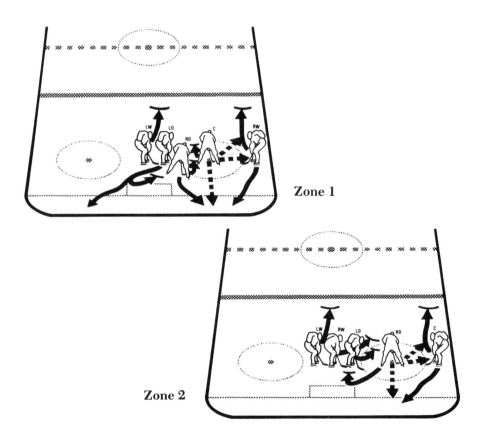

Zone 1

Zone 2

DEFENSIVE ZONE FACEOFFS

Zone 1: 4-3, 4-4, 4-5, 4-6 formation. With one man short, line up the 4 players in a row, overloading the middle with the 2 defensemen. The defense is outside the circle, while the winger is near the boards.

The diagram shows 3 options for movement of the puck and the centerman if the team wins the draw. If the team does not get the faceoff, players may move in the direction of the crossed arrows to set up defensive zone coverage and attempt to regain control of the puck.

Zone 2: 3-3, 3-4, 3-5 formation. When the team is two men short, the remaining skaters—center and 2 defense—position themselves in line at the faceoff circle. The defenders are outside the circle, flanking the centerman. There are 3 options for movement of the puck if the team wins the faceoff and prepares to break out of the zone. If the team fails to win the draw, players chose from the options indicated to get into position for defense of the zone.

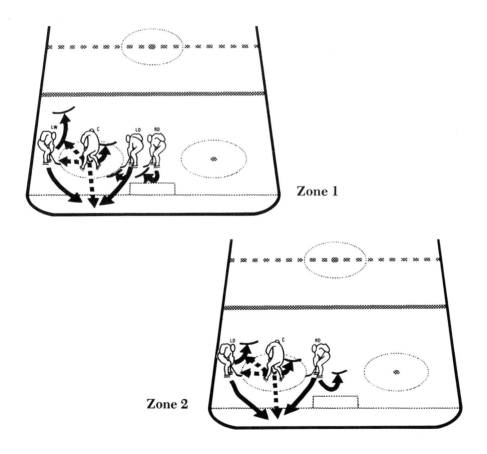

Zone 1

Zone 2

Thought Provokers

1. Is work on faceoff strategy and execution part of your practices?
2. On a crucial faceoff in your own end near the end of the period, would you send your small, quick centerman against their big man?
3. Give your centers a system and give them ice time to practice faceoffs.
4. Consider having someone keep track of faceoffs won and lost over the course of the game.
5. The most important place to win faceoffs consistently is in your own zone. Check this out by recording wins and losses during a game.
6. Advise your centerman to relax at the faceoff. While it's important to be alert and ready, being tense and tight can slow you up.
7. Use other players on the faceoff in certain situations. Give everyone some time in practice to work on strategy and technique.
8. The farther down the shaft the stick is held, the more leverage the player has on the faceoff.
9. Each faceoff in the game is a new opportunity to go on the attack— and score!
10. Concentration, positioning, timing and anticipation are important skills to develop in faceoff situations.
11. The player taking the draw should be prepared to charge off the mark the second the puck goes into play, thereby taking his man out of the play.
12. When you lose a faceoff, it's like a walk in baseball—you give away the momentum.

CHAPTER 10 *The Goaltender's Game*

Goaltending is something of a game within a game and, as such, requires the coach's constant attention. There is no such thing as a textbook goalie. Each tender must work within his abilities and limitations and develop his own style, avoiding the temptation to pattern himself after a Plante, Dryden, Tretjak or Parent. If he is a scrambler, flopper or stand-up stylist, it should be because it is the mode of operation that suits him best.

The goalie must be a master of balance and every bit as fast on his skates as the other players, despite his heavy padding and special skates. In addition, he must have good eyesight, agility, coordination and reflexes, great courage, poise and self-confidence, and an even temperament. This is a lot to ask of any athlete, but on the other hand, consider what is asked of the goaltender! His is probably the most demanding job on the team. The pressure and physical demands are constant: concentration is tested for sixty playing minutes. The rewards are largely internal: self-satisfaction, increased confidence and more experience. Even if the goaltender has a good night, he is rarely credited with a win. And when he has a bad night, he is bound to be tagged with the loss, even if his defensemen packed up and went home in the middle of the game.

Goaltending, nevertheless, is far from a thankless job. Goalies have been called the "backbone of the team" and "half the hockey team" and the "most important player on the ice." And a solid, consistent goaltender is a commodity cherished by the coach, revered by the players, who gain confidence knowing he is in the net, and idolized by fans, who recognize a hero when they see one. Good goalies are like quarterbacks in football. They see what's going on in their defensive zone and help their teammates. They talk, holler, cheer, direct and exhort. They can get the offense going and can be a third defenseman.

This chapter includes drills and ideas geared to sharpen the movements, reactions and skills of goaltenders. While there are many things he can do for himself, on his own, to develop and improve, special drills for the goalie should be a regular part of team practices. Many drills included in earlier chapters, particularly chapters 2, 3 and 4, are excellent exercises for goaltenders.

Drills

SHOOTING DRILL (3 angles, 6 shots)

1. Players line up along the boards in the neutral zone on one side of the rink. Everyone has a puck.

2. Players skate single file on one side, about 15 feet apart, and take a wrist or snap shot at the net. They keep skating, making a swing to the opposite boards, take a second puck at center ice and go in on the goalie in the other end for a second shot on goal. After shooting, players skate toward the middle, take another puck at center ice and continue on to the opposite end for their third shot to be taken from the slot area. To complete the drill, the players reverse the pattern of skating, in order to take their next three shots on goal, starting with the shot from the slot area, as illustrated in the diagram.

VARIATION

Split the team into 2 groups, with a group on each side at center ice facing a different goal. The exercise follows the same pattern outlined above.

NOTE

Pucks are situated in 3 separate groups in the neutral zone, 1 group on each side and a third group in the middle.

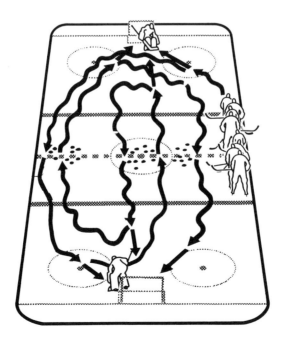

SHOOTING DRILLS

Zone 1: This drill employs 4 players in the zone with a number of pucks. One player is situated on the point on one side of the blue line. He is the first shooter. Another player (second shooter) is placed on the other side of the rink by the boards. The third shooter is at the top of the circle on the same side, and a fourth shooter is located in the slot.

Players rotate shooting from 1 to 4, then are replaced by the next group of 4 shooters. Drill goes on until everyone has participated.

VARIATION

The coach can reverse the arrangement of players' shooting order and rearrange the position of the shooters in the zone.

Zone 2: In this exercise, 2 players are situated in the zone as shooters; each has a number of pucks. The first shooter arranges his pucks in a straight line (as illustrated), while the second shooter has his pucks at an angle to the net. Shooters alternate shots at the goal until both have used up all of their pucks.

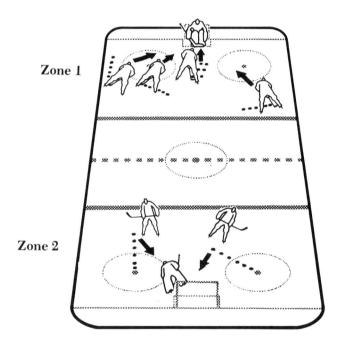

VARIATION

One shooter may complete all of his shots before the second shooter takes over.

NOTE

These drills may be run simultaneously, with part of the team in each end as shooters.

SHOOTING DRILLS

These drills combine work in shooting, passing and stopping pucks for goaltenders. The drills may be executed individually, using 1 zone, or may be run simultaneously in both ends.

Zone 1: Groups of players are situated along the boards at the blue line facing into the zone. The coach or a player is in the slot area with a quantity of pucks.

The person in the slot starts the drill with a shot at the goalie, who in turn stops the puck and makes a pass to a player coming in along the boards and getting ready to break out of the zone. The pass can either be a pass around the boards or a straight pass. After one player received the pass, he goes back into line and the next player comes out from the other side.

VARIATION

After the player in the slot shoots at the goalie to begin the drill, players can come in from each side along the boards. The goaltender passes to one of the skaters; the players turn and break out of the zone 2 on 0 and skate the length of the ice to take a shot on the opposite goal.

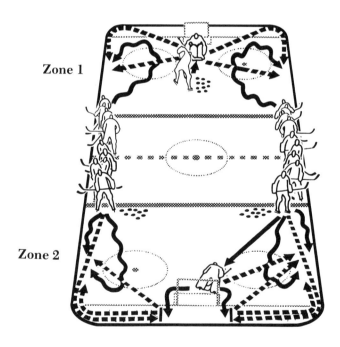

Zone 2: Two groups of players are situated at the blue line along the boards with pucks. The drill starts with one player making 1 of 2 moves: he either takes a shot on goal from the point, or he shoots along the boards behind the net. The goalie has to stop either shot, and then passes back to the shooter, who is coming in along the boards in the zone and taking a winger's position. (As a wing, he would be in position to break out of the zone.)

NOTE

The shooting drill rotates from one side to the other.

SHOOTING DRILL

Zone 1: The players form a shallow semicircle by the blue line; each shooter has several pucks. Two players take up positions in front of the goal to try to screen the goalie. They will face each shooter, with their sticks on the ice in front of them.

Beginning at one end of the line, each player shoots his pucks at the net. All shots must be on the ice! For the goalie, this provides practice in stopping tip-ins, deflections and screen shots. At the same time, it gives the players in front of the net experience in deflections and tip-ins.

VARIATIONS

A. Shooting may go from one side to the other, or may alternate from one end to the other, working toward the middle. Players may take 1 shot at a time, instead of shooting all the pucks at once.

B. Have the goaltender play without a stick.

C. Stagger the depth of the players in the shooting arc. Every other player would be closer to the net giving variation in shooting distance.

D. Require that on one run-through, shooters will make only wrist shots (or snap or slap shots), at the coach's option.

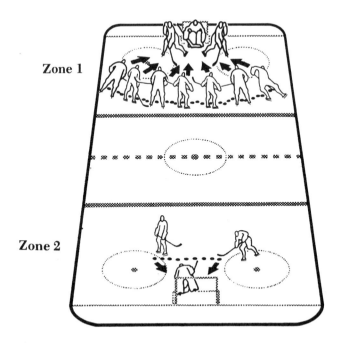

Zone 1

Zone 2

Zone 2: Situate 2 players with a line of pucks parallel to the goal line, as illustrated. The players alternate in shooting on the net.

VARIATIONS

A. Specify a particular shot for each round of shooting.
B. Vary the range on each shift of shooters.

NOTE

These drills may be done simultaneously in each end by dividing players into units.

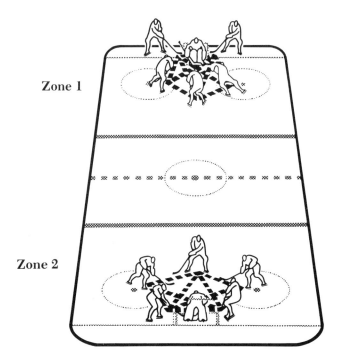

Zone 1

Zone 2

SHOOTING DRILL

Zone 1: Five players work as a unit in this exercise. Two players are situated behind the net and 3 in front, as shown. The players pass a puck around among themselves and try to score. Close-in work trains the goalie to keep his eyes on the puck and gives him practice on such essentials as cutting down angles, lateral movement in the crease, footwork and agility, quickness in going down and getting up, playing rebounds, moving in and out of the crease and cutting off passes from behind the net.

Zone 2: This is a variation of the drill in Zone 1. In this version, the 5-player unit is in front and to the sides of the goal, as diagramed. Players pass a puck around and try to score on the goaltender.

NOTE

These drills may be done at the same time using both ends of the ice.

SHOOTING DRILL

Zone 1: Players are situated with pucks in both corners on one end of the rink. The 2 players in the line nearest the goal start the drill by passing the puck back and forth behind the net. After a couple of passes, one of them breaks out in front of the goal to receive a pass from his partner and tries to score at close range. After the play, the players go to the end of their lines as the next pair begins the exercise.

Zone 2: Players with pucks line up by the boards on both sides of the net. The first skater on one side will try to either go behind the net or around on his near side in order to score on the goalie. This is a close-range play, giving the goaltender work on covering the posts and poke checking the puck away from the net. Play alternates from side to side as the drill continues.

NOTE

The drills may be executed at the same time utilizing both ends of the ice. Have the groups switch drills after a certain period of time.

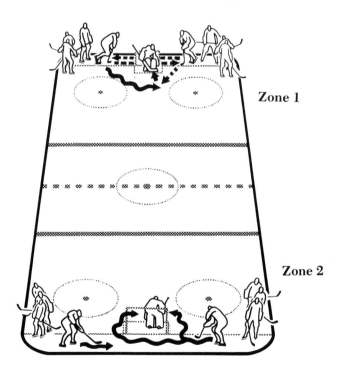

Zone 1

Zone 2

SHOOTING DRILLS: 2 HALF-ICE DRILLS
(shots from the slot, 2 zones)

Split the players into 2 groups and set 1 group up in each zone as diagramed.

Zone 1: Two players are situated in the corners; the remaining players line up at the blue line on either side of the ice.

Starting on one side, the first player in line gets a pass from the opposite corner, skates into the slot and shoots a wrist or backhand shot on goal. After shooting, he skates into the corner where the pass came from to replace the previous passer, and makes the pass to the following player from his side of the ice. After making the pass, the player skates to the end of the line on the same side of the ice.

The sides alternate shooting at the net. It is important that the players use good judgment in timing their passing and shooting so that the drill goes along smoothly and quickly.

Zone 2: Players are grouped in the corners of the zone. Each player has a puck. Alternating sides, the first player in line skates around the faceoff circle and takes a quick wrist or backhand shot on goal. He then

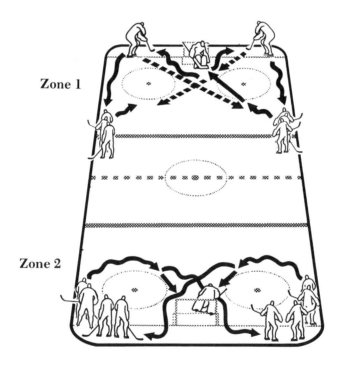

Zone 1

Zone 2

skates to the end of the line in the opposite corner as the first player in that line comes out.

As this drill moves very quickly, it's best to stop after four or five minutes to give the goaltender a brief rest. After a minute or so of rest, start the drill up again.

VARIATION

Have only one puck in play. The skater receives a pass from the opposite corner at the top of the circle and then shoots. This variation emphasizes quick release of the puck immediately after receiving a pass, and still affords the opportunity to work on forehand and backhand shots.

SHOOTING DRILLS: 2 HALF-ICE DRILLS
(2 passes, 2 shots, utilizing 2 zones)

Divide the team and set up each group at center ice facing into the zone (see diagram).

Zone 1: Locate 1 player in each of the faceoff circles with the remaining players lined up along the boards on both sides of the ice outside the blue line. At the coach's signal, 1 player starts skating from the blue line, gets a pass from the player in the circle on the opposite side of the ice, and takes a wrist shot from the slot area. He keeps on skating to the point of the net, receives a second pass from the faceoff circle and tries to flip or tip the puck into the net from close range. He then goes to take the passer's position in the circle, while the passer goes to the end of the line by the boards.

The next skater comes from the opposite line and the drill goes on alternating sides of the ice.

Zone 2: Players line up along the boards at the blue line on both sides of the rink; 1 player takes up a position in the slot. The drill starts with 1 player from one side receiving a pass from the other side and skating in on the goalie with a wrist shot. After taking the shot, he goes around the net, takes a loose puck and passes it to the player in the slot, who in turn takes a shot at the net. The player who took the shot from the slot goes back to the end of the line, replacing the first skater, who takes up the position in the slot.

The drill continues as the first player in line on the other side of the ice gets a pass from across the ice and moves in for a wrist shot, and so on, with sides alternating.

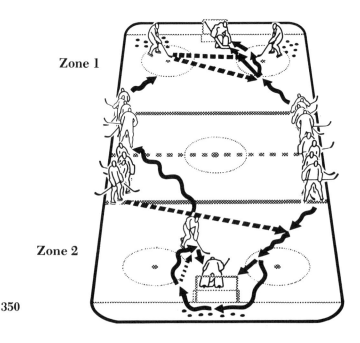

Zone 1

Zone 2

SHOOTING DRILLS: 2 HALF-ICE DRILLS
(utilizing 2 zones)

Divide the team with a group in each zone, or put the forwards in one end and the defensemen in the other end, as shown in the diagram.

Zone 1: Forwards are set up at mid-ice, each with a puck. One line skates toward the net and the players shoot one after another (left wing, right wing and center in order) on goal, and then skate back along the boards to the end of the line at mid-ice.

The wingers should shoot from the top of the circle, while the centers should go either left or right of a player (or the coach) located in the middle of the slot. The shot should be a forehand or backhand shot.

NOTE

It is important for the players to look up and time themselves according to the situation.

Zone 2: Defensemen are situated at the blue line, with 2 players in the corners. Players in the corners make a variety of passes (board passes, off-ice passes, off-the glass passes, and so forth) to the defensemen, who shoot from the blue line. Alternate right and left sides in passing and shooting. Players should rotate positions from time to time.

Defensemen at the blue line have the options of either passing to a partner in the middle or taking the shot themselves. Another option could be for a defenseman to move in on the net before receiving a pass from the corner and taking the shot on goal.

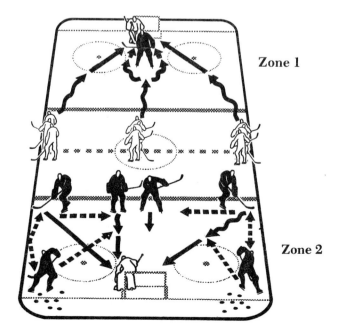

Zone 1

Zone 2

SHOOTING DRILLS: 2 HALF-ICE DRILLS
(utilizing 2 zones)

Divide the team into 2 groups and assign each group to a zone.

Zone 1: Players are set up as shown in the diagram with 2 defensemen at the blue line and 1 player by the boards near the faceoff circle.

The drill begins in the corner as 1 player passes to the player along the boards. The second pass goes to the defense at the point, who passes to the defenseman in the middle. The player who passed from the corner moves to the boards by the faceoff circle to receive the fourth pass, and the player who was at the boards skates a half-circle figure to the slot, receives a pass from the boards and takes a shot on goal.

NOTE

This 5-pass drill requires the players to move quickly and shoot accurately if it is to be effective. For a greater challenge, run this drill on the other side of the zone with 6 or 7 more players. The key to the procedure is timing in shooting.

Zone 2: Players are grouped as indicated in the diagram with two defensemen at the blue line. The drill opens with a player from one corner passing the puck to the defenseman at the blue line. The defenseman shoots as a player from the other corner of the ice moves in to deflect the puck. Alternate sides of the ice in performing the drill. After each player comes out of the corner to try to deflect the puck, he skates to the end of the line on the other side.

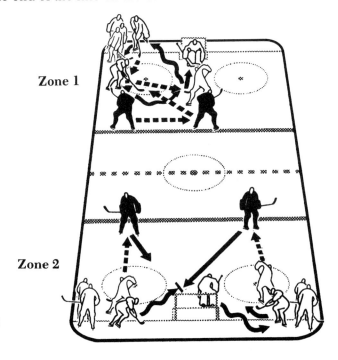

Zone 1

Zone 2

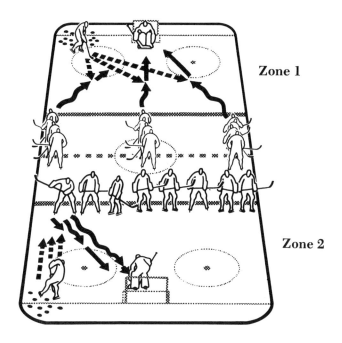

Zone 1

Zone 2

SHOOTING DRILLS: 2 HALF-ICE DRILLS
(shooting, 2 zones)

Split the team into 2 groups and situate each group in 1 zone. If the coach wishes, he can have the defense in 1 zone and the forwards in the other, as illustrated.

Zone 1: Players form 3 lines at mid-ice; 1 player is in the corner with the pucks. The player in the corner passes to the player first in line on the left side, then to the middle and then to the right side. As the players receive the pass, they skate in for a shot on goal. At some point in the drill, change passers.

VARIATION

Have all the players on one side. They move to the middle and then to the right side to receive the pass from the corner before shooting, and so on.

Zone 2: Players line up across the blue line and 1 player positions himself in the corner with a quantity of pucks. The player in the corner passes to the first player at the blue line, who takes a slap shot on goal, then to the second player, and so on. On the second run-through, players take a wrist shot, and on the third round, they use a backhand shot or make a deke on the goaltender. Keeping the players spread across the blue line gives the goalie good practice in handling shots from different angles. Change the passer midway in the drill.

VARIATION

Have the passer pass 2 or 3 pucks to a player before going to the next player in line. If 2 pucks, the player would shoot a slap and a wrist shot on goal before relinquishing his turn. If 3 pucks, player would use slap, wrist and backhand shots in that order.

SHOOTING DRILLS: 2 HALF-ICE DRILLS
(2 shots utilizing 2 zones)

Divide the team and put each group in 1 zone. Players in both zones line up in 2 lines—1 at center ice and 1 along the boards, as diagramed.

Zone 1: One player (or the coach) is positioned in the corner with a quantity of pucks. The player in the corner opens the drill by passing from the corner to the first player by the boards. He in turn passes laterally to the player first in line at mid-ice, who takes a slap shot on goal. A second pass from the corner goes behind the net and is picked up at the boards by the player who has just shot. He passes the puck to the player who skates from the line along the boards on the opposite side of the ice into the slot for the second shot, a wrist shot. After shooting, both players go to the end of lines at mid-ice, but switch lines so that they participate in a different play the second time through the drill.

Zone 2: The coach or player who will do the passing is situated in the corner opposite the lines at mid-ice. The first pass from the corner goes to the first player in the middle, who in turn passes to the first player along the boards. This player takes a slap shot on goal, then goes up along the boards to receive a pass from behind the net. He passes to the player in the middle who is skating into the slot for the second shot, a wrist shot. The players go to the end of the lines, switching groups for the next run-through.

NOTE

Have the groups change sides, and drills, after a period of time.

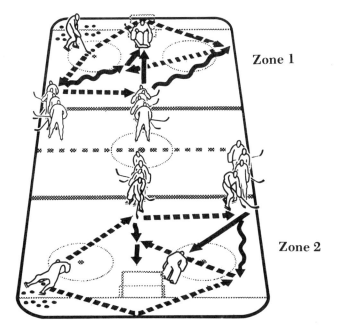

Zone 1

Zone 2

SHOOTING DRILLS: 2 HALF-ICE DRILLS
(shooting from the slot, 2 zones)

Split the team into 2 groups and situate each group in 1 zone.

Zone 1: Players line up at the blue line along the boards on both sides of the rink. The first player in each line takes a puck, skates into the slot, and one after the other takes either a wrist or backhand shot on goal. They continue skating into the corners, pick up pucks and skate back to the end of the line opposite that from which they came, making a pass at the blue line across ice to start the next skater in each line.

The timing of the skating and passing between players is important as the purpose of the drill is to keep the players moving, passing and shooting quickly and smoothly.

Zone 2: Players form a line along the boards on the left side, as shown. The first player takes a puck and skates into the slot for either a wrist or backhand shot on goal. After taking the shot, he skates to the corner, picks up a second puck and passes to the next skater coming into the slot. After shooting, the player goes to the opposite side of the blue line. After everyone has gone through the drill, it is repeated, starting from the right side.

NOTE

Groups could switch zones so that everyone will participate in both drills.

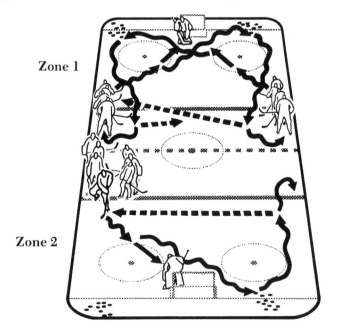

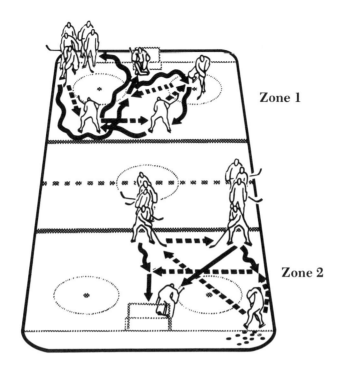

Zone 1

Zone 2

SHOOTING DRILLS: 2 HALF-ICE DRILLS
(utilizing 2 zones)

Split the team into 2 groups and situate each group in a zone, as diagramed.

Zone 1: Two players are positioned at the blue line, 1 player is in the faceoff circle to the left of the goal and the remaining players are grouped in the right corner.

The drill begins when a player in the corner passes to the player near the boards at the blue line. In quick successive passes, the puck goes to the player in the middle, to the player in the faceoff circle and into the slot, where the pass is taken by the player from the corner, who has skated along the boards, around the player at the blue line and into the slot. He takes a shot on goal, then goes to the faceoff circle to replace his teammate. The other players rotate positions, i.e., the player in the faceoff circle goes to the middle, the player in the middle moves to the boards and the player at the boards at the blue line follows the shooter to the net for a possible rebound, then skates back to join the players grouped in the corner. This rotation continues until all of the players have taken part in the drill.

Zone 2: Players form 2 lines at the blue line, one line in the middle and the other along the boards. The coach or a player is in the corner to make 2 passes. The first pass, which opens the drill, is to the first player in line in the middle, who in turn passes to the first player in line by the boards. This player takes a couple of strides and shoots at the net. The second pass from the corner goes along the boards to the player who has just shot. He passes to the player in the middle, who is skating into the slot, and who takes a shot on goal. The 2 players then go to the end of the line opposite that from which they started.

NOTE

In both drills, switch sides of the ice halfway through the drill.

SHOOTING DRILLS: 2 HALF-ICE DRILLS
(utilizing 2 zones)

Divide the team with the forwards in 1 zone and the defensemen in the second zone.

Zone 1 (forwards): The puck is shot from the blue line, either into the corner or around the boards, and the first line skates out to make a play for it. As illustrated, there are several alternatives in making the play. After completion, the line goes back to center ice, and the second line goes through the drill.

NOTE

Notice the positioning of the 2 forwards in front of the net inside the faceoff circles while the third player is behind the goal line.

Zone 2 (defense): Defensemen form 2 lines, one at center ice and one along the boards on the left side. The first shot is taken by the defenseman in the middle (a slap shot) and the second shot is taken by the player along the boards, who skates with the puck to the top of the circle and shoots. The timing of the shots should be close so that the goaltender has to react quickly.

NOTE

Change lines to the middle and right side of the ice halfway through the drill.

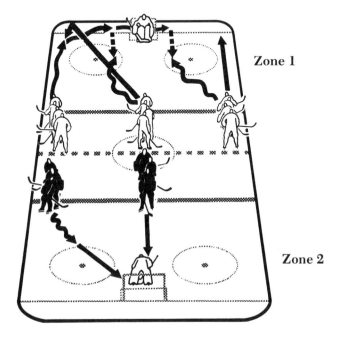

Zone 1

Zone 2

SHOOTING DRILLS: 2 HALF-ICE DRILLS
(utilizing 2 zones)

Five players are positioned in 1 zone with the remainder situated in the second zone (see diagram).

Zone 1: The basic format for positioning is 2 players at the blue line, 1 player roaming in front of the net or in the slot area, and 1 player on each side or in the corner areas. Players pass the puck 5 on 0 and shoot, changing positions in the zone regardless of where the puck is located. None of the positions should be left uncovered.

Zone 2: Have the players form 2 lines at the blue line, one group along the boards and the other in the middle. The coach or 1 player is located in the left corner. The player in the corner passes behind the net and along the boards and is received by the first player in line at center ice, who skates quickly to take the pass before it goes out of the zone. He in turn passes to the first player from the group by the boards, who is skating to the middle to receive the pass and take the first shot on the net. The player who got the first pass skates into the slot to receive a second pass from the corner and takes the second shot on goal.

NOTE

Switch sides of the ice and reverse the skating and passing pattern halfway through the drill.

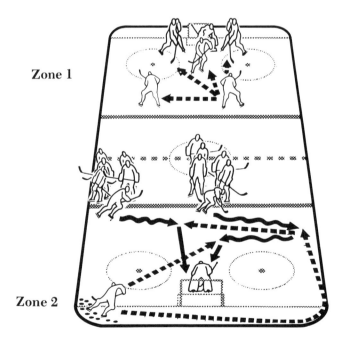

Zone 1

Zone 2

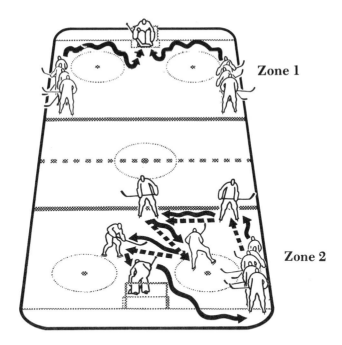

Zone 1

Zone 2

SHOOTING DRILLS: 2 HALF-ICE DRILLS
(utilizing 2 zones)

Divide the players into 2 groups and set up each group in one end of the rink, as illustrated.

Zone 1: Players form lines along the boards on either side of the ice at the blue line.

The drill starts on one side when the first player in line takes a puck, skates outside the circle to the goal and tries to score on the goaltender from close range with a wrist or backhand shot or by deking the goalie. The next shooter comes from the opposite side of the ice. After shooting, players switch the line from which they started.

VARIATION

Instead of having the player carry the puck around the circle, a player from the other side can pass the puck to the player at the goal mouth after he has skated from the boards around the circle.

Zone 2: Two players are set up as defense, 1 inside the faceoff circle and 1 in the slot area by the other circle; 2 players take positions inside the blue line—1 by the boards and the other in the middle. The remaining players line up in the corner, as shown.

The drill begins when the player in the corner passes the puck to the player along the boards at the blue line. He passes to the player in the middle, who in turn passes to the skater in the faceoff circle. The player in the circle passes to the player in the slot, who takes a shot on goal.

After the shot is taken, each player advances one position in the passing pattern. In other words, he goes to the position to which he made the play in the previous run-through. Rotation continues until all players have had a turn in all positions.

NOTE

After a specified length of time, groups switch sides and zones.

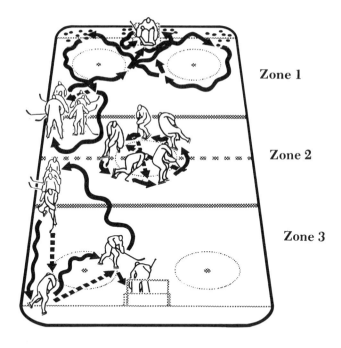

Zone 1

Zone 2

Zone 3

SHOOTING DRILLS: 3 DRILLS
(utilizing 3 zones)

Split the team into 3 units and set up each group in 1 zone (see diagram).

Zone 1: Players are grouped at the blue line on one side with a number of pucks placed in each corner and behind the net.

The drill begins when the first skater takes a puck and skates in on the goalie for a wrist shot. He either gets his own rebound or picks up a puck behind the net and tries to deke the goalie from close range. Then he goes to either one of the corners, takes another puck, skates around the faceoff circle and takes a third shot on goal. The player finishes by going into the opposite corner of the previous play for a puck, which he passes to the next skater in line before going out of the zone and to the end of the line. The object is to do the drill as quickly as possible and to see how well players can do with 3 chances to score.

Switch players at the blue line to the other side midway in the drill.

Zone 2: Players in the neutral zone skate around the center circle passing a puck between them while skating. They can skate forwards or backwards, or alternate directions. Vary this drill by using a second puck or by having a player in the middle of the circle to try to intercept passes.

Zone 3: Players line up at the blue line at the left boards with 1 player positioned in the corner and 1 player in the slot. The first player in line at the blue line passes to the cornerman, who passes to the man in the slot, who turns and takes a quick shot on the net. As they pass and shoot, the 3 players rotate positions so that the point man goes to the corner, the cornerman to the slot and the slot man to the end of the line. Switch sides of the ice halfway through the drill.

NOTE

Allow time so that units can rotate zones and participate in each of the 3 drills.

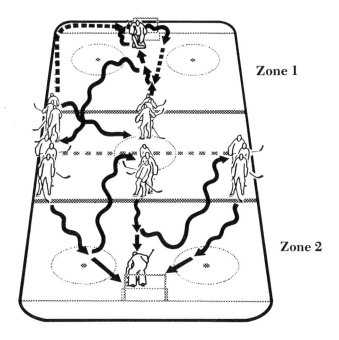

Zone 1

Zone 2

SHOOTING DRILLS: 1 ON 0 DRILL
(1 shot)

Split the team into 2 groups for a 2-zone exercise.

Zone 1: Players form 2 lines at the blue line, one line in the middle and the other along the boards, as illustrated. Players along the boards have pucks.

The drill in this zone starts with one player in the group along the boards shooting the puck around the boards. The goaltender comes out of the net, stops the puck and makes a pass to a player who has come from the line in the middle to break into the slot area for the pass followed by a shot on goal. Players finish by going to the end of the line, but switch lines (i.e., the player from the middle goes to the line by the boards and vice versa).

Drill continues as the next 2 skaters come out. Halfway through the drill, have the players in the middle move to the left side of the ice, while the players on the right boards come to the middle.

Zone 2: Players form 3 lines, as shown, at the blue line. Each player has a puck.

The line on the left side starts out and one after the other they get off quick wrist shots on goal. The group in the middle go out, and the first group skates to that position for the next run-through. When the second unit has taken its shots, the group on the right side leaves (and is replaced by the unit that was in the middle) and shoots. This group goes to the left side.

The drill continues from the right side as that unit skates in for shots on goal. The rotation from position to position, and from left to right starting sides continues throughout the drill.

NOTE

After a certain amount of time, ends switch drills.

SHOOTING DRILLS: 1 ON 0 DRILL
(2 passes, 2 shots)

1. Split the players into 2 groups and position the groups in opposite corners of the rink, as illustrated. One player from each group is situated, with a quantity of pucks, at the red line.

2. The drill begins with the first player in line in each corner. He comes out, skates along the boards and cuts toward the slot area, where he receives a pass from the player at the red line. The skater gets off a shot on the net, circles and takes a second pass from the red line. He takes another shot on goal, then skates into the corner of the rink across from where he started.

3. The drill is run the same way in both ends of the rink. When everybody has gone through the exercise, the drill is repeated with the players at the red line changing the direction of their passes, as indicated.

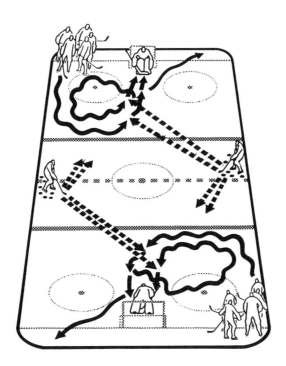

SHOOTING DRILLS: 1 ON 0 DRILL
(5 shots)

1. Split the players into 2 units and situate each group along the red line facing into the opposite zone. All of the players have pucks.
2. Five players from each group start out stickhandling into the offensive zone. They should be evenly spread out as they cross the blue line.
3. Skaters go in 1 on 0 and take 5 consecutive shots on goal from different angles. Shots could be wrist or slap shots.
4. After shots have been completed, the next group of 5 go out and the drill continues.

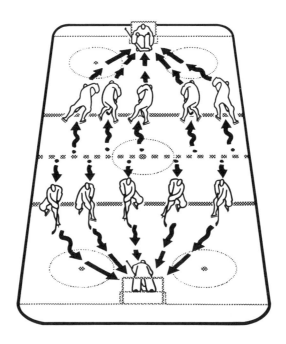

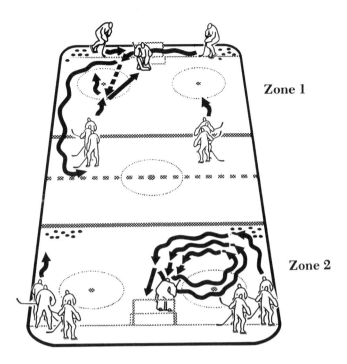

Zone 1

Zone 2

SHOOTING DRILLS: 1 ON 0 DRILL
(2 zones)

Divide the team and assign each group to a zone.

Zone 1: Players form 2 lines, as shown, at the blue line, facing the goal. Two players take up positions in the corners; each has a quantity of pucks.

The drill begins with 1 player in the corner carrying the puck behind the net and then passing it to the player who has moved in from the blue line to the faceoff circle. This player takes a shot on the net and goes into the near corner to replace that player, who becomes the next puck carrier.

Play alternates from side to side, and players rotate positions throughout.

Zone 2: Players split into units in each corner. Pucks are placed on each side of the ice at the blue line.

The drill begins when the first player in one corner skates to the blue line and picks up a puck. He wheels in the zone and takes a shot on the net, circles back to the blue line for a second puck and takes a second shot, and finishes by making another circle, taking a third puck and getting off a third shot on goal.

After the first skater completes his shots, the next skater comes from the other side. Sides alternate throughout the exercise.

VARIATION

This drill can be run from both sides at once without interference.

NOTE

After a specified time, groups should switch drills.

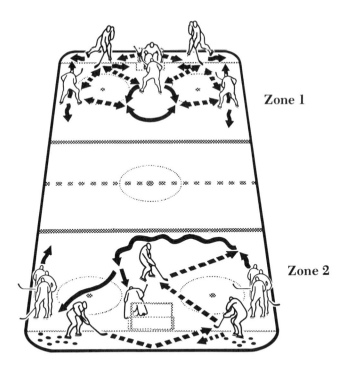

Zone 1

Zone 2

SHOOTING DRILLS: HALF-ICE DRILLS

Divide the team into groups in the two end zones. Zone 1 has a group of
5 players; the remainder of the team is situated in Zone 2.

Zone 1: Three forwards and 2 defensemen set up with the defense
behind the goal and the forwards at the side boards and in the slot area.

The object of this drill is to work on breaking out of the zone and move
the puck around as a unit while staying in the zone. Player movement is
shown by the arrows in the diagram. The puck should be in motion
continually during the drill. Shots should be taken at the goalie while
keeping the puck in motion also.

Zone 2: Situate 2 defensemen behind the goal line and a centerman
in the slot area, as shown. Forwards are located on each side along the
boards.

The drill begins with 1 defense passing the puck to his partner, who
in turn passes to the center in the slot. As the puck goes to the center, a
forward breaks from the corner. The centerman passes to the forward,
who controls the puck as he makes a swing inside the blue line and
skates in for a shot on goal. After taking the shot, the forward goes to the
side opposite that from which he started.

Alternate sides as the drill continues, with skaters coming from opposite sides and defensemen changing direction of their passes. Rotate defense and centers.

NOTE

If the drills are being run simultaneously, have the units switch drills after a certain amount of time on the exercises.

SHOOTING DRILLS: 3 ON 0 DRILL
(passing, half ice)

1. Divide the team and set up each group in 1 zone as illustrated in the diagram.
2. At the coach's signal, a unit of 3 skaters (or a line) starts out in each zone, skating from center ice to the net, passing the puck and finishing with a shot on goal or play until they score a goal.
3. After taking the shot or scoring, the lines return to their original positions at center ice.

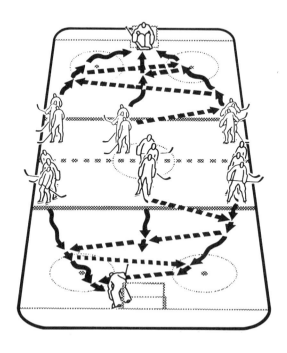

SHOOTING DRILLS: 1 ON 0 DRILLS
(2 zones)

The team is divided into groups along the boards on either side of the blue lines, as illustrated.

Zone 1: To get the drill started, 1 player from each side starts out (every player has a puck). The player on one side carries the puck and takes a shot on the net from an angle near the top of the circle. He moves in on the net while the player from the other side cuts across the middle and shoots from the slot area. He also has the option of passing to the player who took the first shot. The player who shoots first should get in position to take a pass, tip the other shooter's shot, or get a rebound.

The coach may have all the players on the left side take the first shot and all the players on the right make the second move. Halfway through the drill, have the groups switch assignments.

Zone 2: The player from one side skates in the zone with a puck toward the slot area. At the same time, another player comes over from the group at the other side and skates behind the puck carrier, looking for a drop pass. When he gets the pass he can either take a shot on the net, or return the puck to his partner in the play.

Sides should rotate turns in acting as the puck carrier and in taking the drop pass and making a play.

NOTE

Players in the zones may switch drills after a designated amount of time on the exercise.

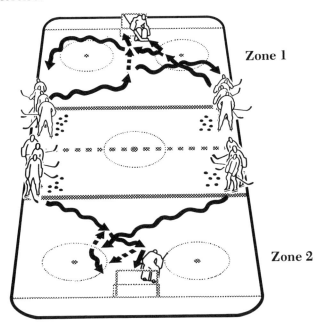

Zone 1

Zone 2

Goaltender's Worksheet

DRILLS (use of equipment and body parts)

FEET: Shots along the ice to low corners with and without a stick.

Both sides, full blade on ice.

HAND (GLOVE SIDE): Rebounds.

Neat (not juggling catches).

Flip shots in close.

Long hard shots.

Catching thrown pucks.

HAND (STICK SIDE): Use of glove instead of stick.

Try to bring trapper across.

Flips and long shots (deflect to corner).

STICK: Deflecting and batting down pass outs.

Sliders to glove side.

Shooting pucks (flip and hard shots).

Stick saves only.

PADS: Backup on low shots.

Close in shots where glove cannot be used.

Deflections.

CHEST: Backup on all shots, especially long shots and high shots.

SITUATIONS

Shot from wing (cut off short side; stay out of crease, don't leave post too soon).

Shot from corner or behind net (heel of skate against post; watch puck).

Screen shots (cut angle; stay low, legs together, stick on ice).

Tip-ins (play the puck; move out on the puck).

Bouncers (stick on ice, pads together; get to puck before or as it bounces).

Faceoffs.

Backhands (cut angle and stay low).

OTHER SITUATIONS

Breakaways (poke checking; keep eye on puck; let puck carrier make the first move).

Faceoffs in your end (know your players' moves; check their center's shooting).

1 on 1, 2 on 1, 3 on 2—keep eye on puck.

Deking (backing in is acceptable; do not back into goal line; don't make first move).

Puck checking dekes or shots from the side (keep eye on puck; don't lean, slide hand up the stick handle).

Rebounds (use trapper if possible; clear toward corner or free ice).

EXERCISES AND SOLITARY DRILLS

Kicking legs to side on command.
Shooting and passing pucks.
Behind the net and back.
Post to post.
Kicking pucks (no stick).
Leg kicks.
Leg raises with pads.
Mirror drills.
Stretching.
Soccer dribbling.
Playing Ping-Pong, squash, handball, tennis, racquetball.
2 pads slide right and left.
Dropping down and getting up.
V sprawl with stick between legs.
Arm raises with stick (wrist curls).
Stopping tennis or Ping-Pong balls thrown at him.

Dos and Don'ts for Goaltenders

DO

Yell—be the team leader.

Stay on your feet as much as possible.

Keep your eye on the puck.

Practice cutting down angles by moving in and out of the net with the attackers.

Work on your own style.

Skating drills with the forwards.

Have confidence in your own ability and that of your defenders.

Get your body and some equipment behind every shot.

Practice without a goal stick.

Keep your knees bent.

Study the opposition.

Clear to a teammate, to the corner or to free ice.

Keep pads together and centered on the puck.

Regain position quickly after a save.

Freeze the puck only when necessary.

Watch for rebounds off the boards and glass.

Catch the puck whenever possible.

Keep your cool and relax.

DON'T

Worry about goals scored against you.

Take your eyes off the puck.

Make the first move (let your opponent commit himself first).

Anticipate movement of the puck.

Blame your teammates for goals.

Drop continuously.

Back in more than you have to.

Hesitate to be aggressive.

Forget to check your stance.

Listen to the crowd behind you.

Go out of the crease during an altercation on the ice.

Roam after loose pucks unless you know you can get to the puck before an opponent.

Stop talking!

Thought Provokers

1. Consider using 2 or 3 goalies in a game (1 each period or 1 each 30 minutes of play).
2. How can you help your goalie develop confidence and poise?
3. If you have an extra goaltender at practice, have him take off the pads and participate in drills (rotate this duty among goaltenders).
4. Top goaltenders don't stand in goal, they play around it.
5. Suggest that the goalie watch the blade of the puck carrier's stick as he keeps track of the puck. The blade will reveal where the shot will go.
6. Consider getting help for your goalies from an expert. Have a goaltender or ex-goalie watch practice and/or games from time to time and work with the goaltenders on the specifics he notes.
7. Emphasize physical conditioning for goaltenders; don't allow a goaltender to put on weight.
8. Try your goaltenders with weighted sticks.
9. Does your goalie ever go through drills without a stick?
10. Do you have special shooting drills to help your goaltender work on angles, close-in and long-range shots, dekes, deflections, tip-ins, breakaways and rebounds?

CHART 1—HELPFUL COACHING IDEAS/CHALLENGES/ TECHNIQUES

- Behind the bench, make criticism constructive.
- Keep harmony among players and be positive in your comments.
- Matching lines for home and away games.
- How do you play against a strongly performing line? (Use two lines against one for one-minute shifts or just your best checking line.)
- How do you play if you have the game lead?
- How do you play if you are down by one or two goals?
- What do you do with your hot goaltender?
- How do you keep the atmosphere in the locker room between periods?
- In forechecking, when should you use the one-man-in, or two-men-in?
- How do you work your power play and who should you use (*i.e.*, on defense, up front)?
- How do you handle your penalty killing unit (*i.e.*, have two units of four; use four defensemen)? How long should the shift be?
- How do you handle your team with five minutes to play at the end of each period?
- How do you cope with flagrant mistakes by the team or by an individual during the course of a game?
- As a coach, what are your priorities at the beginning of each period? (Suggestion: analyze how the opposition is forechecking against your team.)
- What do you do with a player who is having a "hot" night?
- What do you do with a line that is having a "hot" night?
- What do you do with a star or a line that is having a bad night?
- What do you do in your important faceoffs (*i.e.*, at the end of a period or game) and who should be on the ice?
- Do you emphasize the first goal of the game and of each period?
- As a coach, try to acquaint yourself with the strengths and weaknesses of the opposing team, especially in the area of defense.
- How do you arrange your defensive pairings? What side should your best defense play?
- Do you emphasize the job of the "trailer"?
- If things are going wrong, don't be afraid to make changes to generate new life.
- Don't be afraid to give credit to those who deserve it.
- How do you handle stupid penalties?
- Make sure your team always stays balanced.
- Your team must play "position" and must have both offensive and defensive systems.
- How do you direct your line changes?
- How do you handle your goaltender?
- How quick are you to analyze, in a game, the team play of the opposition? (Considerations: are the defense standing up or backing in? Do they play a free style or a close-checking style?)

- Do you ask the players' opinions on how the opposition is playing against them?
- How do you generate life and hustle when the game is dull?
- What should you do with a big lead in a game?
- What should you do if you are down by four or five goals?
- How do you handle your team in a close, tight-checking game?
- Are you prepared for your practices? Do you take into consideration in planning practice the style of play of your next opponent?
- Keep your cool behind the bench.
- Try to always make general remarks in front of everybody in the locker room.
- Make sure when you instruct the player or players are ready to listen, not exhausted or distracted.
- You should be friendly at all times toward your players.
- How quick are you in a game to detect your team's weaknesses as the game progresses.
- Are your practices monotonous?
- Are your practices too long?
- Do you demonstrate to your players what you want from them?
- Coach should always remember not to stay too long on one drill. Better to leave it and come back to it in the next practice.
- Can you detect when your players are tired?
- Do your players know exactly what you are trying to accomplish in practice? Give them direction and answers.
- Are your practices challenging, interesting and fun?
- Do you know when to give time off to your players?
- How do you motivate your players in a game?
- How do you motivate your players in a practice?
- Maintain a consistent pattern of discipline, philosophy and attitude.
- Discipline should be well-defined, clearly understood by players, and consistently implemented by coach.

CHART 2—GAME REPORT

GAME # _____

DATE _____ HOME _____ AWAY _____

_____ _____ VS. _____ _____
　　(Team)　　　　　　(Score)　　　　　　(Team)　　　　　　(Score)

REMARKS about the Team (as the game progresses)

Weaknesses Check List Period	One	Two	Three
Skating			
Passing (good/bad)			
Shooting (close/far, good/bad)			
Visiting Team's shots (good/bad)			
Hitting (body checking/bumping)			
Getting beaten to the puck			
Losing control of puck along boards			
Taking our eyes off the puck			
Fail to pressure puck carrier			
Carrying puck rather than passing			
Fail to pick up trailer			
Standing around too much			
Defensive mistakes by forwards			
Defensive mistakes by defense			
Point covering in our zone			
Deflected shots from point			
Slot covering in our zone			
Team balance			
Shifts are too long			
Break-out system			
Defensive zone play			
Shots blocked by defense			
Checking in defensive zone			
Giveaways in defensive zone			
Rebounds in defensive zone			
Neutral zone play			
Checking in neutral zone			
Giveaways in neutral zone			
Offensive zone play			
Offensive attacks (broke/complete)			
Forechecking of visiting team 1, 2 or 3 men in			
Checking in offensive zone			
Giveaways in neutral zone			
Rebounds in offensive zone			
Faceoffs controlled (good/bad)			
Bad goals from face-off			
Bad goals beg./end of period			
Penalties (good/bad)			
Bad angle goals			
Goalies weaknesses or fault			
Penalty-killing unit			
Power-play unit			
Number of good scoring chances			

CONTROLLED FACE-OFFS

Players' Names		First Period				
		Def.	Neut.	Off.	Total	Remarks
1.	Won					
	Lost					
2.	Won					
	Lost					
3.	Won					
	Lost					
4.	Won					
	Lost					
Team Total	Won					
	Lost					

Players' Names		Second Period				
		Def.	Neut.	Off.	Total	Remarks
1.	Won					
	Lost					
2.	Won					
	Lost					
3.	Won					
	Lost					
4.	Won					
	Lost					
Team Total	Won					
	Lost					

Players' Names		Third Period				
		Def.	Neut.	Off.	Total	Remarks
1.	Won					
	Lost					
2.	Won					
	Lost					
3.	Won					
	Lost					
4.	Won					
	Lost					
Team Total	Won					
	Lost					

HOW EACH GOAL AGAINST THE TEAM WAS SCORED

First Period				Remarks
1. Area where goal was scored from: Players on ice:	R	M	L	
2. Area where goal was scored from: Players on ice:	R	M	L	
3. Area where goal was scored from: Players on ice:	R	M	L	
4. Area where goal was scored from: Players on ice:	R	M	L	

TOTAL GOALS FOR_____

    TOTAL GOALS AGAINST_____

Second Period				Remarks
1. Area where goal was scored from: Players on ice:	R	M	L	
2. Area where goal was scored from: Players on ice:	R	M	L	
3. Area where goal was scored from: Players on ice:	R	M	L	
4. Area where goal was scored from: Players on ice:	R	M	L	

TOTAL GOALS FOR_____

    TOTAL GOALS AGAINST_____

Third Period				Remarks
1. Area where goal was scored from: Players on ice:	R	M	L	
2. Area where goal was scored from: Players on ice:	R	M	L	
3. Area where goal was scored from: Players on ice:	R	M	L	
4. Area where goal was scored from: Players on ice:	R	M	L	

TOTAL GOALS FOR_____

    TOTAL GOALS AGAINST_____

R = right side   M = middle   L = left side

WHO SCORED FOR OUR TEAM

First Period

Players' Names

1.		PPG	SHG	ESG
2.		PPG	SHG	ESG
3.		PPG	SHG	ESG
4.		PPG	SHG	ESG

Second Period

Players' Names

1.		PPG	SHG	ESG
2.		PPG	SHG	ESG
3.		PPG	SHG	ESG
4.		PPG	SHG	ESG

Third Period

Players' Names

1.		PPG	SHG	ESG
2.		PPG	SHG	ESG
3.		PPG	SHG	ESG
4.		PPG	SHG	ESG

PPG = power play goal   SHG = short hand goal   ESG = even strength goal

GAME LINEUPS

Home Team	Visiting Team
Forwards (Player's name and number)	Forwards (Player's name and number)
( ) LW ( ) C ( ) RW	( ) LW ( ) C ( ) RW
( ) LW ( ) C ( ) RW	( ) LW ( ) C ( ) RW
( ) LW ( ) C ( ) RW	( ) LW ( ) C ( ) RW
Defenses (Player's name and number)	Defenses (Player's name and number)
( ) LD ( ) RD	( ) LD ( ) RD
( ) LD ( ) RD	( ) LD ( ) RD
( ) LD ( ) RD	( ) LD ( ) RD
Extras (Player's name and number)	
( ) ( )	( ) ( )

Opposition Power Play (Player's name and number)

( ) LW   ( ) C   ( ) RW   ( ) LD   ( ) RD

Home Power Play (Player's name and number)

( ) LW   ( ) C   ( ) RW   ( ) LD   ( ) RD

Opposition Penalty Killing (Player's name and number)

( ) C   ( ) W   ( ) LD   ( ) RD

Home Penalty Killing (Player's name and number)

( ) C   ( ) W   ( ) LD   ( ) RD

Team injured players_____   _____   _____

Visitors injured players_____   _____   _____

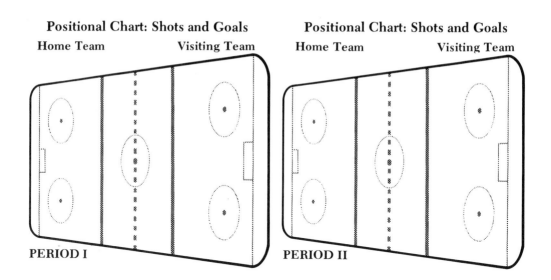

Positional Chart: Shots and Goals

Home Team   Visiting Team

PERIOD I

Positional Chart: Shots and Goals

Home Team   Visiting Team

PERIOD II

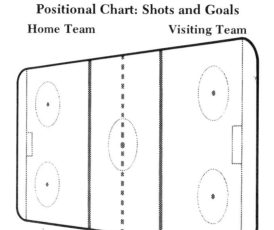

Positional Chart: Shots and Goals

Home Team   Visiting Team

PERIOD III

	Team	Per. 1	Per. 2	Per. 3	Total Shots	Goalies' Names
Shots						

	Goals For	Goals Against
Power Play Goals		
Shorthanded Goals		
Even Strength Goals		

GAME SUMMARY: